DOWNSTAIRS, the kids are really rockin' the joint, but upstairs Mom and Dad are quietly reading. The secret is the suspended acoustical ceiling. For complete information on "quietizing" your home, see the article on acoustics on page 14

NO HUNTING THRILLS can top those of the archer who takes to the field or forest. For tips on camouflage, stalking and proper sighting, see "Bag It With a Bow," page 114

WHEN THE FAMILY GROWS, the house must grow too, and the easiest place to find room is in an unfinished attic. Above and below right you'll find ideas for finishing off boys' rooms. And note the exciting attic ceiling below; for details on its easy construction, see the article on page 130

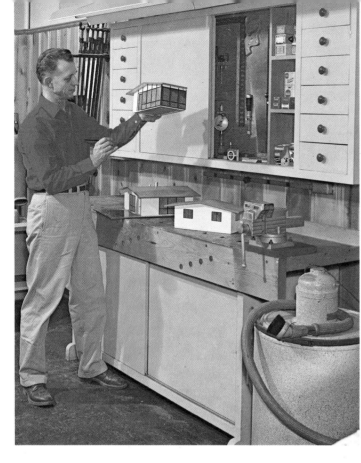

YOU CAN FIND space in a basement, too, whether it's for a fine workshop or a family recreation center. What's that? Water in your basement? This is one of the stubbornest problems the homeowner faces. For information on solving every kind of moisture problem, see page 180

BEST CATCHIN' FISH in the world, according to a big percentage of all anglers, is the bass. He'll strike when you least expect it, and fight your lure with cold fury. He's wily and wicked, yet surprisingly he'll bite on almost anything. For some of fishing's strangest lures (and some you can try yourself, to the delight of your fellow anglers), see the article "What Won't Catch Bass?" on page 188

Popular Mechanics
Do-It-Yourself Encyclopedia

in 16 volumes

A complete guide to

- home maintenance
- home improvement
- hand-tool skills
- craft projects
- power-tool know-how
- hobbies
- automotive upkeep
- automotive repair
- shop shortcuts
- boating
- fishing
- hunting
- model making
- outdoor living
- radio, TV and electronics

Volume 1

Book Division, Hearst Magazines, New York, N.Y. 10019

XII

Foreword

Within the 3,136 pages of this Encyclopedia you will find:

More than 700 feature articles on everything from
Abrasives to Zoetropes

More than 10,000 illustrations telling you precisely
what to do and how to do it

More than 1,000 "Clever Ideas" for solving home
problems and making shop work easier

Hundreds of projects to improve your home

Scores of articles that will enhance your enjoyment
of your hobbies and sports

An "Instant Index" of more than 6,000 entries that
will enable you to find the information you seek

The editors of *Popular Mechanics* have supervised the preparation of material for the Encyclopedia.

For more than 65 years, *Popular Mechanics* has been the world's most authoritative source for how-to-do-it information.

Any Encyclopedia bearing the famous *Popular Mechanics* name must be equally authoritative.

That has been our goal in the preparation of every page in these volumes.

THE EDITORS

VOLUME 1

abrasives
Sanding—start to finish 7
acoustics
Wrap yourself in quiet 14
aeolian harp
Build an ancient window harp 22
air car model
Model air car skims the ground 24
air conditioners
How to buy a good air conditioner 28
Cool your whole house 32
air conditioners, auto
You can have the coolest car in town 37
airplane models
Free-flight parasol plane 42
For a real eye-stopper, build "Hoopskirt" 46
air system, shop
An air supply for your shop 50
alarms, burglar
Prowler alarm 54
Let your telephone tattle on burglars 56
alarms, piggy bank
Piggy bank squeals on thief 62
alarms, power failure
Build a power-failure-alarm 64
alarms, temperature
Cold triggers this alarm 66
alphabets
Anyone can letter signs 68
alternators, auto
Getting to know your alternator 70
ammunition
Load your own shotshells 76
Blast away indoors with wax bullets 80
anchors, boat
Learn the ABCs of anchoring 84
Drift sock for fishermen 89
animal pin-ups
Animal plaques 90
antifreeze, auto
How permanent is permanent anti-freeze? 93
antique finishes
Antiquing furniture—old over new 97
antique guns
That antique gun—fortune or forgery? 100

appliances
When you buy a new appliance . . . 106
Ohm's law 109
aquaplane
Build a boat designed for fun 110
archery
Bag it with a bow 114
arc welding
Arc welding basics 118
attic remodeling
Studio bedroom in the attic 130
auto repair
Eight common car problems—and their solutions 132
Stalled? Here's how to get rolling again 137
You can do your own body repair 142
bait, fishing
When nothing else works, try worms 148
ball joints, auto
Bad ball joints are dangerous 150
band grinder
Build a band grinder for your shop 154
band sander
Band sander for your bench saw 157
bandsaws
Table enlarges your bandsaw 160
bandsaws, blades
Brazing fixture for bandsaw blades 162
Filing jig 163
banjos
Make your own banjo 164
barbecues
Gas-fired barbecue 169
"Old Smoky" barbecue 170
Hide a barbecue pit under your patio 172
Barbecue firemanship 173
bars
Throwaway bar for a one-night stand 174
Rolling patio bar 176
baseball
Pitching target 178
basements
Wet basement? Here's the solution 180
bass fiddle
Washtub bass fiddle carries the beat 186
bass fishing
What won't catch bass? 188
Project-a-plans 191

How to use your Encyclopedia

Browse. Glance through this volume, or any other volume of the Encyclopedia. Likely you will find the solution to a particular home-maintenance problem that has been bothering you, or a shop project so appealing that you will immediately head for your bench. Browsing not only is enjoyable, but is a source of ideas.

Seek specific information. Perhaps you want to find out how to cure that leak in your basement, how to keep the exterior paint from peeling, or how to tune and set the carburetor on your car.

Four reader aids, all cross-referenced, will enable you to find specific information:

1. *Alphabetical headings.* Located at the top of the page, these headings cover broad classifications of information. If you are looking for information on how to keep paint from peeling, for example, look up "Paints" alphabetically, then find the particular section dealing with peeling paint.

2. *Alphabetical cross-references.* These are shown in a box at the bottom of the page. Some material can logically be classified under more than one alphabetical heading, so if you don't find what you are seeking alphabetically (as described above), be sure to check the *alphabetical cross-references* at the bottom of the page; there you may find precisely the classification you are seeking. For example, you and your son decide to build a model airplane, and are looking for plans. You look up "Model airplanes" and find nothing under that alphabetical heading. However, if you glance at the bottom *of that same page* you will find an alphabetical cross-reference that reads: **model airplanes,** see airplane models.

3. *See also references.* These are shown at the end of many articles. They refer you to related articles which may also be of interest.

4. *Instant index.* Located at the end of Volume 16, it is thoroughly cross-referenced to help you find information under any heading.

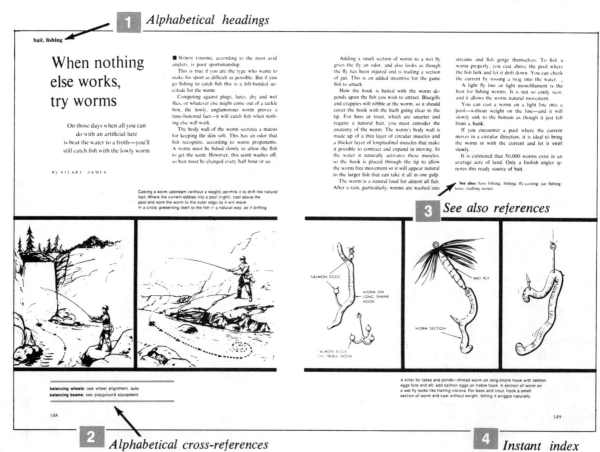

1 *Alphabetical headings*

3 *See also references*

2 *Alphabetical cross-references*

4 *Instant index*

Thorough sanding is one
of the hallmarks of the
master craftsman—that
all-important first step

Sanding from start to finish

BY W. CLYDE LAMMEY

■ GOOD FINISHING begins with good sanding. On new work sanding brings out the best in the wood. On old work which has been previously finished sanding should do two things: preserve the aged color of the wood and smooth the surface to take a new finish. Working from new-rough or old-rough is a repeat-step procedure, using sandpaper from coarse to fine through several successive steps. This applies to both hand and power sanding. In power-sanding new work you may produce an acceptable surface in three successive steps. In hand sanding it may take as many as five successive steps, using five grades of sandpaper, to end up with a surface of equal quality. Each time over must remove the "scratch" marks of the step preceding, as otherwise these marks, will show under any finish.

On old work preservation of the color, or pa-

tina, of fine woods usually is desirable. Take off the old finish, either transparent or opaque, with a wash-off type remover. Then sand lightly with a medium to fine grade paper and note results closely as you go. Don't use a hand scraper or power sander to remove the finish on old work when you wish to preserve the aged color. Finish with the finest grade of paper, normally 8-0 grade.

The best test you have of smoothness is simply

abdominal board: see exercise equipment
abrasive cut-off wheel: see cut-off wheel
absorbers, shock: see shock absorbers
accordion organ: see organ
accordion screen: see remodeling
accordion wall: see bedroom furniture

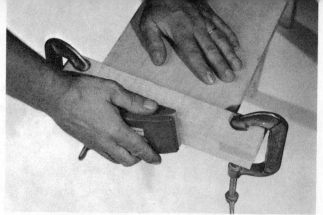

To sand end grain by hand, clamp waste strips to work as pictured. This not only keeps end square but prevents rounding edges. Or, use an unpadded block

Photo courtesy Behr-Manning

Pad sanders are of two types, orbital and straight-line, and are used mainly for the finish steps with the finer grades of sandpaper

"Shoeshine" sanding is usually best for rounding corners and sanding turnings. Method maintains desired radius and leaves smooth surface

Unpadded sanding block usually saves time and work on rough surfaces. It cuts down high spots, sands out hollows and leaves a true surface

to draw your forefinger lightly over the sanded surface diagonally or at right angles to the direction of sanding. Thus you can detect any minor depressions, or even slight roughness. Give these places, if any, a little more attention. But be careful not to cut through that old color acquired only by the aging of the wood.

New work can be handled a little more vigorously. If you are hand-sanding and you discover any slight ups and downs on the surface, make a special sanding block from a 5-in. length of 2 x 4. Cut the ends at an angle of 5 degrees or so, cut a strip of sandpaper to the exact width of the block and to such length that the ends will fold

up on the ends of the block where each can be attached with tacks. Don't pad with felt.

Purpose of such a block is to cut down the high spots, ridges and the like and level the surface the first time over. Use a uniform pressure, overlap each stroke about one fourth the width and be especially careful not to round the edges of the workpiece. Don't allow the block to overrun the edges more than about one-fourth its length or width. If there are knots in the surface, to be retained as a decorative feature of the grain, remember these usually are of a different texture, harder than the surrounding wood, causing the abrasive to cut somewhat slower. Such areas usually call for a few extra strokes in each sanding step to hold them flush. Keep a close watch when sanding certain softwoods having a coarse, flat grain. There may be especially soft areas which tend to cut down faster, producing a surface of low ridges and shallow hollows. Changing sanding strokes to a slight angle with the grain usually disposes of this problem. Keep a close check on progress with the finger-tip test.

Should the project you are working on be of

Something new in "sandpapering." Perforated sheet metal forms edges that cut in all directions. Sheet is self-cleaning, removes stock very fast

For boat-hull sanding there's nothing quite like a portable belt sander of husky size with a belt at least 3 in. wide. It saves hours of labor

Use a coarse grade of sandpaper to bare wood after removing old finish, except on old work where it is desirable to preserve age color, or patina. Use uniform pressure and don't allow block to tilt

With few exceptions sanding should be done with the grain, even though latter is at angle with workpiece

On open-grained woods, such as oak, sanding at a slight angle with grain will prevent enlarging pores

veneer construction, either plywood or solid-core type, either old or new, be especially careful not to over-run the edges and cut down to the core stock. On new work the veneers used are likely to be quite thin, usually only about $\frac{1}{28}$ in., and may have already been machine-sanded, so you haven't much of the veneer left for the finishing steps. On older work the veneers are usually thicker, but as a rule they've been sanded pretty thoroughly when prepared for finishing.

One disadvantage of the unpadded block is its tendency to score the work more deeply than will a padded block and also it may tilt and slightly ridge the work along the length of the strokes if you don't keep close tab on the uniformity of the pressure you are applying. But it does level the work the first time over, cuts down the more resistant areas, such as knots and vertical grain, and in the end it's a timesaver. After using an unpadded block the first time over most craftsmen go to the padded block (the bottom of the block padded with felt or other soft, flexible material) or they use a flexible rubber block such as supplied by manufacturers of sand-

Hand sanding from medium to fine grade is usually done with a felt-padded block unless surface is rough or ridged. Strokes should follow grain and overlap slightly as sanding progresses

Photo courtesy Behr-Manning

Flexible rubber sanding block is often preferred for sanding surfaces originally in good condition. Care must be taken to apply uniform pressure throughout the stroke, also to prevent block from tilting

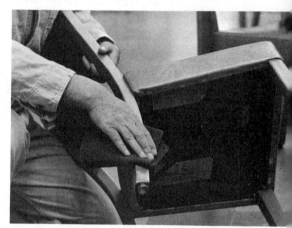

On square parts with rounded corners a nylon abrasive pad or fine steel wool often is used for that final finishing touch

paper. Some even prefer to wrap the sandpaper around a piece of thick, hard felt for the final finish sanding. But in using flexible blocks of any type one should keep in mind that they have a tendency to round the edges and corners of any workpiece which is narrower than the block. For such work, also sanding end grain, a small un-padded block is generally best, especially if the finished job calls for sharp, straight corners with no waves or wobbles.

As a rule blocks don't work well on any type of curved surface that must be hand-sanded. Some types of straight moldings can be sanded quite accurately with flexible blocks but on mold-ings having irregular or curved shapes such as those on scalloped edges, one generally finds it best to cut sandpaper into small squares, fold once over and use the thumb or forefinger as the "block." Such a simple method is quite effective and much faster than one might suppose. Wear a glove or finger cot if there's much of this kind of thing to do.

The "shoeshine" method of sanding usually works best on turnings, either in the lathe im-mediately after turning to finish size or with the workpiece held in a vise, or on turnings already assembled, as in old pieces or unfinished furni-ture. Just tear or cut strips of cloth-backed abra-sive from ½ to 1 in. wide, pass the strip around the work and pull on the ends in a back-and-

forth stroke. When sanding in this fashion in the lathe operate the machine at a slower speed and keep the abrasive strip moving back and forth and simultaneously along the work to prevent undue heating and discoloration of the wood. As a rule you use only the medium to fine grades of abrasives in shoeshine sanding, but you use descending grades from medium to fine to eliminate scratches as you go.

Only the bulb and vase shapes and the con-cavities of turnings should be sanded by the shoeshine method. Don't pass the strip over nar-row beads as it tends to flatten them; use in-stead a fine V-file or 3-cornered file, touching it lightly to the work in a back-and-forth stroke and rolling it simultaneously to retain the curva-ture of the bead. In many cases a strip of sand-paper wrapped around a dowel of small diameter

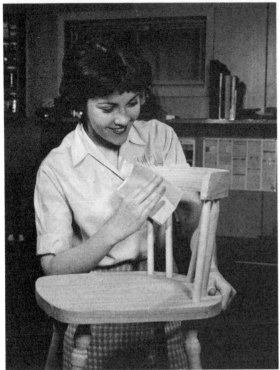

For hand-sanding curves of short radius, a sheet of sandpaper folded several times is quite effective. Flexibility of folded "pad" allows it to follow contour of surface without digging in or scoring too deeply

Photo courtesy Behr-Manning

Disc sander of swiveling type makes short work of truing a butt joint such as that pictured. Disc cuts very fast and leaves a smooth, swirl-free surface. Use only light, uniform pressure

is handy for getting into flutes, round-bottom cuts, also on straight moldings where short-radius shapes are involved. Spread glue on the dowel and wrap the sandpaper strip diagonally with the meeting edges of the strip butted, not overlapped.

how to clean sandpaper

Sometimes there's trouble with the finer grades of paper clogging or glazing, especially on woods of resinous content, or on "oily" woods such as teak. Usually you can clean the abrading surface effectively with a brush having metal bristles; a brush of the type used for cleaning suede shoes is just the thing. When sanding old work preparatory to refinishing, residues of old fillers may tend to glaze the sandpaper and resist cleaning with the brush. When this problem develops just spill a little turpentine onto the work surface. This will usually cut the glaze and "re-sharpen" the abrasive. The turps will evaporate quickly and won't discolor the wood, but one should keep in mind that turpentine is rather highly flammable, that there is always some hazard in its use. Move the job outdoors when possible or have your home fire extinguisher handy. And don't smoke.

Once the initial rough sanding has been finished go to a finer grade of sandpaper, a grade

that will remove the scratch marks of the first, and then continue the step-by-step procedure, going to a finer grade of abrasive each time, until the finger test turns up a glass-smoothness over the entire surface. Many craftsmen dampen the sanded surface after initial sandings from coarse to medium grades of sandpaper. Dampening the surface raises the grain, causes surface fibers to stand vertically, or near vertically. In this position they are easily cut off in the next step. On very fine work this procedure is often carried through several steps, to properly condition the wood for a "piano" finish.

sanding by machine

Machine sanding with a portable electric sander is much the same thing except that it's faster and requires a little closer attention to control of the tool. Generally a portable belt sander is best for average work on flat surfaces, one having a 3-in., or wider, belt being somewhat easier to control when using fast cutting abrasives in the coarser grades. If the surface to be sanded is in reasonably good condition, no digs, gouges, dips, or ridges, then use of a coarse-grade abrasive may not be necessary. Make sure that the belt you use tracks properly when in place on the sander and be sure to check to see that it's running in the right direction. All sander

Photos courtesy Minn. Mining & Mfg. Co.

Nylon abrasive pad works on either metal or wood with equal effectiveness. Just the thing for cleaning and "shining" up aluminum canoes, boat brasswork, door kick plates, also metal turnings. Fold or cut the nylon pad to a convenient size and use as you would sandpaper

belts are marked with an arrow indicating the direction they are to be run.

Start the sander before lowering it onto the surface to be sanded and keep it moving after contact in slow, back-and-forth strokes much the same as in hand sanding, the strokes overlapping slightly and working either to right or left. Don't allow the unit to stop on the surface, even for an instant, and be especially careful to prevent it from tipping sidewise. If the unit is stopped momentarily, or permitted to tilt slightly, the coarser-grade abrasives can cut through thin veneers in the wink of an eye, or form a depression that's difficult to sand out. Just as in hand sanding with a block, be doubly alert to avoid over-running the edges and ends of the work.

Don't bear down on a belt sander. Usually the weight of the unit is sufficient to keep the belt cutting freely. If it seems necessary to urge it a little, as in sanding end grain perhaps, bear down only very lightly and keep close watch of results. Bearing down heavily may cause the belt to heat unduly and glaze, thereby greatly reducing its efficiency. Once the surface has been

leveled satisfactorily—use that finger test again —change to a finer grade belt, continuing to step down until you finish with the finest belt.

Pad sanders are of two types, the terms, or names, used referring to the action of the pad. In the orbital type the pad moves in a circular stroke. On the second type known as the straight-line sander the pad moves in a straight, back-and-forth stroke. On some later-model pad sanders the stroke can be changed from straight to orbital as desired. Pad sanders are generally used for the finishing steps with fine-grade abrasives as they are capable of sanding to a very smooth surface.

In general, stance is of some importance in both hand and machine sanding. Some prefer to stand at the side of the work when hand sanding as they can keep pressure and stroke more uniform on a relatively large surface. Working with a portable belt sander can be done in much the same position. Hand pressure is not necessary with the power unit, leaving the hands free to control direction and limits of the stroke. On some woods, especially those with a coarse, open grain, you'll get a somewhat smoother job by directing the strokes slightly diagonal to the grain through all the steps from coarse to fine. This will be true of both hand and power sanding. Also, it's advisable to do a little experimenting to determine the grades of sandpaper that do the best job from start to finish on a given wood.

See also: cut-off wheel; finishes, removing; floor finishing; grinding; tumbling machines.

Your memo pad and pencil won't wander when you need them in the shop if you keep them together with a large paper clamp. Any pencil or marker with a pocket clip can be snapped onto the clamp's thumbpiece. Hang the clip from a cup hook screwed into your toolboard or bench.

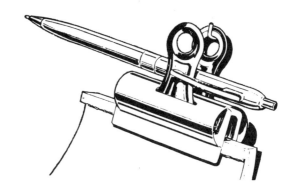

A child's felt markers are easy to make from large plastic drinking straws. Insert a felt tip (oilcup wicking is ideal) in the straw, and fill the straw with marking ink. Then bend back the end of the straw and secure it with tape.

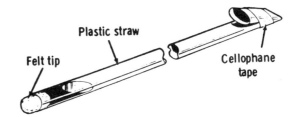

Plastic straw

Felt tip

Cellophane tape

A tiny twist drill can be straightened quickly if you chuck it in a hand drill and then snug a metal-jaw vise on it just enough so that it still turns. Grasp the drill firmly enough to put a little side pressure on the bit and crank it slowly.

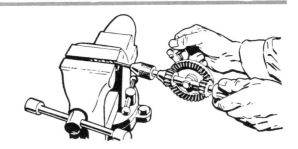

Thermostat squint is a common winter complaint. The markings on the temperature scale are often too small to be read easily. One solution is to add an inexpensive plastic magnifier. Remove the thermostat cover and drill a hole in it. Pass a self-tapping screw through the magnifier and into the hole. Don't allow the screw to protrude so far inside that it interferes with the mechanism.

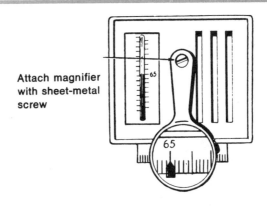

Attach magnifier with sheet-metal screw

By pocketing your fishhooks and sinkers, you can keep them handy no matter how far you roam from your tackle box. Use an empty shotgun shell to protect you and your clothing. Slip the sinkers inside the shell and cap the end with a cork. Now embed the points of the hooks firmly in the cork.

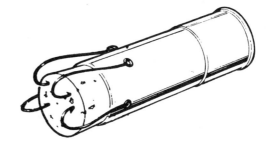

Wrap yourself in quiet

Today's homes are plagued with
new noises—but even in your present
home, you can use new soundproofing
techniques to silence them,
once you know the three ways
that noise spreads through the house

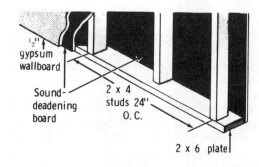

New partitions become sound barriers when 2 x 4s
are staggered so wall faces won't have studs in common.
The two face panels cut the airborne sound

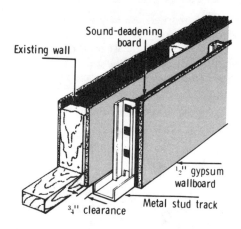

A sound barrier can be erected alongside an existing partition without much loss of floor space.
One method uses metal studs erected in a special track

Panel board drinks noise like a sponge soaks up water,
and lets you erect effective sound barriers.
After nailing to studs, apply wallboard with adhesive

additions, home: see home additions
adhesives: see glues
adult games: see games, adult

Stop airborne noise

■ PROGRESS! Think what the modern home can
offer at the flick of a switch: the swelling burst
of a symphony orchestra—in higher "fi" than
you'd hear in a concert hall . . . the angry screech
of a power saw biting through wood . . . the in-
sistent buzz of appliances that turns the kitchen
into a wasps' nest. However necessary (or even
pleasant) such sounds may be to the person
causing them, mixed together they spell *noise*.

Noise sweeps through your house in three
main ways, the most common of which is *airborne transmission*. Sound waves spread out
from their source like ripples from a stone tossed
in a quiet pond. When they strike hard surfaces,
they reverberate back, but also set the wall surface vibrating. The opposite wall-face vibrates
to match—like the skins of a drum—and thus
the sound moves right on through the wall.

Acoustical ceilings are effective in absorbing sound within a room but do little to stop passage to adjacent rooms. For that, apply tile over suspended gypsum board or use foil-backed tile

Meanwhile, the sound *within* the source room is amplified by being reflected back and forth between hard surfaces, extending its life and reinforcing itself. This is *reverberation* sound. Absorbent surfaces, such as rugs, drapes, upholstered furniture, soak up sound like a blotter, greatly reducing this multiple bounce. You've had a good demonstration of what such materials can do if you've ever moved into an unfurnished house or apartment. Remember how the bare walls and floor sent sounds ricocheting like bullets from a machine gun fired in a steel-plated cell? Once your soft, absorbent materials were brought in, however, these sound "bullets" had no "steel plate" to ricochet from; instead, when they struck the drapes or rug, they *sank in.* That's the principle behind acoustical material such as perforated ceiling tile. Those holes are noise traps that keep many of the sound waves from bouncing back at you. To offer effective traps, however, such material must be *permeable,* so sound can leak on through. That's why acoustical materials have little effect on sound *transmission* from one room to another.

To halt this, you must erect a sound *barrier,* and sound-deadening board is designed for this purpose. It's a special ½-in.-thick insulation-type wallboard made from wood fibers, and comes in panels 4 ft. wide and 8 or 9 ft. tall. When nailed to studs with a layer of ½- or ⅝-in. gypsum board cemented on top, it creates the best sound barrier you can wrap a room in. But just like a *vapor* barrier, it must be continuous,

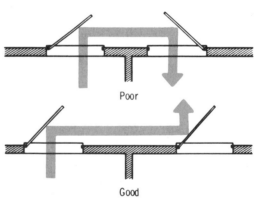

Poor

Good

Careless details can wreck any sound-proofing system. No matter how effective a barrier you have between rooms, close-spaced casement windows opening toward each other (top) will provide an easy detour. But when they open parallel, the second may act as a baffle to bounce sound away from the house. Caulked and weather-stripped windows and doors reduce airborne transmission. No sound barrier should be pierced unnecessarily: insert units such as electrical outlets, heat ducts or medicine cabinets should not be placed back-to-back in the same stud bay, but spaced apart as shown in sketch at left with as few "leaks" as possible. A 1-sq.-in. hole in a plain nonsoundproofed wall will let through as much noise as nearly 100 sq. ft. of the wall itself. So don't try to create a sound barrier with a loose-fitting hollow door in the wall!

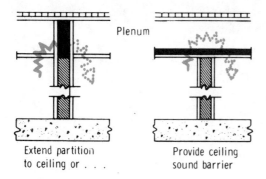

Plenum

Extend partition to ceiling or . . .

Provide ceiling sound barrier

To keep noise from leap-frogging to the next room, either run partitions all the way up to the underside of the floor (as in the left sketch above and the photo at the right) or create a barrier above the ceiling by applying tile over sound-deadening board. Note in the photo that both the sound-deadening and gypsum board layers are notched up between the joists

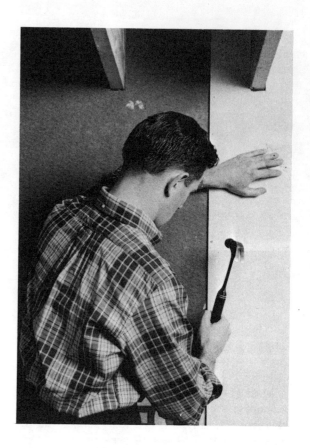

Stop structure-borne noise

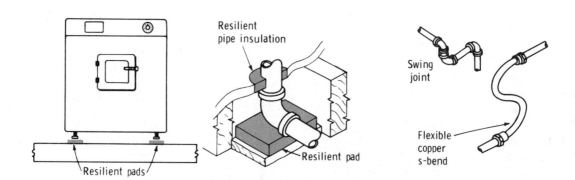

Resilient pipe insulation

Resilient pad

Resilient pads

Swing joint

Flexible copper s-bend

Some noise sources transmit sound directly to the structure of the house. Mount machines such as washers and pumps on pads (left) to absorb vibrations. Pad points where pipes contact framing, and put expansion joints in copper hot water pipes

THE SECOND WAY noise travels from room to room is through the structural members of the house—the studs and joists. As an example of this type of sound transmission, just remember how tenants in old apartment buildings used to rap on radiators to tell the furnace room —many floors below—that they wanted more heat.

The way sound travels along a pipe—or a structural member—presents one of the biggest problems in soundproofing. Obviously you have to rest walls solidly on floors—you can't isolate one from the other with a spongy sound trap. But there *are* ways to isolate noise sources *from* the structure, and a few of these are shown on the previous page. Resilient material between pipe fittings and their structural supports lets the pipe move without creaking or binding. Pumps, washers and air conditioners should not only float free of their support on rubber or cork pads, but should be tied into water lines with a section of flexible piping. Rooms separated by a sound barrier should not share a heating duct.

These are details. Even more important in stopping structural transmission are the basic techniques of *constructing* sound barriers. Staggered studs isolate the two faces of a partition wall so that sound vibrations can't pass directly from member to member. And ceilings can be suspended below floor joists so as not to "pass along" structure-borne sound. Special resilient clips let furring strips "float" out of contact with the joists they're hung from, creating a structural gap (as shown in the sketch). A floating ceiling provides double sound protection.

Stop impact noise

EVER WAIT beneath a bedroom for the person up there to drop that other shoe? Here's an example of a home's third noise problem: *impact* sound. It's that noise that jabs at you when a floor or wall in an adjacent room is struck or a door is slammed. Actually, it's another type of structure-borne noise, but since it's mainly concerned with floor-through-ceiling transmission, the special silencing techniques demand a separate category.

The most common impact irritants are footsteps or furniture scraping on the floor above you. The most obvious means of dampening such sound is at the source: by cushioning the floor with carpet or resilient flooring. But the floor surface can also be isolated from the supporting structure (the joists, or the concrete slab in modern apartment construction) by sandwiching sound-deadening board between the subfloor and finish flooring. Or you can attack the problem from the opposite side by isolating the ceiling— that is, suspending it on either resilient clips, as shown below, or on independent joists. Where access to the joist spaces is available, you can further dampen both impact and airborne noise by stapling insulation across them, as shown.

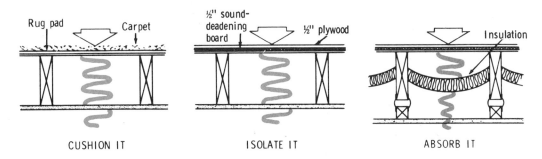

CUSHION IT   ISOLATE IT   ABSORB IT

Three ways to dampen overhead noise are: (left) with a resilient floor covering; (center) with a sound barrier to isolate finish floor from joists; and (right) with a porous blanket between joists and "floating" ceiling

Caging a roaring workshop

CERTAIN AREAS of the house are a noise-nuisance by nature: the kitchen and bath, the playroom, and—worst of all, especially if you have power tools—the basement workshop. Here, experts in acoustics show how sound-deadening board used in conjunction with an acoustical ceiling can tame this noisiest corner of the average home. The basic ideas illustrated here can be adapted to other locations. Keep in mind that you are trying to absorb noise and also to prevent its transmission.

As the photo shows, the "cage" is the staggered-stud framing we've already discussed, double-faced with sound-deadening board and gypsum wallboard, each ½-in. thick. The joints of these board layers must never align. Attach the

The sound from these power tools will no longer have the run of the house. The cage that will confine their snarls is of 2 x 4 studs, staggered 24 in. o.c.

wrap yourself in silence, continued

Sound barrier walls must be thorough. Joints of the first layer are offset from those of the second; this calls for opposite L-shapes around the doorway

sound-deadening panels vertically, with nails spaced 24 in. o.c. along the edges. Stagger the joints on opposite sides of the framing. Now attach the wall board panels with 8d coated nails spaced 12 in. o.c. and driven through the sound-deadening layer and into the studs. (An alternate method is to *cement* the wallboard in place by applying vertical stripes of laminating compound to the face of the sound board.) Stagger the wallboard joints on opposite sides of the wall, and offset them 24 in. from the sound board joints.

Finish all the wallboard joints with joint compound and perforated tape. Now, seal all joints between the new partitions and the floor and sidewalls with ordinary calking, and calk also around any outlets or pipes that pierce the wall.

The floating ceiling cross-sectioned above right is an automatic system that's easier to install than it looks. You tack furring strips temporarily along the bottom edges of the joists—*before* applying the finish wallboard layer inside the room. Next, fit the special clips over the furring and nail one leg to each side of the joist. The spacing is determined by the joist spacing. For joists 16 in. o.c., you'll need clips only every 24 in., but if the joists are 24 in. o.c., clips should be 20 in. apart. After applying them, remove the temporary nails from the furring and

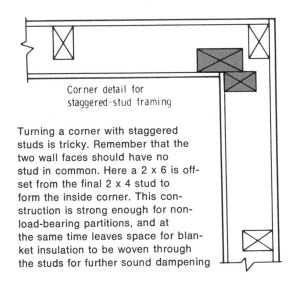

Corner detail for
staggered-stud framing

Turning a corner with staggered studs is tricky. Remember that the two wall faces should have no stud in common. Here a 2 x 6 is off-set from the final 2 x 4 stud to form the inside corner. This construction is strong enough for non-load-bearing partitions, and at the same time leaves space for blanket insulation to be woven through the studs for further sound dampening

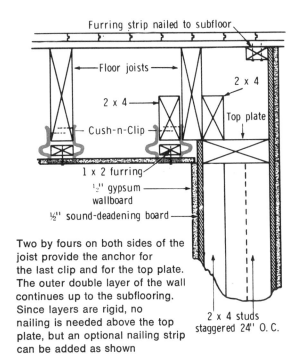

Furring strip nailed to subfloor

Floor joists

2 x 4

2 x 4

Top plate

Cush-n-Clip

1 x 2 furring

½" gypsum wallboard

½" sound-deadening board

2 x 4 studs staggered 24" O. C.

Two by fours on both sides of the joist provide the anchor for the last clip and for the top plate. The outer double layer of the wall continues up to the subflooring. Since layers are rigid, no nailing is needed above the top plate, but an optional nailing strip can be added as shown

nail ½-in. gypsum wallboard to the strips with gypsum nails 6 in. o.c. (Nails can't be more than ⅛ in. longer than combined thickness of board and furring.) The perimeter of the wallboard ceiling should stop about ⅛ in. short of the face of the sound board.

Now apply your wallboard facing, cutting the panels short enough to fit between floor and floating ceiling without forcing. Apply molding at the ceiling line to finish the job.

Now: switch on those growling, screeching beasts you've caged. Sound louder than ever? That's because much less noise is *escaping* to adjacent areas. To control this confined sound, you may want to add acoustical tile to the wallboard ceiling. If so, install these before you add that inner gypsum layer.

The point where the wall joins the floor should be sealed with caulking before the base molding is nailed through to the sole plate. Don't leave gaps

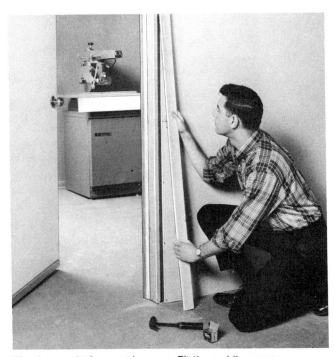

The door and trim must be snug. Fit the molding carefully to seal cracks between the frame and the wall. The retractable weatherstrip drops as the door closes

19

Sealing a ceiling

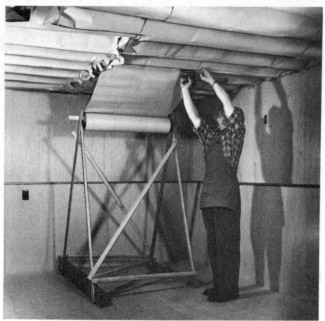

One man can apply rolled building felt if you make a rough rack of 1 x 2s to push across the room. The roll spins on the top bar

wrap yourself in silence, continued

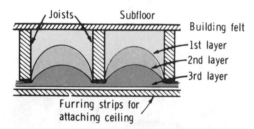

The final layer of felt is stretched flat across the bottoms of the joists, then standard furring is added at right angles to joists or along their edges

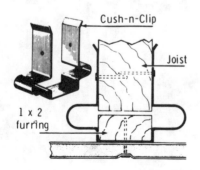

MOST PEOPLE'S idea of "sound treating" a ceiling is to apply acoustical tile. But as we've pointed out, this material is designed to dampen noise originating *within* the room, not to prevent passage upward *from* the room, or downward from a noisy room overhead. Yet most ceiling treatments are concerned with keeping sound that originates in downstairs areas, such as rumpus rooms or workshops, from surging up into the living or bedrooms above.

One method of "sealing ceilings" against sound passage was discussed previously, and is further illustrated in the sketch and the photo below. A different treatment is demonstrated at left. Home remodelers have found that curved layers of building felt between overhead joists cut down considerably on sound transmission. The heavier the paper and the more layers of trapped air, the more effective the treatment. The first strip is merely unrolled across the joists and bellied up into each bay until the apex of the curve is within an inch or two of the subfloor. Staples into the joists hold the scalloped shape. The next layer is bellied less deep, to leave an air pocket between it and the first—and so on. At cross-braces and walls, lap, clip, fold and staple the felt to create a seal. After furring is nailed over the flat final layer, a finish ceiling of wallboard or tile can be added for a neat, low-cost way to put the lid on basement noise.

See also: building; insulation.

Special clips that "float" acoustical ceilings come in two sizes: for standard 1⅝-in. joists and for 3¼-in. double joists. They are available from building supply dealers. When wallboard is nailed to the furring, as shown in the photo, it drops into suspension by its own weight, creating a gap between the furring and joist

An easy-grip switch for a desk lamp is made by pushing a wedge-type pencil eraser over the regular switch.

Jar rubbers taped to the window sill make excellent mats for small potted plants.

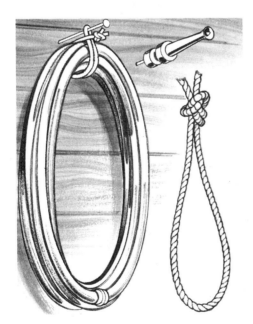

Form a loop in a 20-in. length of cord, and use this to hang your hose from a nail.

Your teapot spout can be made drip-proof if you wrap it with a pipe cleaner just below the tip.

Build an ancient window harp

BY DENNIS D. DOROGI

■ ALMOST UNKNOWN TODAY, the aeolian harp works on a principle that was familiar as far back as biblical times. It is recorded that King David was fond of hanging his harp over his bed when retiring so that he would be lulled to deep slumber by the sound produced as the night breezes played lightly over the strings, setting up varying patterns of tuneful vibration.

Basically, the harp illustrated on these pages consists of a long narrow sound box over which a dozen nylon guitar strings are stretched—four Gs, four Bs and four Es. The strings are attached to headless nails at one end and tuning pins at the other. These pins are designed for use in auto-harps and zithers, and can be ordered at most music stores. Order a tuning wrench at the same time, since you will need one to turn the pins. If desired, brass screws, drilled crosswise to hold the strings, may be substituted for the pins. All strings should be tuned to the same note, usually a low G on the musical scale.

The length of the sound box is not important, so the instrument can be designed to fit any window of your house. Simply place the harp on the sill and lower the window so that it rests on the cover, holding the instrument firmly in position. You will find that the raised cover directs a strong air current over the harp strings, producing an ethereal sound that varies with the intensity of the wind.

See also: banjo; bass fiddle; guitars; organ; pianos.

African violets: see plant stand

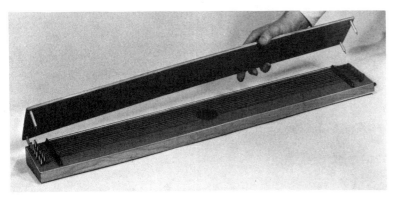

The removable cover directs wind over the box's surface. Pins in the posts fit into holes

The strings are attached at one end to headless nails driven into the block

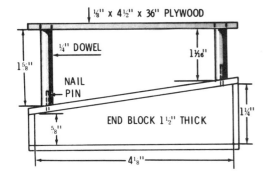

¹⁄₈" x 4¹⁄₂" x 36" PLYWOOD

¹⁄₄" DOWEL

1¹¹⁄₁₆"

1⁵⁄₈"

NAIL
PIN

END BLOCK 1¹⁄₂" THICK

1¹⁄₄"

⁵⁄₈"

4¹⁄₈"

At the other end the strings are held by tuning pins, which can be adjusted

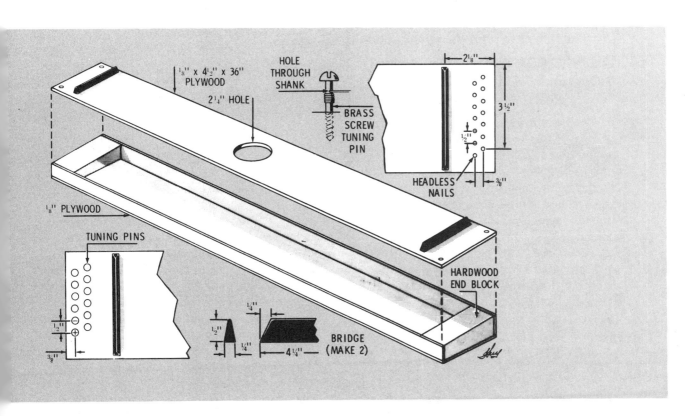

¹⁄₈" x 4¹⁄₂" x 36" PLYWOOD

2¹⁄₄" HOLE

HOLE THROUGH SHANK

BRASS SCREW TUNING PIN

2¹⁄₈"

3¹⁄₂"

¹⁄₂"

HEADLESS NAILS

³⁄₈"

¹⁄₈" PLYWOOD

TUNING PINS

¹⁄₂"

³⁄₈"

HARDWOOD END BLOCK

¹⁄₄"

¹⁄₂"

¹⁄₄"

4¹⁄₄"

BRIDGE (MAKE 2)

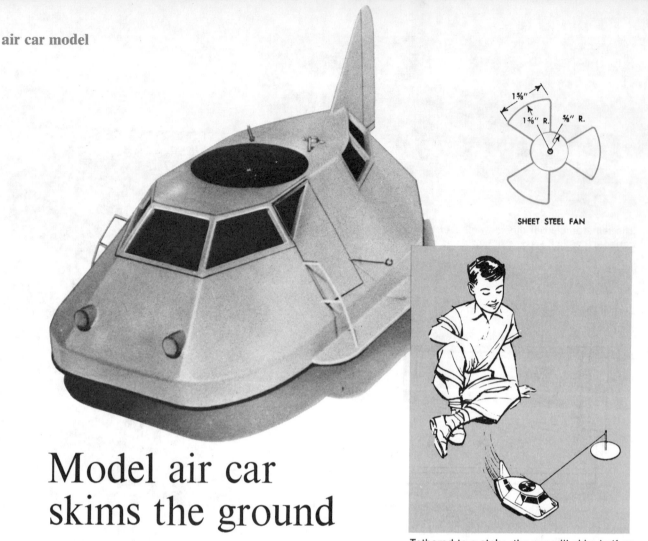

SHEET STEEL FAN

Tethered to a stake, the car will skim half an inch or so off the ground, around and around until it runs out of fuel

Model air car skims the ground

BY ROY L. CLOUGH, JR.

Working model of a ground-effect
vehicle rides on a cushion of air
from a model-airplane engine

■ WITH A hollow whistling note audible over the whine of its tiny engine, this advanced working model of a ground-effect vehicle skims across the floor supported on a cushion of air. What makes it go?

Air is supplied by a prop to a peripheral slot which produces a high-speed wall of air around the edge of the model to retain the lift. A separate propulsion-system tube bleeds off air for reactive propulsion—from the blower section, not the skirt. Supporting pressure is not reduced —a major fault of ground-effect vehicles which

propel by dumping air pressure and lifting the skirt on the opposite side from the desired direction of travel. Stabilizers on each side act somewhat like the dihedralled wings of an airplane— if the model tilts to either side, air pressure escaping from the skirt builds up under the vane and returns it to even keel. The result is a model which can buzz along at a good clip on any level surface with a minimum of sideslip due to minor irregularities on the surface. Attached to a tether it will whizz merrily around in a circle until the fuel runs out. It rides a half inch or so off the floor even when running free. Any small airplane engine can be used to power it. If you use the engine installed in the original model, which is

air cleaners, auto: see filters, auto

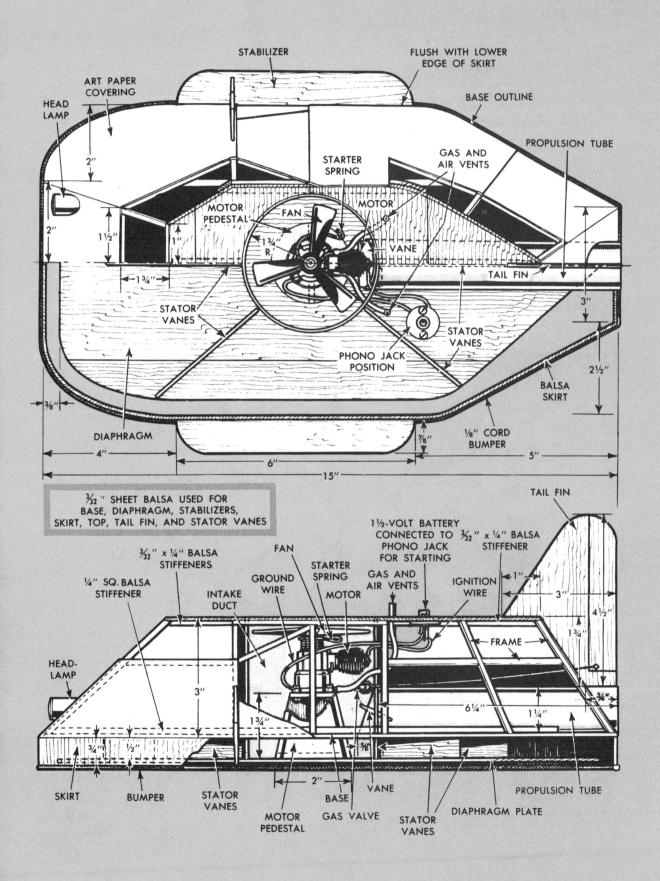

STABILIZER

FLUSH WITH LOWER
EDGE OF SKIRT

BASE OUTLINE

ART PAPER
COVERING

HEAD
LAMP

2"

STARTER
SPRING

GAS AND
AIR VENTS

PROPULSION TUBE

MOTOR
PEDESTAL

FAN

MOTOR

2"

1½"

1"

1¾"
R.

VANE

TAIL FIN

3"

1¾"

STATOR
VANES

STATOR
VANES

PHONO JACK
POSITION

2½"

BALSA
SKIRT

3⁄8"

DIAPHRAGM

⅛" CORD
BUMPER

7⁄8"

4"

6"

5"

15"

3⁄32" SHEET BALSA USED FOR
BASE, DIAPHRAGM, STABILIZERS,
SKIRT, TOP, TAIL FIN, AND STATOR VANES

TAIL FIN

3⁄32" x ¼" BALSA
STIFFENERS

FAN

1½-VOLT BATTERY
CONNECTED TO
PHONO JACK
FOR STARTING

3⁄32" x ¼" BALSA
STIFFENER

¼" SQ. BALSA
STIFFENER

INTAKE
DUCT

GROUND
WIRE

STARTER
SPRING

MOTOR

GAS AND
AIR VENTS

IGNITION
WIRE

1"

3"

FRAME

4½"

1¾"

HEAD-
LAMP

3"

1¾"

6¼"

1¼"

¾"

¾"

½"

3⁄8"

2"

SKIRT

BUMPER

STATOR
VANES

MOTOR
PEDESTAL

BASE

GAS VALVE

VANE

STATOR
VANES

DIAPHRAGM PLATE

PROPULSION TUBE

25

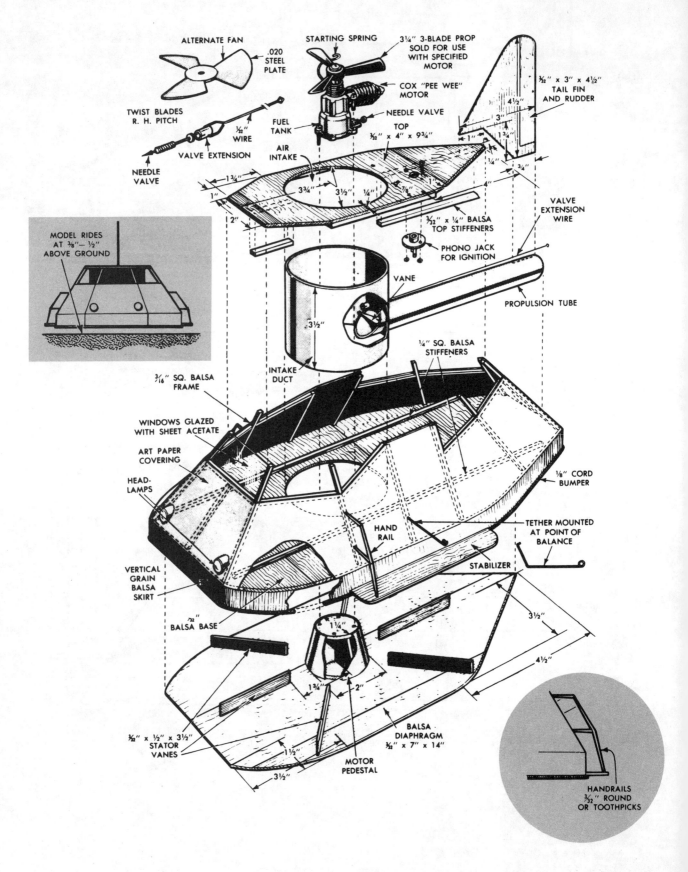

ALTERNATE FAN

.020 STEEL PLATE

TWIST BLADES R. H. PITCH

NEEDLE VALVE

VALVE EXTENSION

$\frac{1}{32}$" WIRE

STARTING SPRING

3¼" 3-BLADE PROP SOLD FOR USE WITH SPECIFIED MOTOR

COX "PEE WEE" MOTOR

FUEL TANK

AIR INTAKE

NEEDLE VALVE

TOP $\frac{3}{32}$" x 4" x 9¾"

$\frac{3}{32}$" x 3" x 4½" TAIL FIN AND RUDDER

4½"

3"

1¾"

1"

¼"

¾"

1¾"

1"

3¾"

3½"

¼"

$\frac{7}{8}$"

4"

$\frac{3}{32}$" x ¼" BALSA TOP STIFFENERS

2"

VALVE EXTENSION WIRE

MODEL RIDES AT $\frac{3}{8}$"—½" ABOVE GROUND

PHONO JACK FOR IGNITION

VANE

PROPULSION TUBE

3½"

¼" SQ. BALSA STIFFENERS

INTAKE DUCT

$\frac{7}{16}$" SQ. BALSA FRAME

WINDOWS GLAZED WITH SHEET ACETATE

ART PAPER COVERING

HEAD-LAMPS

$\frac{1}{8}$" CORD BUMPER

HAND RAIL

TETHER MOUNTED AT POINT OF BALANCE

STABILIZER

VERTICAL GRAIN BALSA SKIRT

3½"

$\frac{7}{32}$" BALSA BASE

4½"

$\frac{3}{32}$" x ½" x 3½" STATOR VANES

1¼"

1¾"

2"

1½"

3½"

MOTOR PEDESTAL

BALSA DIAPHRAGM $\frac{3}{32}$" x 7" x 14"

HANDRAILS $\frac{3}{32}$" ROUND OR TOOTHPICKS

26

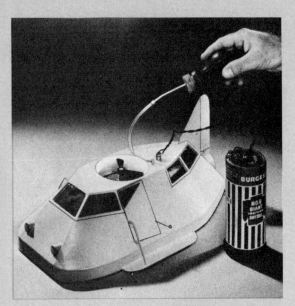

A squeeze bulb feeds fuel through the plastic fuel line connected to the tank. The dry cell plugs into the phono jack

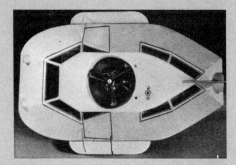

Top and rear views above and below show the engine mounted in the intake duct and the propulsion tube outlet at the rear. Note the wire hook on the door for tethering

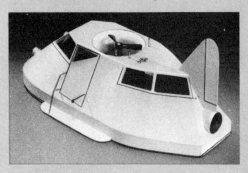

supplied with a three-blade prop, you won't have to make a prop of sheet metal, a pattern of which is given. If the engine is new, break it in by running on a test stand for 15 or 20 minutes.

First study the cutaway drawings given to become familiar with the various parts. Then begin construction by making up the base, top and diaphragm plate from edge-glued 3/32-in. balsa sheet. Use stiffeners where shown and allow to dry on a flat surface. Make up the 3½-in. intake duct from art paper and use this as the first structural member to hold the top and base together. When dry, add the 3/16-in. uprights which form the supports for the side covering. Next install the paper propulsion tube. Note the vane to direct airflow within it.

The skirt is vertical grained 3/32-in. stock glued around the bottom edge of the base. Use basswood or balsawood and there will be no difficulty in making the bends. Cover the framework of the car body with art paper, one section at a time, beginning at the rear. Add dummy headlights and fin, stabilizing vanes and handrails. Windows may be glazed with sheet acetate or left open. Finally turn the model over and install stator vanes. Coat the interior with at least two coats of hot fuelproof dope (clear). Dope the exterior in your favorite color. The original was

painted light blue outside, fire red inside.

Make up the engine pedestal, mount the engine and cement the pedestal to the diaphragm plate. Three coats of clear hot fuelproof dope are advisable here. Attach leadout wires to the glow plug. Cut out a 3¼-in. disk of cardboard and use this as a guide in centering the engine. Actual installation is made by cementing the diaphragm plate to the stators. Use a slow-drying cement to allow time to even up the slot around the skirt and center the engine shaft.

Run out the fuel filler tubes and engine leadout wires and make up a needle valve extension shaft. The glow-plug wires lead to a phonograph jack—a great convenience in starting. A recoil spring starter is a must and is installed before the prop.

A length of ⅛-in. cord is cemented around the skirt as a buffer. (A round shoestring works very nicely.) Suspend the model by the engine shaft and balance it so that it hangs evenly. Small bits of solder, coated with cement and dropped inside the body on the light side or end will do the trick. If tethered operation is desired, cement a wire hook through the covering to the upright on the center line.

See also: airplane models; glider model; gyroplane model; jet plane model.

27

How to buy a good air conditioner

Knowing what to look for is half the job in buying a good air conditioner. Here's a basic guide,

along with a handy estimating chart to give you a head start

BY GORDON L. WILLIAMS

■ THE BEST TIME to buy an air conditioner is after August 1, when prices drop, but before you go shopping anytime, consider these points about the unit:

1. **Size.** The British Thermal Unit is the stand-ard. The more BTUs, the greater the cooling power. Measure the area you want cooled, then use the chart on page 31 to find the size you need. Remember, too small a unit won't do the cooling job; too large a unit won't dehumidify.

2. **Voltage.** Units under 8500 BTUs can go on a 115-volt line; anything larger will need 220 volts.

3. **Amps.** You'll avoid overloads and be able

Louvers come in all types, shapes and sizes. Make sure they will move vertically and horizontally and can be moved individually to send air in several different directions at once

EFFECTIVE COOLING

WINDOW CAN BE CLOSED
FOR CLEANING
WITH UNIT IN PLACE

Controls are mounted in a number of places. Pull knobs to see if they are sturdy, that they won't come off in your hand. Make sure controls for window units extend out far enough so that a lowered blind will not block them. Check click stops for audible, positive action

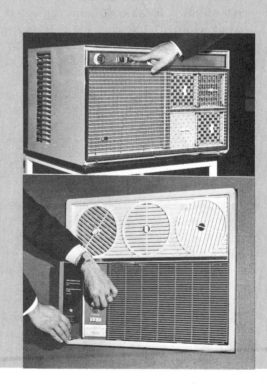

air conditioners

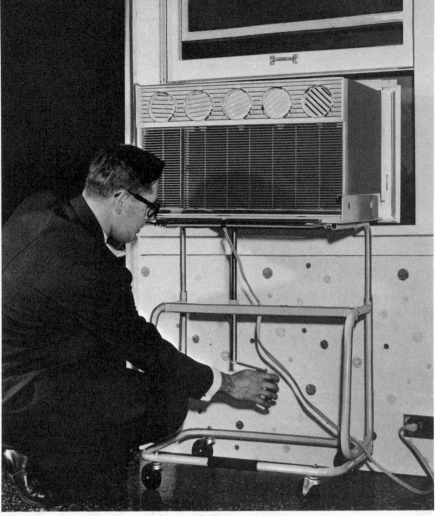

Portable cooler, rolled from window to window and room to room,
requires no installation, but usually lacks top cooling power

buying an air conditioner, continued

to use the more efficient 10, 12, or 15-amp. units if you run the conditioner on a separate circuit. Otherwise, you'll have to stick with a unit of 7.5 amps. or less.

4. Installation. You'll have the widest choice of models with a window installation, and it is cheaper. However, you can't mount a conditioner in every window; some windows can't be closed with the unit in place, and window units frequently must be removed in winter or will require an extra-cost cover. Portables rarely match the cooling power of a permanent installation.

5. Dimensions. Measure the height, width and depth of the spot where you want to install the conditioner. Units vary in size.

Which make is best? To be safe:

—Check with a dealer you trust or shop two or three stores.

—Stick with well-known brand names.

Now you're ready to buy. If you want to set a spending limit, tell it to the salesman and remember that your limit must include the cost of the unit, installation (if you're not installing

it yourself) plus any rewiring or structural changes.

Complete this check-list before choosing:

1. If the BTU rating isn't stamped on the unit, insist on seeing the manufacturer's specification sheet.

2. Listen to the unit at all speeds. If it sounds unduly loud in the store, it will sound louder in the bedroom.

3. Controls should be readily accessible, legible and easy to understand. Knobs should be sturdy and secure. You should be able to reach all controls without much bending or fumbling.

4. The unit should distribute air evenly over a wide area, without strong drafts. You should be able to adjust louvers individually, both horizontally and vertically, so that air can be aimed in several different directions at once.

5. Better air conditioners offer at least two operating speeds—a high for normal cooling, a low for nighttime use, plus, occasionally, a third speed for superfast cooling. The unit should have at least two speeds.

6. Is the thermostat adjustable? Some can't

30

Filters should be easy to remove without the use of tools or the need for removing control knobs

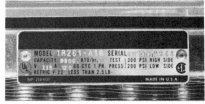

BTU rating should be stamped on the unit along with the amp and voltage rating

be adjusted; others offer up to 10 or 12 temperature-control settings. There should be at least two adjustments.

7. Any conditioner should ventilate a room or exhaust stale air, though not necessarily both. Don't buy a unit which can do neither as you will lose a major benefit of air conditioning.

8. Both the replaceable glass-wool filter or the metal mesh or plastic permanent type are about equally effective. But find out how often a replaceable filter must be replaced and how much a replacement costs. If it's a permanent filter, is it easy to remove and replace and, above all, is it washable? You should be able to remove filters without using tools or having to remove control knobs.

9. Better units tackle the rust problem by using metal parts made of aluminum, plastic, or galvanized steel, the metals usually being coated with baked-on enamel. To find if metal parts are rustproof, consult the manufacturer's specification sheet. Look into the unit's interior to determine rustproofing treatment of parts.

10. When service is needed, must the complete unit be removed from its mounting or can the chassis alone be lifted out of the shell?

11. Standard warranties cover the entire unit for a year, the sealed refrigeration system for five years. Better warranties include labor charges for the first year.

See also: air conditioners, auto; caulking; condensation; humidifiers; insulation.

ROOM AIR CONDITIONER ESTIMATING CHART

If the area to be cooled is:	Use this size unit:
100 to 200 sq. ft.	5500 to 6000 BTU
200 to 300 sq. ft.	6000 to 7500 BTU
300 to 400 sq. ft.	7500 to 9000 BTU
400 to 500 sq. ft.	9000 to 11,000 BTU
500 to 750 sq. ft.	11,000 to 14,500 BTU
750 to 900 sq. ft.	14,500 to 16,500 BTU
900 to 1000 sq. ft.	16,500 to 18,000 BTU
1000 sq. ft. and over	18,000 BTU and over

In certain situations your computations will have to be altered. Add 10 percent to your total BTU requirement for each of these conditions that apply to you: Picture window or several unusually large windows exposed to the sun; roof or ceiling not insulated; summer temperature in area is consistently above 90 degrees F. Also, a single room air conditioner can cool several rooms in a home which has an open floor plan. Be sure to include the dimensions of all rooms you want cooled.

Cool your whole house

BY HARVEY A. BURLEY

Follow these simple steps
for installing a central
air-conditioning system

2 If a basement window is not handy it will be
necessary to cut a suitable opening in the wall

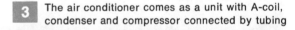

3 The air conditioner comes as a unit with A-coil,
condenser and compressor connected by tubing

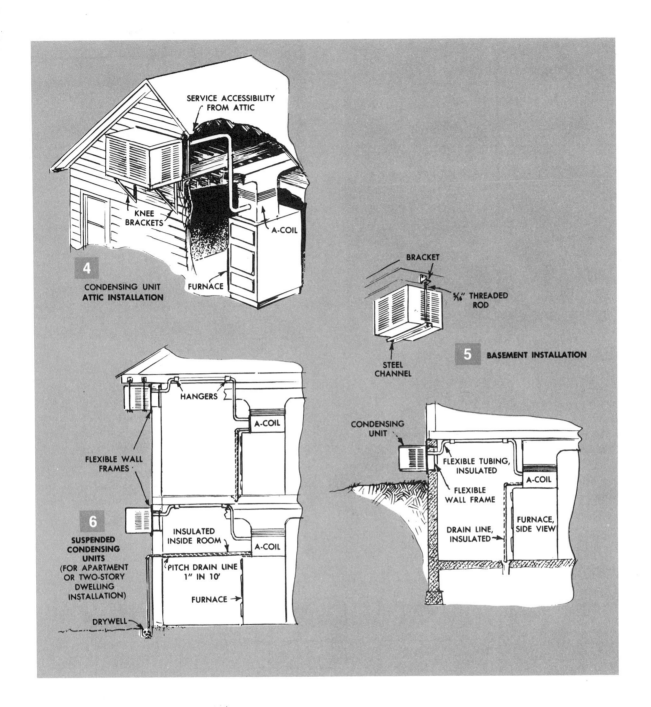

4 CONDENSING UNIT ATTIC INSTALLATION

SERVICE ACCESSIBILITY FROM ATTIC

KNEE BRACKETS

A-COIL

FURNACE

BRACKET

5/16" THREADED ROD

STEEL CHANNEL

5 BASEMENT INSTALLATION

HANGERS

A-COIL

FLEXIBLE WALL FRAMES

6 SUSPENDED CONDENSING UNITS (FOR APARTMENT OR TWO-STORY DWELLING INSTALLATION)

INSULATED INSIDE ROOM

A-COIL

PITCH DRAIN LINE 1" IN 10'

FURNACE

DRYWELL

CONDENSING UNIT

FLEXIBLE TUBING, INSULATED

FLEXIBLE WALL FRAME

A-COIL

FURNACE, SIDE VIEW

DRAIN LINE, INSULATED

■ MANY HOMEOWNERS think of air conditioning as cooling one room for sleeping comfort. It's true that room air conditioners do a nice job of pumping cool, dry air into a bedroom. By getting one this summer and one or two more next summer you can eventually cool the whole house. But this is the long way 'round and is more expensive than installing central air conditioning and cooling the house with one unit. And you'd be surprised how simple and easy it is to install your own central system. The conditioner comes as a unit consisting of the air-cooled condenser and an A-coil or evaporator,

connected with about 18 ft. of flexible tubing. The unit has been evacuated and filled at the factory and is ready to operate as soon as it has been installed. The condenser must be located outside the house, Fig. 1, as it is air cooled. Locations are preferably on the east or north side where it will be shaded during the hottest part of the day. The A-coil is placed in the warm-air plenum of the furnace, Figs. 7, 8 and 9, the flexible connecting line being uncoiled and attached with hangers to the floor joists.

Average sized, self-contained conditioning units of the type pictured will effectively cool

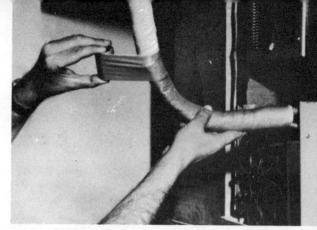

8 For insulation and protection the flexible tubing should be wrapped throughout its length

7 The A-coil is installed in the furnace, and the unit is connected with the compressor outside

central air conditioning, continued

built and properly insulated structure. This rule is fairly accurate for average capacity calculations.

In a basement installation like that in Fig. 5, the compressor-condenser unit can be located just outside the basement wall and about 18 ft. from the furnace. If a basement window is not handy, or is not the required size, then you must cut an opening in the wall as in Fig. 2. A steel unit is available for framing this opening, making the mounting of the compressor unit much easier, Figs. 1, 3 and 11. In locating this outside unit you'll get much more efficient cooling if the compressor is placed where it will not be exposed directly to the sun.

Although the operational noise level of the compressor is very low, it still may be objectionable to a next-door neighbor under some condi-

one-floor homes of 1200 sq. ft. floor area or even more if the structure is well insulated and other factors are favorable. One rule of thumb that some air-conditioning men use is that a capacity of 15 BTU's per sq. ft. will lower inside temperatures from 12 to 15 degrees in a well

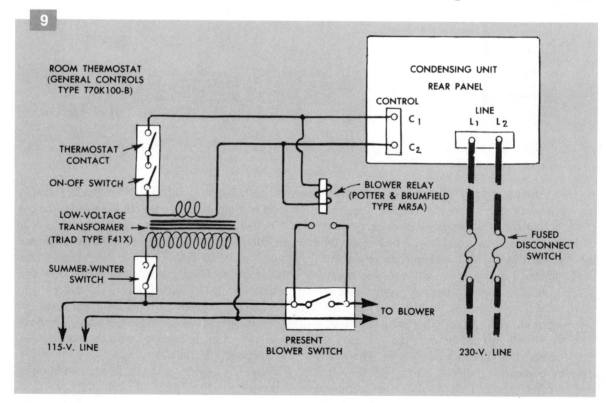

tions. Take this possibility into account when planning location. Noise from the unit is directional, which makes it somewhat easier to control. Often this can be accomplished by placing a low-growing shrub in the sound path. But remember that the unit is air cooled and requires a clear breathing space of 2 to 3 ft. on the three exposed sides. Finally, in choosing the location make sure that when installed the rear of the unit is accessible from inside the basement. Figs. 4 and 6 show installations made in an attic, Fig. 4, and in an apartment, Fig. 6, where it is necessary to hang units above grade level.

There are thermostats available for controlling both heating and cooling units but if you don't already have one installed, then you'll probably be better off to install a separate thermostat to control the air conditioning unit. The control unit specified in the wiring diagram, Fig. 9, does the job nicely. This unit is fitted with an anticipator which prevents wide temperature variations as the conditioner goes through its on-off cycles. To turn the furnace blower on and off along with the conditioner, another 24-volt relay is wired in parallel with the one in the compressor and its normally open contacts are connected in parallel with the blower on-off switch. To operate the compressor you will need to connect it to a 230-volt line and unless you are an experienced electrician, you'll need outside help for this installation.

11 Place the unit on 2 x 4s level with the opening and slide it into the frame. Then bolt it down

If you have warm-air registers that deflect the air downward or straight out from the wall, it's a good idea to replace these with the type that deflect the warm air upward. This gives a more comfortable distribution of cool air. In basement installations it is permissible to install a similar register in the furnace plenum, Fig. 7, to allow basement air to be drawn into the system. Due to reduced vacuum in the returns the blower will then deliver more cooled air.

Some improvisation may be necessary when installing the A-coil (evaporator) in the plenum. Keep the opening out in the plenum to the minimum size required, Fig. 7, and provide some means of rigid support for the unit. Insulate and wrap the flexible tubing as in Fig. 8. Finally, cover the opening with a tight-fitting sheet-metal cover as in Fig. 10. This usually must be made with an offset to fit over the projection of the A-coil. Attach with sheet-metal screws.

Now a bit of simple plumbing and your central air-conditioning unit is ready to cool your home on the hottest summer day. To carry away condensate there must be a drain line from the tap on the A-coil to the nearest drain, or, in some installations, to a dry well. If you lead the drain pipe to a floor drain, you can use plastic pipe or tubing, attaching it to the A-coil with a special fitting made for the purpose. Or, if it's more convenient, use ordinary ¾-in. steel pipe. Insulate that portion of the drain line which is exposed in the basement.

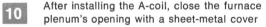

10 After installing the A-coil, close the furnace plenum's opening with a sheet-metal cover

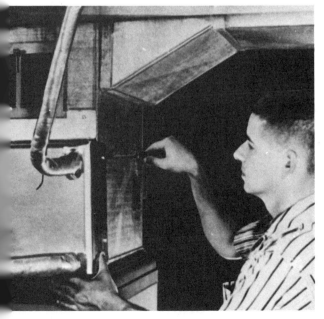

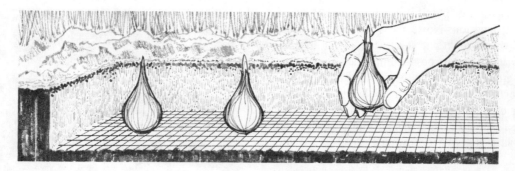

Plant your flower bulbs over wire mesh, and you can find them by pulling up the mesh.

Legs from worn-out slacks make good carry-all bags. Sew the uncuffed ends and run ropes through the cuffs.

Mount a bleach bottle on your ladder to use as a holster for your drill.

Keep food in a dish drainer to prevent it from sticking to your freezer walls.

You can have
the coolest car in town

This 'option,' so popular it has almost become standard, preserves comfort throughout the hottest days of summer. But understanding and care are important

BY MORTON J. SCHULTZ

■ AN AUTO AIRCONDITIONER is great! By now, many millions of car owners are eager to testify to its hot-weather benefits. But, like any mechanical device, it carries the potential for giving you trouble. Let's take a closer look at this increasingly popular option.

Happily, airconditioner failure reports are relatively few; mechanics said a/c is one automotive system that might most often be called "trouble-free." Nevertheless, airconditioners do require reasonable care and maintenance, and we'll get to that shortly. First, let's see how the system actually works.

All automobile airconditioners are basically the same. All are governed by the same principles of refrigeration and cooling as the airconditioner in your home. All operate on the natural law that heat always moves from a warm object to a cold object. And all are continuous-

air layering: see propagating, shrubs
air mattress: see camping
airplane float: see parade floats

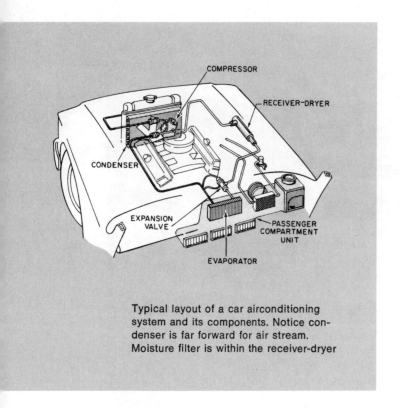

Typical layout of a car airconditioning system and its components. Notice condenser is far forward for air stream. Moisture filter is within the receiver-dryer

forced into the receiver-dryer—which is nothing more than a reservoir. Its job is to insure that an adequate supply of liquid Freon is always present to flow to the expansion valve.

The expansion valve is used to regulate the flow of the refrigerant in proportion to the amount of liquid coming from the receiver. The valve bleeds refrigerant into the evaporator—the second major component of the system—at pressure that is substantially reduced.

Hot, humid air from the passenger compartment is blown around the evaporator core so the liquid Freon within the core can pick up the heat, begin to boil, and vaporize. The air, without the heat, is blown back into the car—and you feel it as a cool, refreshing breeze. The heat is picked up and carried along by the refrigerant. Eventually it will pass to the outside air.

The Freon, now in the form of a gas, leaves the evaporator carrying its load of heat, drawn toward the compressor—the third major part of the system—by a suction line. After it passes through the compressor, the hot vapor is shoved

auto air conditioning, continued

cycle types that use the same refrigerant over and over again.

Here, briefly, is how an airconditioning system works in your car:

Heat in the car is drawn to the airconditioner's evaporator unit through which the liquid refrigerant (Freon) circulates. As the Freon absorbs heat it exceeds its boiling point and is transformed into a vapor. When it reaches the condenser, the refrigerant cools off, drops below its boiling point, and returns to a liquid state to start the cycle all over again.

Let's imagine the cycle starting at one of the three major units of a car's airconditioning system—the condenser.

The condenser receives the heat-laden, vaporized refrigerant after the latter has done its cooling job. It swamps the condenser coils with cool, circulating air that brings the coolant below its boiling point, where it reverts to liquid form. Simultaneously, the hot, humid air pulled out of the car's interior by the refrigerant is dried out as it is blown across the cooling core. Water condenses on the core and is drained away.

From the condenser, the liquid refrigerant is

If the magnetic clutch (indicated) is shot, it can't drive the a/c system compressor

on toward the condenser, completing its cycle around the system.

Your home airconditioner concentrates all these parts in one big box. Their jobs are the same in each case, but in your car the parts are widely separated. The engine drives the compressor, so that part must line up with the engine drive belt. The condenser needs a blast of fresh outside air, so it's usually up near the radiator. The evaporator is in the passenger compartment near the firewall so it can pick up unwanted heat from the inside air.

Even without exotic special tools, there are a number of troubleshooting jobs you can handle, although a stem-to-stern servicing job is beyond most home mechanics. It's easy to tell when something has gone haywire; you push the button and the blower doesn't blow or the cooler doesn't cool.

Most blower failures can be traced to the fuse concerned. Sometimes the system will start after two or three tries, but replace the fuse anyway. A bad switch, loose electrical connection, broken wire, or defective blower motor can also cause you to "lose your cool."

If the blower motor is okay but air output is low, chances are the trouble is a clogged air-distribution system. Maybe you forgot to open the air-output valves, so check 'em.

Valves okay? Then look for an obstruction in one of the blower outlets. Sometimes a leaf or twig gets caught in the blower inlet between the fan and housing. You'll have to remove the blower to clean it out.

Other reasons for low air output when the blower motor is working properly are:

—A low charge in the battery.
—A loose wire connection.
—Short, dirty or loose switch contacts.
—Binding shaft or blower blades.

If air circulation is great, the trouble almost certainly is in the refrigeration circuit. And a prime suspect is the belt that drives the compressor. To check, start the engine and turn on the a/c, then watch the compressor pulley. A slipping belt must be tightened; a worn one must be replaced.

While you're at it, check to make sure the compressor's magnetic clutch is working. It activates the compressor when the system is turned on. A bad clutch can't drive the compressor, so cooling stops.

When condenser fins are choked with bugs or leaves, the unit can't do its job; blow them out with an air hose. But blow from the engine side.

A propane torch detects refrigerant leaks by color change in its normally blue flame

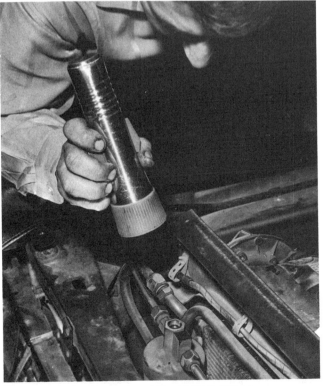

The amount of refrigerant and its condition can be checked through the sight glass on the receiver

Filter may, after a few years, clog up and require, as shown here, replacement of the receiver-dryer

auto air conditioning, continued

Manifold-gauge set, a must for most airconditioner trouble-shooting, tests suction and pressure

a pro's five-point checklist

The following checklist suggests how a pro would trouble-shoot your system. Familiarize yourself with it so you'll understand what's happening next time you have to submit your unit to the tinkering of an expert.

check for refrigerant leaks

A propane torch is often used to do this. It is fitted with a special adapter to which a hose is connected. The bluish flame of the torch is passed along near (but not against) the underside of the a/c lines and connections. At a point in the system where a leak exists the flame will change color. A small leak will turn the flame orange and a big leak will turn the flame a bright green.

Before removing or replacing a leaky hose— or any part of the system through which the coolant passes—all the refrigerant must be removed. To do this, a manifold gauge set (an indispensable tool for airconditioning work) is tied into the compressor at recharging ports.

First connect the inlet-suction line, which goes to the inlet-suction gauge, to the side of the compressor where the refrigerant enters as it comes from the evaporator. The outlet line, which connects to the outlet pressure gauge, is then hooked to the side of the compressor through which refrigerant passes on its way to the condenser.

If you're working inside, a third line—the exhaust—must be connected to an exhaust port which will carry the old coolant safely outside. Freon is dangerous stuff—it can literally freeze your eyeballs. So, a smart mechanic will wear goggles when he does this job.

Okay, the needle and outlet valves of the gauge set are now opened to permit the refrigerant to evacuate through the exhaust line. When the needle of the outlet gauge reads zero, the system is clear.

If a refrigerant leak is coming from a connection, tighten the connection and test the refrigerant, again. If it still leaks, replace the connection.

test for internal malfunctions

If the system still doesn't come up to par after all leaks are fixed, the manifold gauge set is again hooked into the system to test the adequacy of refrigerant pressure and to uncover other possible internal causes of trouble.

Outlet pressure should be high; if it's low, faulty cooling is being caused by a shortage of

With old coolant removed, vacuum pump purges the system of air and moisture before it's recharged

Amount of new refrigerant added is checked with the manifold gauge. It's critical to follow specs

refrigerant, too much moisture in the system, or perhaps a kink or obstruction in one of the circulation lines.

Inlet-suction should normally be low, of course. If it's high and outlet pressure is normal, there's trouble either with the expansion valve or with moisture in the system. Either of these will probably require major work.

Another, although less accurate, way to check on the condition of the refrigerant is to study the sight glass that's usually on the receiver-dryer unit. Start the engine and let it run slowly until the compressor is warm. Then check the sight glass. If there is too little refrigerant or if air has gotten into the system, the Freon will look cloudy or foamy or may even appear to be bubbling somewhat.

vacuuming the system

Once the system has been drained and the necessary repairs made, it is vitally important that it be vacuumed out.

To do this, the manifold-gauge set is left in place and the set's exhaust line hooked up to a vacuum pump. Then all valves of the manifold set are opened and the pump is started. The system should be pumped out for at least 15 minutes to remove all air and moisture. During this process, you'll note that the inlet suction gauge will drop down past zero, indicating the existence of good vacuum within the a/c system.

the receiver-dryer unit

This storage box contains a filter element designed to remove small amounts of moisture and dirt that may work their way into the system. In time, the element can become clogged. A clogged filter may reveal itself by the constant presence of small bubbles in the refrigerant. Check it with a glance at the sight glass. Another clue to filter trouble is a distinct temperature difference between the high-pressure line into the receiver-dryer and its outlet line. You can't get at the filter to clean it, so if that's your trouble, the entire unit will have to be replaced.

recharging the system

When refrigerant has been drained or needs replenishing, your airconditioning system must be recharged. A full load must be put back in the system. Methods vary, but it's vital that you follow manufacturer's instructions and specifications. A plate, normally on the compressor, will tell just how much refrigerant your system needs. Follow it to the letter.

See also: air conditioners; cooling system, auto; starting, auto, hot weather.

Free-flight parasol plane

It may look like a flying dinner plate,
but this way-out model actually is a
rugged performer worth a big hand
at any flying competition

BY ROY L. CLOUGH, JR.

■ ONE OF THE MOST unusual designs in the
history of aircraft is the pancake wing, a weird-
looking bird that actually has a number of features to recommend it.

A circular wing presents little drag at low
angles of attack, making it fine for high-speed
cruising. At high angles of attack the wing develops a great amount of lift and drag, perfect
characteristics for low-speed landings. The
sharply curved leading edge is an effective substi-
tute for stabilizing dihedral angle.

If you want to have some relaxation during a
few evenings that is certain to produce a lot of
fun for you and all the children in the neighborhood—from age six to 60—take on the job of
building this parasol plane. Made mostly of balsa

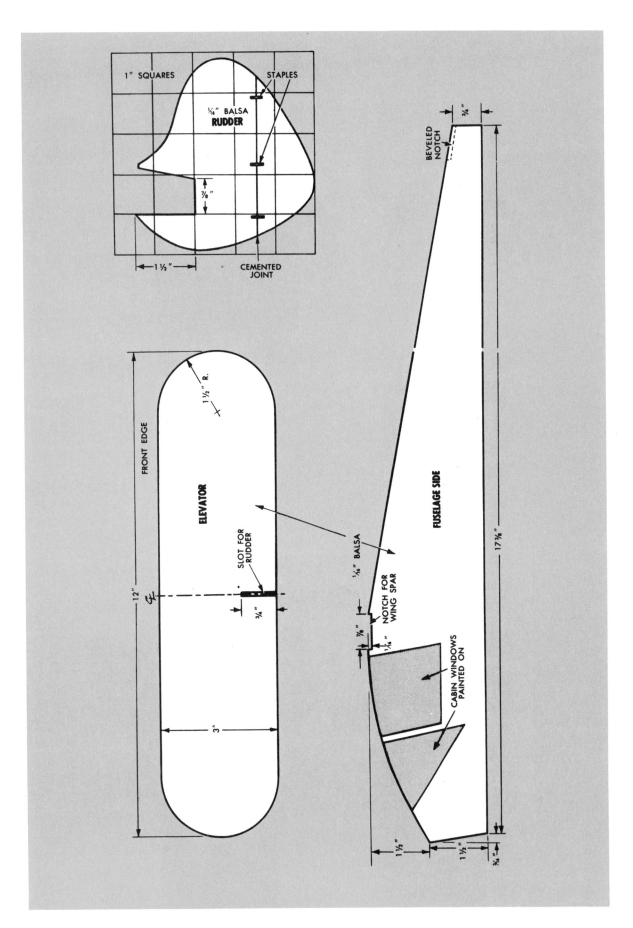

1" SQUARES   STAPLES

1/16" BALSA
RUDDER

7/8"

1 1/2"

CEMENTED
JOINT

BEVELED
NOTCH

3/4"

ELEVATOR

1 1/2" R.

FRONT EDGE

SLOT FOR
RUDDER

3/4"

12"

3"

FUSELAGE SIDE

1/16" BALSA

NOTCH FOR
WING SPAR

7/8"

1/16"

17 3/8"

CABIN WINDOWS
PAINTED ON

1 1/2"

1 1/2"

3/16"

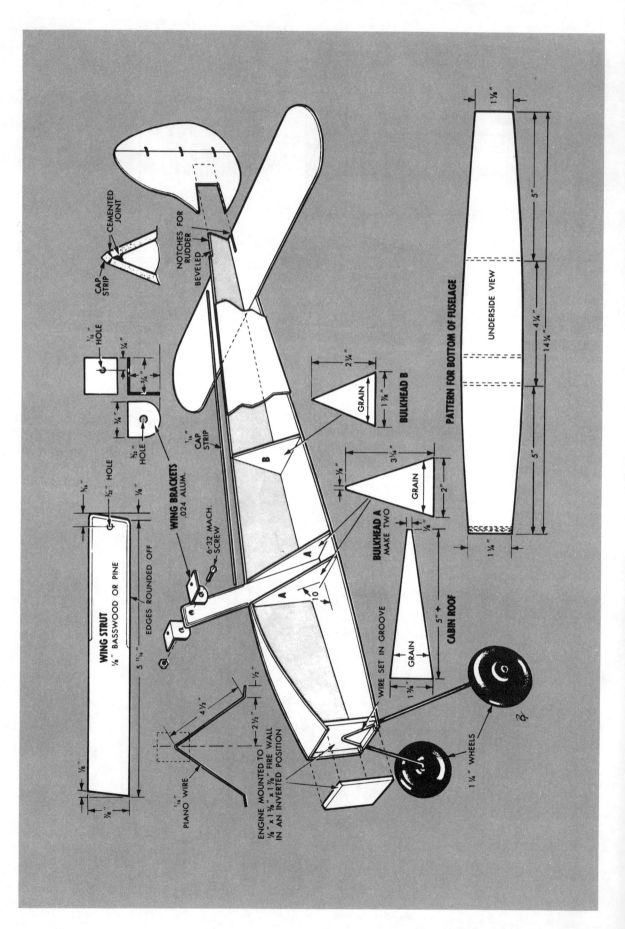

CEMENTED JOINT

CAP STRIP

BEVELED

NOTCHES FOR RUDDER

2 1/4"

1 7/8"

GRAIN

BULKHEAD B

1/8"

3 1/16"

2"

GRAIN

3/8"

BULKHEAD A
MAKE TWO

PATTERN FOR BOTTOM OF FUSELAGE

UNDERSIDE VIEW

1 1/8"

5"

4 1/4"

14 1/4"

5"

1 1/4"

1/16" HOLE

1/4"

3/4"

3/4"

3/32" HOLE

WING BRACKETS
.024 ALUM.

6-32 MACH. SCREW

1/16" CAP STRIP

B

A

A

A

10

WIRE SET IN GROOVE

5" +

GRAIN

1 3/8"

CABIN ROOF

3/16" HOLE

3/32" HOLE

1/8"

EDGES ROUNDED OFF

5 11/16"

3/8"

WING STRUT
1/8" BASSWOOD OR PINE

1/8"

4 1/2"

1/2"

1/16"
PIANO WIRE

2 1/2"

ENGINE MOUNTED TO
1/8" x 1 3/8" x 1 7/8" FIRE WALL
IN AN INVERTED POSITION

1 1/4" WHEELS

44

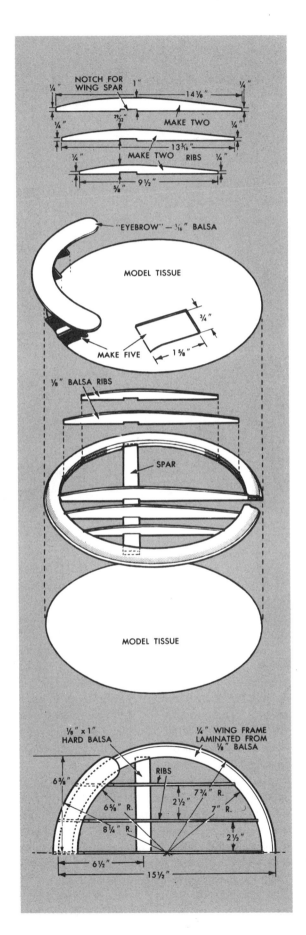

NOTCH FOR WING SPAR

1"

¼"

¼"

14⅛"

²⁹∕₃₂"

MAKE TWO

¼"

¼"

13⅜"

¼"

MAKE TWO   RIBS

¼"

9½"

⅝"

"EYEBROW" — ¹∕₁₆" BALSA

MODEL TISSUE

¾"

MAKE FIVE

1⅝"

⅛" BALSA RIBS

SPAR

MODEL TISSUE

⅛" x 1"
HARD BALSA

¼" WING FRAME
LAMINATED FROM
⅛" BALSA

RIBS

6¾"

7¾" R.

6⅝" R.

2½"

7" R.

8¼" R.

2½"

6½"

15½"

sheet, which is easy to work with, this plane can be made fairly easily in an evening.

As an extra feature on this model, "eyebrow" slots have been added to permit climbing at steep angles without stalling.

Construction begins with the fuselage. Cut out the two sides and cement them together along the top edges, starting at the tail end and working as far forward as the strut. Insert the bulkheads and the wing strut, then add the cabin roof cut from ¹∕₁₆-in. balsa sheet mounted cross-grain. Note that the firewall must be shaped to fit the contour at the top.

When the cement is dry, install the elevator and cover the bottom of the fuselage with balsa sheet laid cross-grain. Slip the rudder into place and capstrip the top fuselage joint with a strip of ¹∕₁₆-in. balsa sanded to the proper contour.

Make up the wing outline from two layers of scrap ⅛-in. balsa sheet. The joints in the bottom layer may be located at random, provided they are lapped with solid balsa in the second layer. Sand this outline to shape before installing the spar and ribs. Next, make the wing brackets and attach them to the underside of the spar with cement and two 2-56 bolts.

Cover the wings with lightweight gas-model tissue, applying it in strips between the ribs in the upper surface, then spray this lightly with water to shrink it and pin the wing to a flat rigid surface to prevent warping during drying. When dry, coat the covered wing with a couple of thin coats of butyrate dope.

The top piece forming the eyebrow slot is cut from ¹∕₁₆-in. sheet balsa and supported on flow separators cemented to the top of the wing. Note that the contour of the wing ribs changes from the center outward. When the eyebrow top is cemented to the separators, the result will be a down twist at the outer ends. This assists in producing the desired airflow condition over the center and prevents the model from tipping.

Attach the wing to the strut with brackets and a 6-32 bolt, then add the decorations and give the whole fuselage a coat of clear butyrate.

To discover the best wing angle, glide the model over long grass until you achieve a smooth, flat glide, then tighten the bolt. Finally, start the motor and test-fly the model to find the rudder adjustment which yields the proper angle of climb.

See also: glider model; gyroplane model; jet plane model; stick-model planes.

For a real eye-stopper, build "Hoopskirt"

BY ROY L. CLOUGH, JR.

Flying barrels have been in the air since Bleriot, but this model proves they can still turn in a top performance

■ TROT THIS MODEL out on the field at your next meet and watch the eyes bug. If anybody snickers, put 'em in their place by reminding them that the annular wing is a very old aeronautical principle. Then launch your Hoopskirt. If its tradition hasn't impressed them, its performance is certain to!

At least a half-dozen full-scale planes (plus innumerable kites and gliders) have been built on the "flying barrel" design. One of the initial aircraft made by Ellehammer—the first Dane to fly—took this form. Louis Bleriot, the daring Frenchman who was the first to fly the English Channel, perched one on floats and tried, with indifferent success, to get it off the water. The French are still at it; their latest attempt at annular-winged aircraft is a tail sitting jet.

One of the big advantages of this design is its propulsive efficiency. Efficiency in a flying system is highest when the velocity of the discharged air is almost as great as the forward speed of the plane. This means that it's better to move a lot of air relatively slowly than a small amount at high speed. (It's rather like matching impedances.) The annular wing with a propeller ahead of it functions as an effective aspirator to increase the amount of air thrust backward.

Such a wing has more *lift* than you might think. The closed-circuit nature of the airfoil eliminates wing-tip vortices. Theoretically, a hoop-wing plane shouldn't have to bank in order to turn. This model does, however, because of the vertical stabilizing fin at the top of the wing. This was added to produce an effect comparable to dihedral.

The Hoopskirt is an extremely stable flying machine. It'll teach you a lot about this off-beat configuration. Don't let the circular wing scare you—it's quite easy to build. Any cylinder with a diameter of about 10 in. (a half inch either way won't hurt) can serve as a mold for the two spars. I used a straight-sided layer-cake pan. The spars can be of any light wood that bends easily when soaked in hot water. Bind these

around the mold with a strip of rag. When dry, trim the ends in long, matching bevels to form the lap shown in the sketch; cement and bind with sewing thread.

You can trace the wing-rib pattern directly onto your balsa, stacking blanks to cut as many at once as you can manage. The slots in each end are $\frac{3}{32}$ in. wide and $\frac{1}{4}$ in. deep. The width should provide a snug fit over the spars. When these hoops are seated in the notches, their outer edges will protrude $\frac{1}{16}$ in. for rounding off.

An easy way to space the ribs accurately is to set the spar-mold cylinder on a piece of cardboard and scribe around it to produce a circle the same diameter as the spars. Mark off sixteen rib positions by means of radius lines and assemble the wing vertically over this pattern.

Cover the frame one section at a time with light model-plane tissue. Sections into which the strut, fin or booms will pass can be left uncovered until assembly is completed—or you can cover the entire wing and then slit the paper

of these sections when you install parts that must be cemented to the ribs. Water-shrink the paper; when dry, give it a coat of clear dope.

Careful alignment of all balsa parts pays off in good performance. Don't diminish the strength of the rock-hard-balsa booms by sanding off the corners—leave them square.

The tail plane has a deeply-notched trailing edge, backed up with parallel pieces of soft wire cemented to the wood. These wires—which can be snipped from a paper clip—will hold any flight-adjustment bends you may give the two elevator sections after trial runs. An annular wing operates at zero incidence, so you'll have to bend the elevators up two or three degrees to get an angle of attack for climb. Bending one elevator up more than the other makes the model turn in that direction. The rudders have no adjustments, and are simply cemented to the sides of the booms after the tail plane is in place.

The engine-pilot nacelle is given a coat of pigmented dope after the motor is fastened on its plywood mount. The color scheme of the model shown is: red nacelle, rudders and fin: natural white wing; silver booms, strut and tail plane— a highly visible combination against a blue sky.

For best performance, be sure the model balances at a point about 1¼-in. ahead of the trailing edge of the wing. An easy way to balance the plane is to stick straight pins into both booms 1¼-in. ahead of the trailing edges. Support the plane on these pins between two stacks of books, and add weight—in the form of bits of clay, small pieces of lead, etc.—to either the nose or the tail until the plane is suspended between the books in a level flight position.

Hand launch the model over tall grass until, by bending the elevators up a little at a time, you get a flat glide. As a check on these adjustments try a flight with the motor running rich, then lean it out and watch your model zoom.

This is a free-flying model, and has not been adapted for control-line operation. It is a stable flyer, and when out of fuel, it will glide gracefully to a landing if you balanced it carefully.

If you're flying it in a limited space, it's a good idea to burn off some of the fuel before turning it loose, because the model travels at a good clip.

In any event, you'll draw a good many curious glances—and perhaps a few snorts of derision —when you take Hoopskirt out for its first flight. Any snickers in your direction, though, will quickly change to whistles of admiration when onlookers see the stability of the "flying barrel," one of the earliest of all aircraft designs.

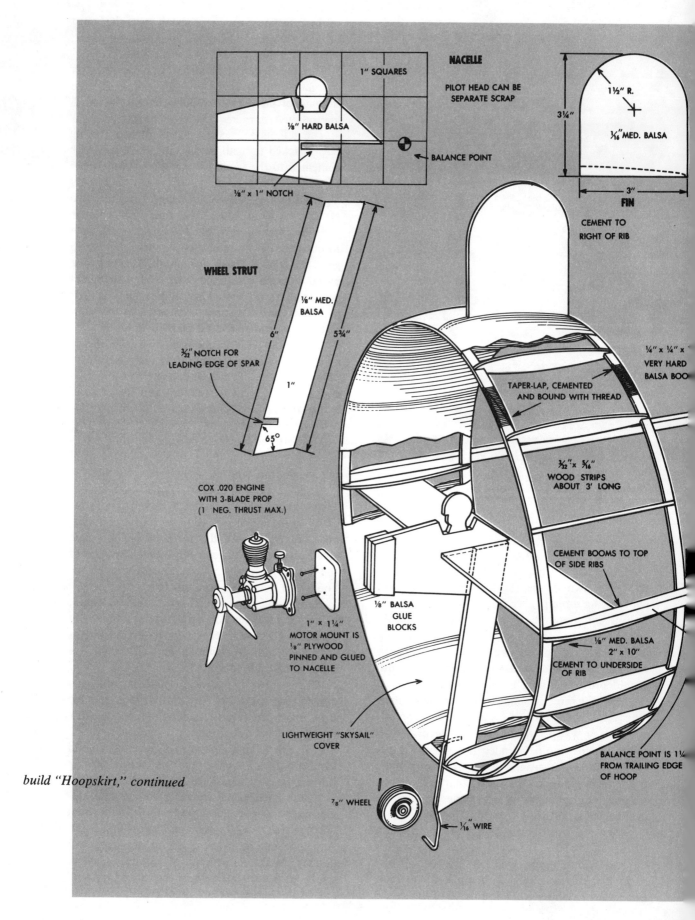

1" SQUARES

NACELLE

PILOT HEAD CAN BE
SEPARATE SCRAP

⅛" HARD BALSA

← BALANCE POINT

⅛" x 1" NOTCH

1½" R.

3¼"

1/16" MED. BALSA

3"

FIN

CEMENT TO
RIGHT OF RIB

WHEEL STRUT

⅛" MED.
BALSA

6"   5¾"

3/32" NOTCH FOR
LEADING EDGE OF SPAR

1"

65°

¼" x ¼" x
VERY HARD
BALSA BOO

TAPER-LAP, CEMENTED
AND BOUND WITH THREAD

3/32" x 5/16"
WOOD STRIPS
ABOUT 3' LONG

COX .020 ENGINE
WITH 3-BLADE PROP
(1 NEG. THRUST MAX.)

CEMENT BOOMS TO TOP
OF SIDE RIBS

⅛" BALSA
GLUE
BLOCKS

1" x 1¼"
MOTOR MOUNT IS
⅛" PLYWOOD
PINNED AND GLUED
TO NACELLE

⅛" MED. BALSA
2" x 10"
CEMENT TO UNDERSIDE
OF RIB

LIGHTWEIGHT "SKYSAIL"
COVER

BALANCE POINT IS 1¼
FROM TRAILING EDGE
OF HOOP

build "Hoopskirt," continued

⅞" WHEEL

1/16" WIRE

"Hoopskirt"

You can trace the wing-rib pattern below, directly onto your balsa, stacking blanks to cut as many at once as you can manage. Note the tail plane, diagrammed at the bottom. The trailing edge must be backed up with parallel pieces of soft wire cemented to the wood. Wire snipped some paper clips will do nicely. The two spars for the circular wing, at left, can be formed in any cylinder with a diameter of about 10 in. such as a layer-cake pan

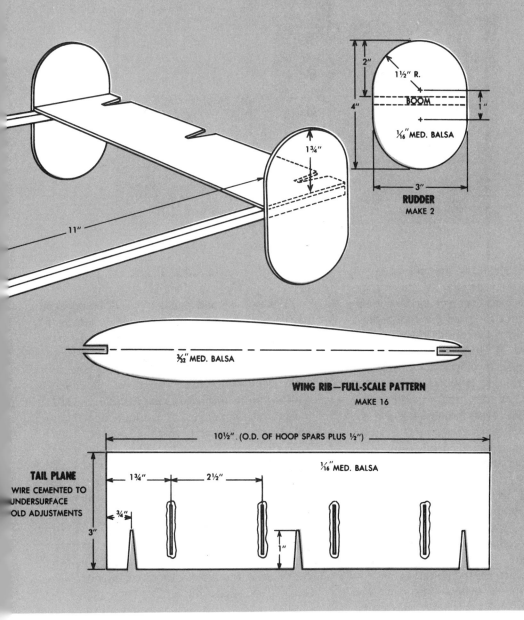

2"

1½" R.

BOOM

4"

1"

1⁄16" MED. BALSA

3"

RUDDER
MAKE 2

1¾"

11"

3⁄32" MED. BALSA

WING RIB—FULL-SCALE PATTERN
MAKE 16

10½" (O.D. OF HOOP SPARS PLUS ½")

1⁄16" MED. BALSA

TAIL PLANE
WIRE CEMENTED TO
UNDERSURFACE
OLD ADJUSTMENTS

1¾"

2½"

¾"

3"

1"

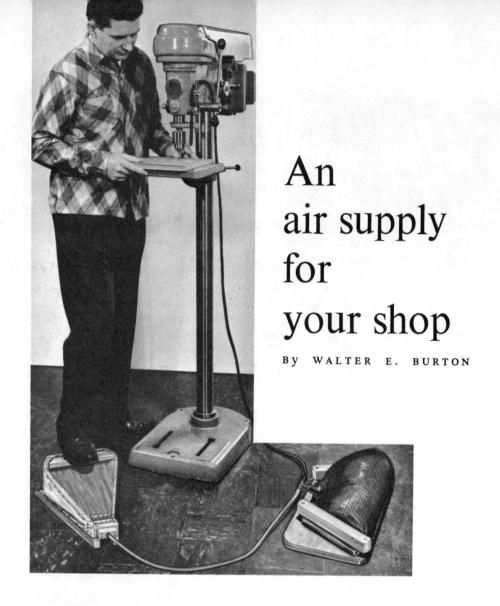

An air supply for your shop

BY WALTER E. BURTON

■ MOST HOME WORKSHOPS are not equipped with an air supply. If your shop is among them you'll wonder how you ever got along without one, once you've built and used this foot-bellows air system. For practical versatility this toe-touch unit is hard to beat. It can be used in a number of ways, for example, to blow out mortises and clear chips while routing to pattern lines (as in the photo above), or to provide an air supply for a small forge, a blowpipe, Bunsen burner, or any similar piece of shop equipment. You'll find that the unit can be called into service on any job around the shop where comparatively low air pressure is required.

The bellows air system, Figs. 1 and 2, consists of two plywood panels that are hinged together. The space between them is enclosed by a diaphragm. A coil spring holds the panels apart until they are forced together. The inlet valve, Fig. 3, is located in the bottom panel and allows air to enter the bellows chamber. The compression stroke closes this valve, forcing air

through the outlet valve, Fig. 4, and carrying it to the expansion air chamber, Fig. 11.

After cutting and drilling the ⅜-in. plywood panels for the bellows, Figs. 5 and 6, attach the end piece, stop blocks, base strips or runners, spring pocket (a fruit jar lid) and spring, Fig. 7. Then the hinge can be installed. To prevent air from leaking out, use a length of piano hinge with a thin leather gasket placed underneath.

Cut the diaphragm from cloth-backed vinyl upholstering material or thin, pliable leather. The diaphragm should enclose the bellows chamber completely with the spring slightly compressed. It is fastened in place with a double row of tacks and glue. If there are pleats at any of the corners, split them and overlap.

The inlet valve is mounted on a 4 x 4-in. square plywood block, Figs. 8 and 9, so that it can be removed if necessary. At this point you'll find a need for a leftover piece of inner tube. Cut a 1⅞-in. disc out of it. Then punch two holes in this disc to accommodate ⅜-in. No. 4

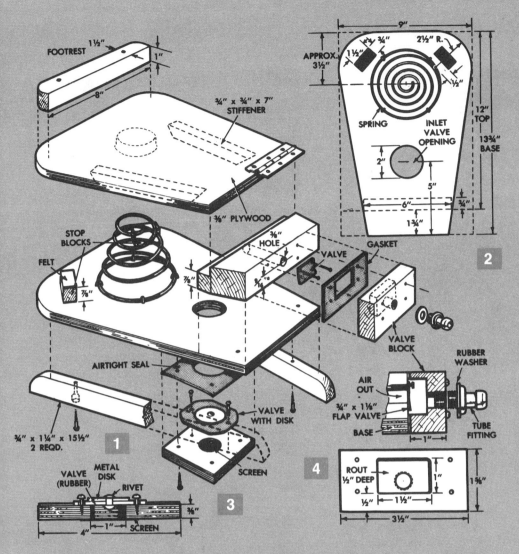

FOOTREST 1½" 1"

8"

¾" x ¾" x 7" STIFFENER

STOP BLOCKS

FELT ⅞"

¾" HOLE

VALVE

3/8" PLYWOOD

AIRTIGHT SEAL

7/8"

¾" x 1¼" x 15½" 2 REQD.

1

VALVE (RUBBER) METAL DISK RIVET

VALVE WITH DISK

SCREEN

3

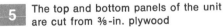

VALVE (RUBBER) METAL DISK RIVET

3/8"

4" 1" SCREEN

9"

APPROX. 3½"

1½" ¾" 2½" R.

1½"

SPRING INLET VALVE OPENING

2"

12" TOP

13¾" BASE

5"

6" ¾"

1¾"

GASKET

2

VALVE BLOCK

RUBBER WASHER

AIR OUT

¾" x 1⅛" FLAP VALVE

BASE 1"

TUBE FITTING

4

ROUT ½" DEEP

1"

½" 1½"

1⅝"

3½"

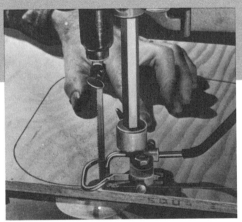

5 The top and bottom panels of the unit are cut from ⅜-in. plywood

6 The ⅜ inlet valve opening is ⅛ in. larger than the inlet valve itself

round-headed wood screws. Make sure that the holes are slightly oversize but smaller than the screw heads. Let the screw heads project approximately ⅟₁₆ in. above the rubber. Next, rivet an aluminum disc in the center to prevent the rubber piece from being forced into the valve opening.

The outlet valve is simply a flap of the same rubber that is fitted over the ⅜-in. hole in the end piece. Install a metal or plastic fitting for syringe tubing in the valve block. Attach the block to the end piece, using a rubber gasket. The air chamber, Figs. 10 and 11, is made from a section of inner tube that must be sound for

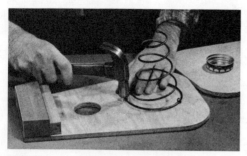

7 The coil spring holding the panels apart is fastened with staples

8 The inlet valve is mounted on a plywood block and can be removed

9 A wire screen is placed over the inlet valve opening to catch any small objects

10 The tee connector is made from a valve cap and a piece of tubing

about 15 in. from the valve in every direction. This measurement is taken along the outer circumference. Seal the ends tightly with the type of cement that is used in repairing inner tubes. Position the section of tube with the valve uppermost on the inner edge, then fold each end under twice so that the length at the outer edge is approximately 14½ in. As a covering for the air chamber, look for a piece of netting. Material cut from an open-mesh sack will serve this purpose. Clamp the air chamber to the plywood base board with a pair of wooden strips. When the chamber is fully inflated, the netting should allow about ½ to 1 in. upward movement of the top of the inner tube.

The last step is making the tee connector, which is fabricated from a tire-valve cap and a piece of brass or copper tubing. First, cut the top off the valve cap. File it concave so that it can fit snugly against the ⁵⁄₁₆-in. tubing, then drill a ³⁄₁₆-in. hole in a 2-in. piece of this tubing, solder the cap over the hole, and you've got a convenient air system for your shop. Just one word of warning: If you want to keep your new air system in your shop, don't let your wife know about it. She will want to use the bellows unit while working on her arts-and-crafts projects,

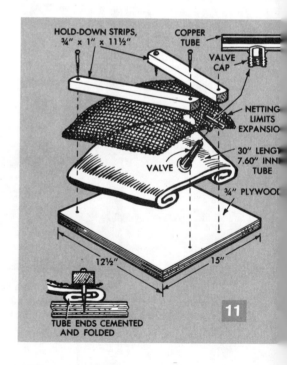

HOLD-DOWN STRIPS, ¾" x 1" x 11½"
COPPER TUBE
VALVE CAP
NETTING LIMITS EXPANSIO
30" LENGT 7.60" INNE TUBE
VALVE
¾" PLYWOOL
12½"
15"
TUBE ENDS CEMENTED AND FOLDED
11

or she may find a use for it in doing some household chore. Once she finds out that you've got an easy-to-operate air system in your shop, the only sensible thing to do is build a duplicate bellows unit.

See also: radial-arm saws; vacuum cleaners, shop.

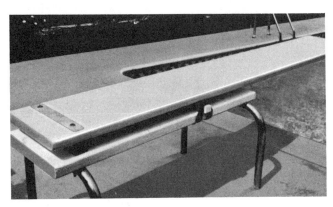

Save money when replacing a diving board by making an adjustable fulcrum. Use the old board as a platform. Cut a 2 x 4 to the width of the board and another 4 in. longer. Bore ½-in. holes in the shorter 2 x 4 to match those in the new board. Install it between the board and the platform with two ½ x 10-in. stovebolts. Slide the longer 2 x 4 under the board to the point where the fulcrum is wanted, and secure it with a bicycle inner tube looped over the ends.

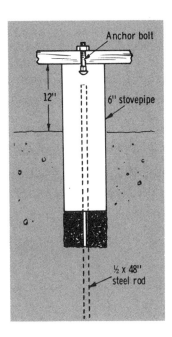

Stovepipe sections are ideal forms for foundation piers. Center a rod in the hole, place a pipe over the rod, and fill.

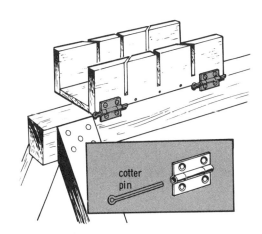

Here's a way to fasten your miterbox to a sawhorse and have it easily removable. Simply mount loose-pin butt hinges on the box and horse, or replace the pins in standard butts with cotter pins. This way, you don't have to clamp the box or keep it mounted.

When welding small butt joints, it's often hard to hold the pieces together for a good weld, while providing a grounding circuit for the arc welder. A clever way is to secure the pieces with C-clamps to a large horseshoe.

Turn on the power, press the reset button and your house and property are safe, even if nobody's home

Prowler alarm

BY RONALD L. IVES

As a burglar discourager, this prowler alarm does a fine job. The unit operates with a trip wire which keeps a relay in a locked position. Should the wire break, the relay opens and whatever you have plugged into the a.c. outlet will then be activated. The alarm can be either a floodlight, a bell, or a combination of these.

As the unit is electrical rather than electronic, there is no serious problem concerning lead dress or parts placement. Keep the leads as short and direct as possible, and avoid short circuits.

The trip wire should be very fine, such as a number 38 enameled. This will be invisible in the dark, yet will break readily under pressure. As line voltage isolation is provided by transformer T1, there is never more than 3.15 volts through the wire. A good source for the wire might be an old radio transformer or the field from a small electric motor.

For stringing the alarm wire around the doors and windows, note the setups suggested in the sketches shown right. If the wire is strung tautly over a partly open window, any attempt to raise the window further to gain entry will break the wire and sound the alarm. Similarly, a door can be protected by looping the wire over the knob. A garage door can be guarded simply by using two nails. Attach them so that in the closed posi-

tion the nail on the door makes contact with the nail in the jamb. Connect one trip lead to each nail, and as long as the door is closed, the alarm will be silent. You will need a switch outside the garage to let yourself in, however. You will probably be able to devise numerous other methods yourself.

Be sure, when connecting the trip wire, that you have removed all the enamel insulation at the terminal points and, in the case of the garage alarm, where it connects with the nails.

In use, turn the power switch on and press the reset button. The unit is now "on guard." When the wire breaks, the a.c. out socket is activated and the internal buzzer sounds, or the floodlight lights, if you are using a light for an alarm.

See also: piggy bank; alarm, power failure; alarm, temperature; electronics; heating systems, home; safe; switches, light.

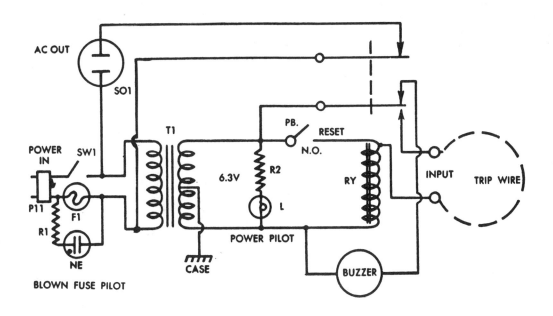

AC OUT — SO1

POWER IN — SW1

P11

R1

F1

NE

BLOWN FUSE PILOT

T1

CASE

6.3V

R2

L

POWER PILOT

PB.

RESET

N.O.

RY

BUZZER

INPUT

TRIP WIRE

under chassis view

top view

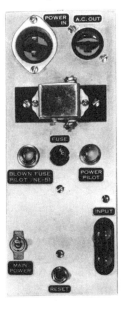

P1—Recessed male a.c. plug
SO1—Flush female a.c. receptacle
Case—Aluminum chassis box 10″ x 4″ x 2½″, LMB No. 144
   or equiv.
R1—100,000-ohm, ½-watt carbon
R2—10-ohm, 2-watt carbon
SW1—SPST toggle switch and plate
F1—1-amp. fuse in holder
RY—6.3-volt DPDT a.c. relay, Potter and Brumfield AP11A
   or equiv.
NE—NE-51 bulb with jewel and socket
L—6.3-volt pilot assembly
T1—6.3 volt, 1.2 amp. filament transformer, Stancor P-6134
   or equiv.
Buzzer—6-volt adjustable buzzer
PB—Push button, normally open
Miscellaneous—2-terminal tie point, 2 terminal binding
   posts, cable ties, etc.

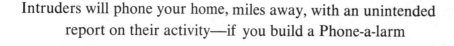

Let your telephone tattle on burglars

BY W. R. KINGEN

Intruders will phone your home, miles away, with an unintended report on their activity—if you build a Phone-a-larm

■ ARE YOU PLAGUED by vandals' or burglars' break-ins at an unattended vacation home, an unoccupied business office, or some other unsupervised and remote building?

You can't be everywhere at once, of course. You can't protect everything. But you can rig your summer cottage, for example, so unsuspecting burglars will telephone you about their activity—without even knowing they've tipped you off.

The Phone-a-larm was developed for just that purpose. Its first use was for the protection of a school building, deserted from late afternoon until the next morning and all during weekends. The device will work just as well to warn you of the unauthorized opening of doors or windows wherever telephone service is available.

alarms, electrical power failure: see
alarms, power failure
alarms, heating system failure: see alarm,
temperature; heating systems, home

If you choose, you can even program the Phone-a-larm to call your home area code and telephone number from a distant city.

When the opening of a door or window triggers a concealed switch, this system lifts a telephone receiver and dials your number. After your home phone rings about three times, Phone-a-larm drops the receiver to break the connection. This lets you telephone police.

Further, it keeps on trying automatically, so if your home phone was busy on the first few tries, the one-minute cycle is repeated. You'll probably wire a timer into the circuit to cut off the entire device after a given number of dialing-and-ringing cycles are completed.

The first Phone-a-larm cost less than $50 to build and took several weeks of spare-time work to design and put together. Depending on the pieces you may have in a scrap box, the parts may cost you less. And since the design is now completed, your work should go faster.

The telephone company's instrument isn't altered in any way—either electrically or mechan-

Tripper finger, made of an old teaspoon handle, rides up at clip in the program drum's dialing track to close switch S3. Switch plungers ride atop fingers

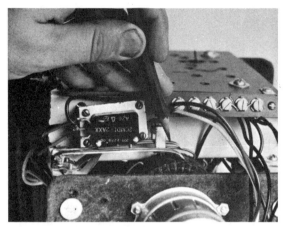

The plunger of solenoid K2 (indicated) pulls the plastic slide carrying dialing motor M2 into position so rubber dialing roller can function

The rubber stopper on the dialing motor shaft serves the function of intruder's finger in dialing you to warn of his unauthorized entry

ically. A metal band is clamped around the receiver to give the device a "grip" so it can start. Otherwise, the telephone instrument is merely clamped in place between rubber bumpers.

It's worth the effort, incidentally, to put together a relatively soundproof box or other enclosure for the whole device, so intruders don't realize they have telephoned their presence.

You could decide, of course, to locate the Phone-a-larm at some location away from the area you're trying to protect.

Start construction by cutting out four hardboard panels, following the exploded view drawing. Then bolt the two shelf brackets in place.

To carry the assembly for the dialing motor (M2), bend two of the 6-in. mending plates 2¼ in. from one end. The included angle should be about 120 degrees. The short legs will be uprights and the long leg—3¾ in. long—will extend up across the telephone dial face, matching its slant. The design varies and you may have to modify the plates' angle to get a good match.

The straight mending plates will be bolted on top of the long legs, extending an inch beyond their upper end and about 1¼ in. below the bend. Use a pressed cardboard spacer (or some other scrap) to keep the two plates separated, providing room for the drilled plastic plate that will slide in, carrying the dialing motor.

Drill the projecting inch of the upper mending plate and bolt to it the aluminum-bar or strap-iron supporting ties shaped as shown in the exploded view. These will hang the upper part of the slide assembly from the shelf brackets. One bolt for each side is adequate.

Mount the 30-rpm dialing motor on a clear plastic slide after you have drilled out a hole for the motor shaft. You'll also need a transverse hole through the motor shaft itself.

Slip a one-hole No. 3 rubber stopper on the motor shaft. You'll need to trim the small end to ¾-in. dia.; the big end should have a 1-in. dia. Be careful, in trimming the small end, that the hole remains well centered. Then push a ¾-in. wire brad through the stopper and the transverse hole in the shaft to pin the stopper to the shaft. Recess the brad head slightly and the dialing roller will be ready.

Slip motor M2 and its plastic slide into the space between the two pairs of mending plates. It must be able to slide freely. Then bolt the sheet metal angle with its rubber bumper to the lower end of the top mending plates. (On the exploded view, this angle is called the "stop plate." It keeps the dialing motor assembly from slipping out of the slide assembly.)

It's time, now, to try this much of the Phone-a-larm onto your telephone instrument for size.

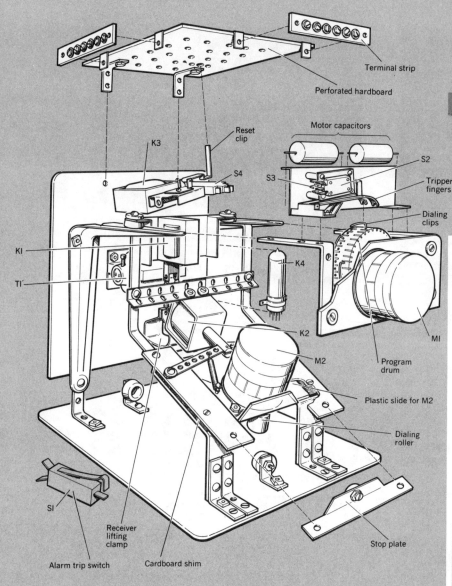

Terminal strip

Perforated hardboard

Reset clip

Motor capacitors

K3

S4

S3

S2

Tripper fingers

Dialing clips

K1

K4

T1

K2

M2

M1

Program drum

Plastic slide for M2

Dialing roller

S1

Receiver lifting clamp

Cardboard shim

Stop plate

Alarm trip switch

A Exploded view shows Phone-a-larm details. Not shown is sheet metal lever from plunger of K3. When the plunger pulls in, the lever presses pin plunger of S4 and reset clip drops lever, holding the actuating switch shut

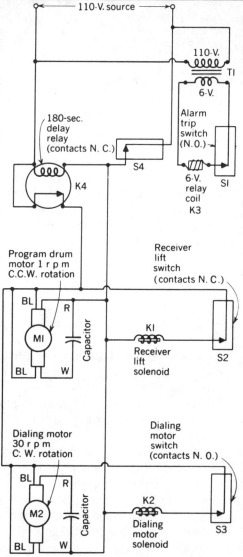

B This schematic diagram shows the alarm's operation. Tripping S1 causes K3 plunger to pull in, closing S4. Power is applied to M1 and its program drum actuates S2 and S3 to lift receiver and dial phone. K4 closes system

Phone-a-larm, continued

Slide the instrument into the rig and push it toward the low end of the slide assembly until the extreme low end of the dial is just about ⅛ in. from the rubber dialing roller. The lower end of the roller must be at least ⅛ in. above the case of the instrument itself. You may, at this point, have to adjust your basic rig to fit. It can be done by redrilling some of the holes in new locations or by elongating some you've already drilled into something of a slot shape to give yourself some leeway.

When you've established the location you want for the instrument, it's time to establish more-or-less permanent locating points for the telephone instrument. Fix rubber bumpers on the small, 1-in. angles. Put them in position in front of and in back of the instrument and mark the base for drilling. The back bumper should be mounted in a short slot in the base, rather than a drilled hole, so that it can be adjusted fore and aft to a limited degree.

Then, with the telephone instrument clamped into its position, complete any necessary adjustment of the various supporting angles of the over-all dialing assembly.

prepare solenoid's mount

Now prepare the sheet-metal angle that will hold solenoid K2. This component will pull the dialing motor assembly up in the slide assembly; return springs pull it back in place when necessary and generally help to improve the slide action. K2, incidentally, must be a version with 10½ oz. lift, at least. It shouldn't be too much stronger than specified in the parts list, because action will become too "snappy." But the 10½-oz. specification must be reached.

For the same reason, you should be sure that the mending plates of which the slide is made are free of burrs or other rough imperfections. And it won't hurt to keep the slide properly lubricated.

You'll find two prethreaded holes at the rear of the top portion of the solenoid's frame. Use these to bolt the solenoid to the underside of the sheet-metal angle. You'll find that bolts for these holes are furnished, but it may be necessary to use longer ones. Rubber washers or some other shims should be placed between the solenoid frame and the underside of the angle to which you mount the solenoid. Note that sheet metal parts should be of heavy $\frac{1}{32}$-in. gauge.

Bolt the angle carrying the solenoid to the support upright so the solenoid plunger clears the plastic slide by ¼ in.

Cut sheet-metal lever arms to spring-pull the dialing motor. Drill a hole for the end bolt and another three or four small holes starting near center and toward plunger end of arm for spring anchors. Be sure to elongate the holes through which the solenoid plunger pin must pass to prevent binding of plunger stroke. Insert rubber washer between the lever-arm ends within the plunger fork; this will greatly reduce solenoid hum and vibration.

Drill and insert anchor bolts for springs in the plastic slide. Clip the other end of the spring into corresponding holes drilled in the lever arm. Work the solenoid plunger with your finger; try

different positions for the spring anchor in the lever arms. Motor and slide should pull up without binding and return to the unengaged position easily by gravity. Use powdered graphite lubricant in the slide grooves.

A hard-rubber toy truck wheel 1 in. wide and of 2½-in. dia. forms the "program" drum, a most important component of the Phone-a-larm. When turned at 1 rpm by motor M1 and rigged with dialing clips, it will dial any number you program onto it by alternately making and breaking the circuit through switch S3. One complete "track" for the dialing clips allows for proper spacing. Now form a second track on the drum, space the wire clips to trip switch S2.

After motor M1 is mounted on its panel, predrill or punch a hole in the wheel hub to match the position and hole in the shaft of the motor. A ¾-in. wire brad (16-ga.) can be inserted as a pin through the wheel hub and shaft, using needle-nosed pliers.

Before mounting the drum motor assembly, be sure to go back to the framework and attach the two 3 x 3-in. angle irons for supports. First, use your drill or router to elongate the two holes in one arm of each angle iron about ¾ in. Then bolt the irons onto the top of the 6-in. arm of the shelf brackets, with the inside angle approximately ¼ in. from the end of the bracket arm.

Next, prepare the sheet-metal panel which serves as front top panel support and switch-mounting panel. Its dimensions are 2 x 7 in. after ½-in., 90° edges have been turned all around. Bolt this into position, flanged side back, 1½ in. from the front of the panel to the inside of the motor and drum panel.

PARTS LIST

K1—Guardian Type 12, 115-v.a.c. solenoid, continuous duty, 1" max. stroke, 22-oz. lift
K2—Guardian Type 2, 115-v.a.c. solenoid, continuous duty, ⅞" max. stroke, 10½-oz. lift
K3—Guardian Type 11, 6-v.d.c. solenoid, continuous duty, 1" max. stroke, 26-oz. lift
K4—Amperite Type 115C180, 180-sec. normally closed delay relay
M1, M2—Hurst CA Series, reversible synchronous motors; 1 and 30 rpm, respectively
S1—Acro Type 2CMD1-2AXX-A24, snap-action flat-leaf actuating switch, 3-amp. rating, 115-v.a.c.
S2, S3—Acro Type 1CMD1-2AXX, snap-action pin-plunger actuating switch, 3-amp. rating, 115-v.a.c.
S4—Acro Type 1MD1-1A, snap-action, pin plunger actuating switch
T1—115 v.a.c. to 6-v.a.c. power transformer
Hardware—2 shelf brackets, 6 x 8"; 6 angle irons, ½ x 1 x 1" 6 angle irons, ½ x 1½ x 1½"; 2 angle irons, ¾ x 3 x 3"; 4 flat mending irons, ⅛ x 1⅛ x 6"; strap iron, ⅛ x ½ x 16" or aluminum bar, ⅛ x ¾ x 16"; heavy-gauge (1/32") sheet metal, 6 x 12"; 2½ doz. flat-head stove bolts, 3/16 x ½"; 2½ doz. round-head stove bolts, 3/16 x ½" 1 doz. machine bolts, 6-32 x ½"; 2 machine bolts, 8-32 x ¾" 6 machine bolts, 4-40 x 1"; 4 machine bolts, 2-40 x ¾"; 6 metal screws, ½"-7; 2 springs, 3/16 x 1½"; 8 to 12 oz. pull; 2 springs, 2¼ x 1", 12 to 16 oz. pull; 3 rubber screw bumpers; 1 doz. washers, ¼"
Miscellaneous—clear plastic box lid, 3¾ x 4 x ⅛"; wide toy truck wheel or disc of hard rubber, plastic or hardwood, 1" wide x 2½"-in. dia., with 3/16" hole for motor shaft; rubber washers; hookup wire, 10'

The tripper finger assembly comes next. Start with a 1¼ x 2-in. piece of sheet metal. Cut and shape it and drill two ³⁄₁₆-in. holes in the base, each on center ⁵⁄₁₆ in. from the edge for mounting. Drill each hinge-pin ear with a ¹⁄₁₆-in. bit for inserting a 1-in. brad (16-ga.) or piece of wire. Bolt this assembly into place.

After trying various materials for tripper fingers, I found that an inexpensive, rigid teaspoon handle was the perfect answer. Use a hacksaw or heavy side-cutting pliers to cut into the bowl. File or grind handles down to a fairly uniform width of ⁵⁄₁₆ in. near the end of the handle. Cut and square off the handle end so that remaining total length is 3⅜ in. Use a ⁵⁄₁₆ x ¾-in. strip of sheet metal to form a hinged support for the trippers. Coil the end of a metal strip around a piece of wire or wire brad about ¹⁄₁₆ in. dia.

hinge needs good fit

To insure a snug hinge-pin fit, fill the coiled end with solder and drill out again with a ¹⁄₁₆-in. bit. Solder the coiled strip into a filed recess on the end of the spoon handle—the final overall handle length should now be 3½ in. Fit the tripper fingers into the mount with a small nut between to separate the fingers about ⅛ in. Insert pin and secure with solder.

Insert a test wire clip into each track of drum. Temporarily connect the drum motor to current supply, wiring as indicated for counterclockwise rotation. As the drum turns, check fingers for proper alignment. With the two tripper fingers riding atop the test wire clips and the motor stopped in this position, hold the assembled switches immediately over the fingers, with pin plungers of the switches near the midpoint. Measure for length of wooden or plastic standoff dowels. Cut the standoffs, reposition switches with pin plungers located over fingers as before, but with plungers pressed in; mark, drill and bolt in this position.

The panel for mounting the receiver-lifting solenoid should now be suspended approximately midway atop the horizontal arm of the shelf bracket. The clamp for lifting the receiver should be attached near its center with the springs attached to the clamp and solenoid plunger. With the plunger held fully inserted into the solenoid, position the mounting panel, including vertical adjustment, until the receiver is raised sufficiently to permit the telephone cradle plungers to rise to maximum height—about ½ in. Bolt and secure panel in this position.

Complete the mounting and locate the remaining electrical components:

1. The delay relay, with its octal tube socket can be mounted vertically on the back panel in the "loft" section.

2. Mount relay K3 and switch S4 in the loft area—near the right side for easy access. Mount the relay with the plunger in a horizontal position, and fabricate a small sheet-metal clip to keep the plunger engaged and switch S4 closed when the alarm trip switch S1 activates the relay. In this manner the Phone-a-larm continues operating until the 180-sec. relay K4 cuts it off. Reset the alarm by lifting the fabricated clip to allow the plunger of K3 to return to the off position and switch S4 to open.

3. Wire the two capacitors supplied with motors M1 and M2 as shown in the schematic. With the black leads connected together and voltage applied to the black and white leads, clockwise rotation results; current to the black and red leads gives counterclockwise rotation.

4. Finally, mount the transformer 5½ in. above the bottom edge of the rear panel, halfway between the brackets.

If terminal strips are not used, solder and tape all connections (see schematic). When completed, mount the top panel.

plan program carefully

Although wire clips on the program drum are approximately ⅛ in. long for each dial fingerhole or digit, the length will vary according to the telephone dial size and circumference of "clutching" point of rubber stopper roller. Be sure the lower edge of the dial fingerhole of each digit of the called number approaches the dial finger stop at the instant of cutoff. Set clips enough apart for return of the dial between dialed digits.

Once the dialing track is complete and accurate, insert a wire clip ½ to ⅝ in. long in the receiver control track. This should drop the receiver about 8 seconds before the dialing cycle.

To set the alarm, operate the drum motor until the tripper finger for the receiver has just dropped off this clip; it will then pick up the receiver the instant the alarm is tripped and approximately three seconds before dialing.

The entire alarm must be concealed and soundproofed if it is to tattle successfully and secretly on unsuspecting burglars. One further note: It's very important that your program drum be constructed very carefully to dial *your* telephone number only. A malfunctioning Phone-a-larm can ring wrong numbers and tie up lines.

A thimble on your finger helps to fasten staples which aren't firmly clinched.

Looking for a mold in which to cast steppingstones for the lawn? A hog feed pan is easy to use, and the fluted edges add a decorative touch.

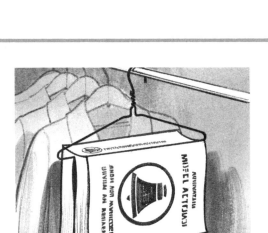

You can save valuable space by hanging that seldom-used phone book on a coat-hanger in the closet.

Artist's brushes can be cleaned and shaped faster if a V-notch is cut in the rim of a plastic or paper cup containing the cleaner.

A shoehorn makes a good improvised doorstop. It can be bent for a better fit.

Piggy bank squeals on thief

BY TOMMY THOMAS

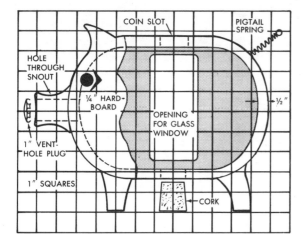

COIN SLOT

PIGTAIL SPRING

HOLE THROUGH SNOUT

¼″ HARD-BOARD

OPENING FOR GLASS WINDOW

½″

1″ VENT-HOLE PLUG

1″ SQUARES

CORK

The pig consists of four rings (two with feet) cut from ¾-in. wood and glued together. Cut the sides of the body from ¼-in. hardboard or plywood. The optional window is held in place with contact cement. After gluing the rings together, drill holes for the cork and the vent-hole plug in the snout

WINDOW

TRY TO FILCH a coin or bill from Mrs. Tattle-tale and you'll be greeted with a loud squeal of protest. Her guarding voice is a buzzer that sounds off when tiny mercury switches, tucked insider her body, are tilted the least bit.

The buzzer, which should be 1½-volt, and no more than 2 in. in diameter, was taken from a bicycle horn. Power is from two 1½-volt pen-light dry cells. Note that the dry cells are connected in series, and that the bottom one stands in a hole in the cork, which also plugs the bank's access hole. A 1-in. pipe clamp under the coin slot protects the batteries from being damaged by falling quarters and half-dollars.

The three mercury switches are glued in "downhill" grooves filed in the sides of a ¾-in. thick triangular wood block, 1½-in. long. To make the switches as sensitive as possible, find out by trial-and-error how close to horizontal the switches can be installed without activating the buzzer. The more gradual the incline of the switches, the more quickly they'll respond to movement. Cement the switch block and buzzer in place with epoxy.

Wire the circuit according to the diagram. After testing, cover the buzzer and switches with heavy mastic to prevent coins from shorting the circuit. Make sure the mastic is the type that dries. The cork holding the dry cells is cemented last, after final sanding and painting. To empty the bank, just break out the cork. You can re-place it when you start the next fund.

See also: alarms, burglar; alarm, power failures; alarm, temperature; electronics; safe; switches, light.

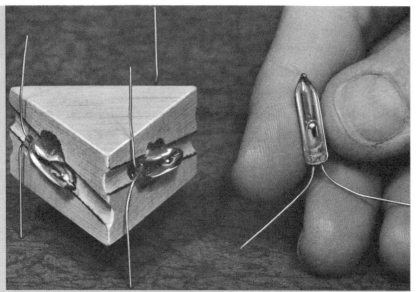

Mount the switches with epoxy. Be sure the longer wire inside each switch is on top. Cement the block inside the body with one switch forward

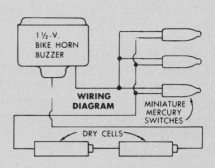

Wiring schematic: Connect the mercury switches in parallel, so that tilting any one of them will activate the buzzer. The batteries are in series. The buzzer must be aimed through the hole in the snout

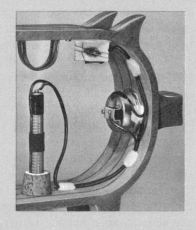

Heavy mastic or cement keeps coins from shorting the circuit or damaging the buzzer and switches. Connecting wires are tacked on with epoxy

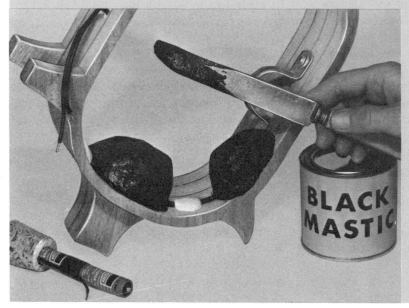

Build a power-failure alarm

BY CHARLES CARINGELLA

■ A POWER FAILURE ALARM? Who needs it? When your a.c. lines go dead, *usually* there are obvious indicators: Your lights go off, the TV picture becomes a tiny dot and disappears, or, at high noon, the electric mixer stops. But there are times when you might be unaware of a complete or partial blackout in your home. A blown fuse or tripped circuit breaker can disrupt power in part of your house. You might not know you have a problem until you lift your freezer lid and find ice cream soup.

If a power failure happens at night, your electric clock becomes useless. At such times, a power-failure alarm will wake you or alert you to the fact that perishables in your freezer or refrigerator are in danger.

You can build a simple, inexpensive power-failure alarm from a handful of parts that cost only a few dollars. It's a self-contained unit that plugs into any a.c. outlet. An internal battery provides power for the warning buzzer, which sounds when power is lost in the a.c. line. The unit can easily pay for itself the first time you have a power loss.

As seen in the schematic diagram, the circuit is extremely simple. A thermal-delay relay is used as the power-sensing device. The delay feature of the relay is insignificant here. The thermal-delay type relay is used because of its low cost as compared to conventional a.c. relays.

The relay is packaged in a small 9-pin glass enclosure, similar to a 9-pin miniature vacuum tube. Internally, the thermal relay consists of a small heater and a set of bimetal contacts. When current flows through the heater, the contacts either open or close, depending on the contact configuration.

A thermal-delay relay with normally closed contacts was chosen for this application. The contacts are normally closed when no power is applied to the relay's internal heater. When power is applied to the heater, the contacts open and remain open until power is removed. The specified relay utilizes a 115-volt heater. In the power-failure alarm, the heater circuit is applied directly across the 115-volt a.c. line. As long as power is present in the a.c. line, the heater is kept in an energized state, and the contacts remain open. The heater, incidentally, consumes only two watts of power, less than that needed to operate most night lights.

A simple battery operated buzzer circuit is connected to the thermal-relay contacts. The moment power is lost in the a.c. line, the relay contacts close, and the buzzer is activated. No power is drawn from the battery until an actual power failure occurs, therefore battery life should be equivalent to its shelf life. A 1.5-volt battery and buzzer are used here, although a six-volt battery arrangement can be used with a six-volt buzzer if you've got one in the scrap box.

Switch S1 turns the buzzer on and off. It can be used to turn the buzzer off when the unit is unplugged from the a.c. line for routine testing and servicing or during a power failure. As far as testing is concerned, the alarm buzzer has another good use—checking power at various a.c. outlets while you label your fuse or circuit breaker box. It's a quick job and once you've finished, you'll put an end to the confusion of wondering which fuse protects what circuit.

Mount the tube socket on ¾-in. spacers. Commercially available spacers are available and called out in the parts list. Suitable homemade spacers can be manufactured from ¼-in. brass or aluminum tubing. The buzzer mounts to the

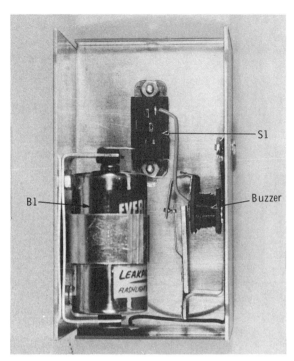

Switch S1, which disconnects buzzer from battery B1 when the alarm is unplugged, mounts on the front

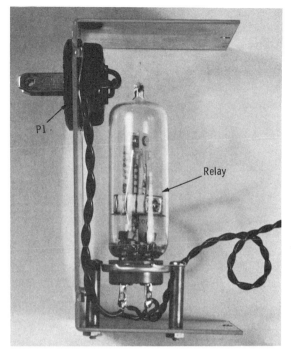

Mount P1 near the top of the back cover so the top outlet receptacle is clear when the alarm is in use

chassis with a single screw. One of the electrical connections to the buzzer is made to its frame; therefore, a solder lug should also be mounted under the screw used to hold down the buzzer. The lug provides a convenient connection point to the frame.

Both halves of the unit are wired separately. And two interconnecting leads are used. They run from pins 3 and 8 on the thermal-relay socket, to the battery and the on-off switch.

The power-failure alarm is self-testing. Once the wiring has been completed, slip the C battery into its holder. Flip the switch to the on position. The unit should buzz loudly. Now, while the unit is still buzzing, plug it into an a.c. outlet. After

two seconds, the relay should open and the buzzing should stop. The two-second delay, in this case, is the delay time of the Amperite relay.

PARTS LIST

B1—1.5-volt flashlight battery, size C
P1—Chassis mounting a.c. plug (Amphenol 61-M or equiv.)
RLY—Thermal-delay relay, normally closed contacts, 115-volt heater (Amperite **115C2T** or equivalent)
S1—S.p.s.t. slide switch
BUZZER—1.5-volt a.c.-d.c. buzzer (CEI type 302, may be ordered directly from the manufacturer, C. E. Inc., Post Office Box 327, Upland, Calif. 91786, $1.00 postpaid)
Misc.—Battery holder, C size (Keystone 173), chassis box (Bud CU-2103A or equiv.), 9-pin miniature tube socket, 2 spacers, ¾" long (H.H. Smith 2373)

See also: alarms, burglar; alarm, piggy bank; alarm, temperature; electrical wiring; electronics; heating systems, home; switches, light.

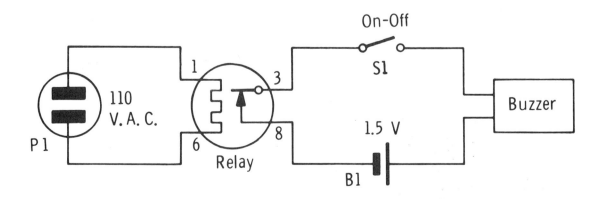

Cold triggers this alarm

BY MORTON J. SCHULTZ

A SIMPLE ELECTRONIC alarm can warn you when an overnight failure of your heating plant or electric power lets house temperature drop below what the heating system's thermostat calls for.

A self-contained thermostat trips the battery-powered alarm at whatever temperature you decide. Set it for about 5 deg. lower than the heating system controls and you'll get ample warning.

The unit consists of an audio oscillator operating at about 400 cycles. When triggered by the built-in thermostat the oscillator output is fed to a small speaker. The resulting tone is quite penetrating and sure to wake almost any sleeper.

Wiring is fully detailed in the pictorial diagram. Work slowly and solder carefully. Do not insert the transistor into its socket until all wiring has been completed. Make sure battery polarity is correct.

You can test the completed alarm in several ways, but the simplest is to set the alarm thermostat to a temperature higher than that in the house. Immediately, the thermostat contacts should close and the alarm sound off. Now lower the alarm thermostat setting, and the signal tone should stop as soon as you get below the room temperature. One last hint: Keep the alarm level on a flat surface or it will not operate properly.

See also: alarms, burglar; alarm, piggy bank; alarm, power failure; electronics; heating systems, home; oil burners; switches, light.

---

alarm, touch: see electronics

alignment, wheel: see wheel alignment, auto

alkaline batteries: see batteries, dry cell

Set the alarm by setting its thermostat 5 deg. below what the heating system controls call for. If heat fails the alarm sounds

In its compact metal case, the alarm speaker is set into the top, the perforated circuit board to the bottom, and controls in the side

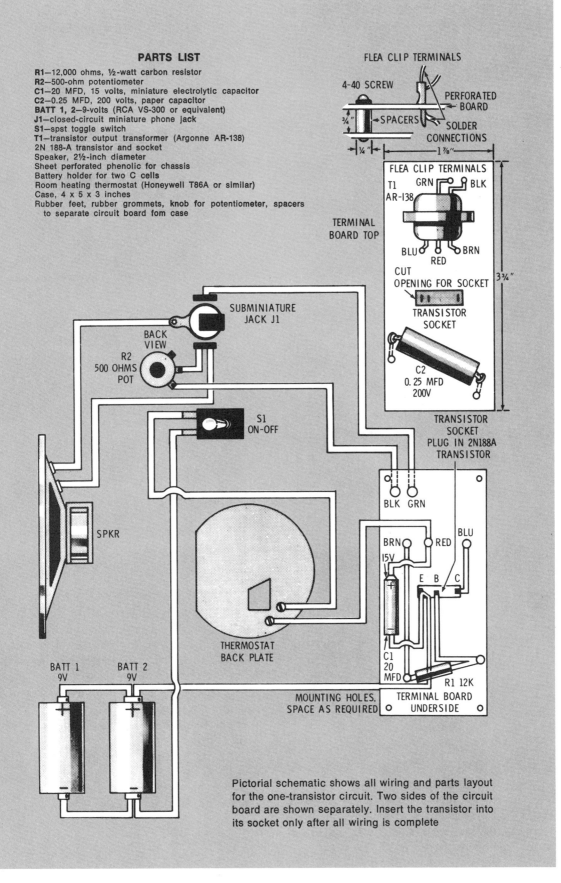

PARTS LIST

R1—12,000 ohms, ½-watt carbon resistor
R2—500-ohm potentiometer
C1—20 MFD, 15 volts, miniature electrolytic capacitor
C2—0.25 MFD, 200 volts, paper capacitor
BATT 1, 2—9-volts (RCA VS-300 or equivalent)
J1—closed-circuit miniature phone jack
S1—spst toggle switch
T1—transistor output transformer (Argonne AR-138)
2N 188-A transistor and socket
Speaker, 2½-inch diameter
Sheet perforated phenolic for chassis
Battery holder for two C cells
Room heating thermostat (Honeywell T86A or similar)
Case, 4 x 5 x 3 inches
Rubber feet, rubber grommets, knob for potentiometer, spacers
  to separate circuit board fom case

FLEA CLIP TERMINALS

4-40 SCREW

PERFORATED BOARD

SPACERS

SOLDER CONNECTIONS

¾"

¼"

1 ⅞"

FLEA CLIP TERMINALS

TERMINAL BOARD TOP

T1 AR-138

GRN   BLK

BLU   BRN

RED

CUT OPENING FOR SOCKET

TRANSISTOR SOCKET

3¾"

C2 0.25 MFD 200V

TRANSISTOR SOCKET PLUG IN 2N188A TRANSISTOR

SUBMINIATURE JACK J1

BACK VIEW

R2 500 OHMS POT

S1 ON-OFF

SPKR

BLK   GRN

BRN   RED   BLU

15V

E B C

C1 20 MFD

R1 12K

THERMOSTAT BACK PLATE

BATT 1 9V

BATT 2 9V

MOUNTING HOLES. SPACE AS REQUIRED

TERMINAL BOARD UNDERSIDE

Pictorial schematic shows all wiring and parts layout for the one-transistor circuit. Two sides of the circuit board are shown separately. Insert the transistor into its socket only after all wiring is complete

Anyone can letter signs

BY DAVID M. SWARTWOUT

Project-a-plan will instantly turn you
into a professional sign and poster maker

■ Do YOU FIND yourself in the business of making posters and signs once in a while? And do you have trouble making the letters come out looking better than the scratching of a mad hen? If so, you need this foolproof method of turning out posters and signs—the Project-a-plan.

You'll find a collection of Project-a-plans on

SOCIAL

EQUAL DISTANCE BETWEEN LETTERS

TONIGHT

POOR SPACING

SOCIAL

BALANCED AREA BETWEEN LETTERS

TONIGHT

GOOD SPACING

page 191 of this volume, on a special page which permits you to clip them out without damaging the reference pages of the book. See the index to find other Project-a-plans.

What is a Project-a-plan? It enables you to enlarge patterns to any size within seconds; in the example shown here, it makes it possible for you to turn out professional lettering even though you've never had art training. All you need is a slide projector and the ability to trace lines with a paint brush or a pencil.

You clip the Project-a-plan "slides" from the book (page 191), coat both sides of the paper with clear nail polish or shellac, and let dry. Then you insert the coated paper in a standard 35-mm. slide mount.

To letter a sign, you simply put the slide in your projector, project on poster board which you have taped to the wall and trace the letters you need. Move the board as you finish each letter. It's as simple as that.

There are a few precautions. You must be careful to set up the projector so that it is exactly perpendicular to the poster board. Otherwise the image of the letters will be distorted. And to make your sign straight, the poster board must be parallel with the floor.

You can vary the size of the letters by moving the projector closer to or farther away from the poster board. After tracing the first letter, simply shift the poster, align it with the row of projected letters, and trace the next letter.

You can increase your stock of lettering styles by purchasing sheets of lettering at an art store and photographing to make 35-mm. slides. You can do the same thing with simple line drawings and cartoons.

See also: drafting equipment; ellipsograph; signs.

Compact, efficient and highly productive—all these describe your car's alternator. In return for its favors, what does it ask of you? Just a little understanding, so you can do right by this reliable friend of your car's charging system

Getting to know your alternator

BY MORTON J. SCHULTZ

■ ALL OF TODAY'S AMERICAN-BUILT cars have an a.c. generator, commonly called the alternator, instead of the old d.c. version. The development isn't new, but it's important.

Alternators have been around since World War II. First they were bought separately and installed in vehicles with telephones or two-way radios. In 1961, they became standard in Chrysler's cars.

Alternators are lighter, smaller, and more reliable than generators. But their big advantage is the ability to keep batteries well charged even if the engine is only idling and even while you run accessories like the radio, heater or aircondioner. It *is* possible, of course, to so overload circuits with accessories that even an alternator

aluminum boats: see boats, used
aluminum calking: see calking
aluminum paints: see roofs
aluminum yard lights: see yard lights

can't maintain a full charge with an idling engine. But the ammeter or troublelight will warn you, just as with an old-fashioned generator.

Both devices produce alternating current, converting it to d.c. for the battery and accessories. The big difference is in *how* they do it.

Generator brushes pick a.c. off a commutator and convert it to d.c. Alternators use silicon diodes to "rectify" the a.c. to d.c. (Don't be confused by the presence of brushes in your alternator; they're quite different, feeding field current to the rotor via a pair of slip rings.)

An alternator rectifier is critical (and delicate). A product of solid-state electronics, it acts like a turnstile, letting current flow "forward" with very little resistance, but blocking any attempt to flow "back." Thus it cuts out the reverse flow of alternating current and leaves what is, in effect, direct current.

So current flows *to* the battery, but, when the alternator, with a slowly idling engine, can't put out enough to overcome electrical pressure from the battery, the diodes also prevent any back flow or discharge from the battery.

Both alternator and generator have regulator units, but the makeup of these differs in one important aspect—the absence of a circuit breaker (the cutout relay) in the alternator regulator.

In the generator regulator, the cutout relay connects and disconnects the generator and battery at the proper time. When generator voltage is higher than battery voltage, such as when the engine is accelerating, the points of the cutout relay close magnetically, causing current to flow

The alternator rotor (left hand) does the same job as a generator's field coil. The other half of an alternator is the stator (far right), corresponding to the generator armature (right hand)

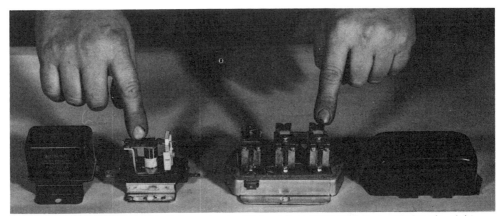

An alternator's regulator, at left, is a simple device when compared to a generator's, right. The one part they have in common is the voltage regulator, indicated

from the generator to the battery. When current in the *battery* is higher than in the *generator,* such as when the engine is idling, the points open. If the points remained closed, the current would flow back into the generator, causing discharge of the battery and possible damage to the generator.

The alternator is self-rectifying, providing a constant, steady flow of current to the battery with no return flow. That's why it allows the battery to maintain a full charge, even when the car is operating at low and idle speeds.

Both the generator regulator and alternator regulator contain a voltage regulator unit that limits the amount of voltage the generator or alternator can produce at any one time. This is needed to prevent an excessive flow of current to the battery, and to keep the alternator or generator from burning itself up.

Regardless of the type of alternator system on your car—Chrysler, Delco-Remy "Delco-

tron," Electric Autolite "Prestolite" or Motorola —troubleshooting and testing are basically the same.

Anyone equipped to test and service generators can easily do the same with an alternator. (Some mechanics even contend that alternator troubleshooting and service are easier. They claim that replacing parts in an alternator is a lot simpler.) When troubleshooting and testing, keep in mind one fact—that in order for an alternator to produce electricity, it must have normal field current, and the stator circuits and rectifiers must function.

As you can see by the troubleshooting chart, nine types of malfunction can occur in an electrical system charged by an alternator. These malfunctions are centered in four areas: the alternator itself, the alternator regulator, the battery and the fan belt.

There are only two periodic tests needed to make sure the alternator and alternator regulator

Alternator repairs in chart include: (A) Replacing brushes—a lot easier than the same job on a generator; they spring out when unscrewed from their sockets (arrows). Numbers show this is a six-rectifier alternator. (B) Replacing stator—just pry from case. (C) Replacing rotor—use pulley tool. In each of these photographs, the needed new parts are shown nearby

WHAT'S WRONG	HOW TO TELL	PROBABLE CAUSE	HOW TO CURE IT
Alternator fails to charge	Ammeter troublelight glows red on idle or acceleration Dead battery	*Fan Belt:* Loose Broken *Alternator:* Brushes sticking Broken stator winding Broken wire in field winding Defective rectifiers Loose connection Worn brushes Worn slip rings *Regulator:* Loose connection Burned or pitted points	Tighten Replace Replace brushes (Photo A) Replace alternator or stator (Photo B) Replace alternator or rotor (Photo C) Replace rectifiers Tighten all connections and terminals Replace brushes Replace rotor Tighten all connections Replace regulator
Unsteady low charging rate	Ammeter troublelight flickers "on" and "off," especially at low engine speed and idle Rundown battery	*Fan belt:* Loose *Battery:* High resistance at terminal posts Poor ground connection *Alternator:* Loose connection Resistance in charging circuit Poor brush contact Open stator windings	Tighten Remove and check condition of cables; clean terminals Tighten ground connection or replace cable Tighten connections Tighten connections Replace brushes and check condition of slip rings Replace stator

WHAT'S WRONG	HOW TO TELL	PROBABLE CAUSE	HOW TO CURE IT
Low voltage output	Ammeter troublelight flickers "on" and "off" at all speeds Rundown battery	Alternator: Resistance in charging circuit Grounded stator Shorted rectifier Regulator: Faulty regulator Low regulator setting	Tighten all connections Replace stator Replace rectifier Test regulator, replace if necessary Adjust regulator
Excessive charging rate	Battery uses excessive amount of electrolyte Excessive amount of acid salts on battery top and hold-down parts	Regulator set too high Regulator contact points stuck Open windings in regulator Poor regulator ground	Adjust regulator Replace regulator Replace regulator Remove regulator, clean mounting surface. Tighten mounting screws and ground wire
Noisy alternator	Noise	Loose mounting bolts or base Improper belt alignment Loose drive pulley Worn shaft bearings Sprung rotor shaft Bent rotor fan blades Open or shorted rectifier Open or shorted windings in stator and rubbing rotor poles	Tighten mounting bolts or replace damaged bolts Make necessary corrections to mounting base attachment. Also make sure alternator is correct one for your car Tighten pulley Replace bearings or replace alternator Replace rotor Straighten blades or replace rotor Replace rectifier Replace alternator
Oxidized regulator points	Battery uses excessive amount of electrolyte Excessive amount of acid salts on battery top and hold-down parts	Regulator: Poor ground connection Improper air gap setting High voltage setting Alternator: Shorted field windings in rotor pole	Tighten ground connection and clean mounting surface Adjust regulator air gap Adjust regulator voltage Replace rotor
Burned voltage regulator points	Battery uses excessive electrolyte Excessive acid salts on battery top and hold-down parts	Regulator: Setting too high Alternator: Shorted field windings in rotor pole	Lower voltage regulator setting Replace rotor
Burned coil winding in voltage regulator	Battery uses excessive electrolyte Excessive acid salts on battery top and hold-down parts	Regulator voltage setting too high	Adjust or replace regulator, depending on extent of damage
Voltage regulator points stuck closed	Rundown battery	Poor ground connection between alternator and voltage regulator	Replace regulator, making sure new one is well-grounded

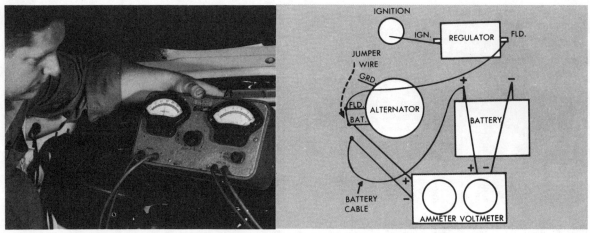

A current output test tells you the overall condition of the charging system. Hooked up as shown, the ammeter shows the alternator condition and the voltmeter reports on the regulator

know your alternator, continued

caution

Before making any test meter connections (as shown in the photos with this article), make certain the ignition switch is off and disconnect the ground cable from the battery. Failure to do this may, if meter leads are hooked up incorrectly, damage the alternator

are operating properly and not developing a malfunction: the current output test and the voltage regulator test. Before conducting either, check the battery with a hydrometer or voltmeter. If less than three-quarters charged, it should be removed and charged or a new one installed. Otherwise test results will not be accurate.

To perform the current output test (photo and diagram at the top of page 74), first disconnect the cable connected to the battery (BAT) terminal of the alternator. Connect the positive lead of an ammeter to the BAT terminal of the alternator, and the negative lead of the ammeter to the cable end you disconnected at the alternator's BAT terminal. (All cars that have alternator systems are negative grounded.) Now, connect a jumper wire between the BAT and field (FLD) terminals at the alternator. (The third terminal you see there is the ground.)

The battery ground cable you disconnected as a precaution must now be reconnected to the negative battery post. Hook up the voltmeter with its positive lead going to the battery's posi-

tive post and its negative lead going to the battery's negative post.

Turn on the car's lights, radio, and other electrical accessories for a few minutes with the ignition off. This drains the battery sufficiently so the alternator will operate at peak output, providing a truer test reading.

Start the engine. The ammeter should read the number of amps at which the alternator is rated —in today's cars, anywhere from 30 to 40 amps. If not, there is a malfunction in the alternator, and the unit should be removed from the car for troubleshooting.

The voltmeter should read about 14.2 to 15 v. for a 12-v. charging system, and 7 to 7.5 v. for a 6-v. charging system. If not, the voltage regulator unit needs replacement.

Test alternator regulator independently by hooking a jumper from the regulator field terminal to its "IGN" terminal and putting a voltmeter across the battery

At the bench, check condition of alternator rectifiers with a special tool or ammeter calibrated in one-amp steps. When touched with a probe (above), each should read at least 1¾ amps. They're wired together within the stator case. Knock out duds with a punch after clipping its leads. Solder the replacement leads

Since most alternators are equipped with pre-lubricated bearings, they require no periodic lubricating service. However, at regular periods —every 5000 miles or so—the outside of the alternator should be wiped clean as shown. Check dirt accumulation that could obstruct the flow of air.

In testing or troubleshooting the alternator, certain precautions must be observed which are unlike those involved in checking a generator:

1. Make sure battery connections are correct when hooking them up, to prevent damage to the rectifiers. If you disconnect your battery cables, check them with a voltmeter to determine battery polarity before hooking them up again. Any reverse in cables—a negative cable put on a positive post or vice versa—can send a flow of electrons back into the alternator, damaging it.

2. Try to avoid the use of a booster battery to start your alternator-equipped car. If the booster is improperly connected, even for a few seconds, electrons will flow back into the alternator, damaging it. If you must use a booster battery, make doubly sure of the connections (plus to plus, minus to minus) before hookup.

3. If you use a fast battery charger, disconnect the battery ground cable before making a hookup. Never use the fast charger as a booster for starting the vehicle—a wrong connection could damage the alternator.

4. The field circuit between the alternator and alternator regulator must never be grounded. Grounding of the field terminal of either the alternator or regulator will damage the regulator.

5. Grounding of the alternator output terminal will damage the alternator. This is true even when the system is not in operation since, on most systems, no circuit breaker is used and battery voltage is applied to the alternator output terminal at all times.

6. The alternator must not be operated on open circuit with the field winding energized. This will cause alternator voltage to be extremely high and may damage the rectifiers.

7. Never attempt to polarize an alternator as you would a generator. No polarization is required and any attempt to do so may result in damage to the alternator, regulator or circuits.

8. Care should be taken when adjusting the voltage regulator to prevent a short circuit from occurring between the voltage regulator relay and the regulator base. The tool you use to make the adjustment should be insulated by tape or with a plastic sleeve.

9. Care should be taken not to spill oil into the air passages of the alternator when servicing the engine.

10. Always turn the ignition switch off when performing work on the alternator. Bear in mind that it is, after all, a power plant.

See also: batteries, auto; electrical system, auto; headlights, auto; spark plugs, auto; **timing, auto engine.**

Load your own shotshells

BY W. CLYDE LAMMEY

An increasingly popular hobby offers
a safe, easy, enjoyable way to cut
your ammunition costs by as much
as 50 percent with only a small
equipment investment

■ RELOADING your own shotshells is a fascinating way not only to save money, but to extend the pleasure of your hunting or trap and skeet shooting.

There's a wide variety of reloading equipment available, suited to the needs of the shooter who uses a box or two of shells during the bird season, and to the requirements of gun clubs, shooting preserves and individuals who fire hundreds of rounds in a single weekend.

Cost of reloading equipment for all common shotgun gauges ranges from a few dollars for the simplest hand-loading kit to a hundred dollars or more for semi-automatic units that reduce shotshell reloading to a few short-reach arm movements. Capacity of the latter units can run as high as 500 reloads per hour in the hands of a skilled operator. Savings in cost per shell may range from 30 to 50 percent, the figure depending on such factors as quantity purchases of reloading components, the type of components used, and the number of reloads made per shell.

In general, shotgunners have three types of reloading equipment to choose from. The first type consists of a number of separate parts which are used manually to deprime, reprime, and resize the shell, insert wads, recharge with powder and shot, and crimp the open end. Such a kit is a good choice for the shotgunner who reloads perhaps 25 to 100 shells for the bird season or occasional rounds of skeet. Used carefully it will

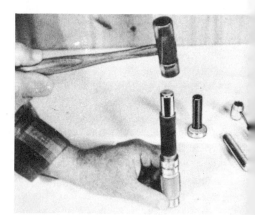

1 With a simple hand loader, the first step is decapping the fired shell. You drive out spent primer after inserting the decapper in the shell

2 To seat a new primer, insert the rammer in the loader, place a live primer on the rammer head, insert the driver and tap it lightly

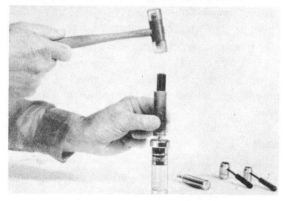

3 Pour in a level-full measure of powder. Select the type of powder from the manufacturer's chart according to the amount of shot you use

4 Insert the wad column. Start the over-powder wad sidewise past the crimp, then straighten. Insert the filler wads with a twisting motion

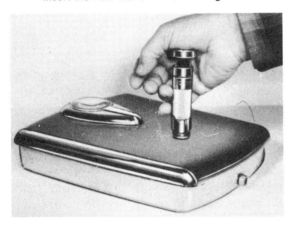

5 Slip shell into the loader, insert the rammer and place on a bathroom scale. Seat the wads to the required pressure, then add shot charge

6 Insert the charged shell in the loader and push all the way down to start the crimp. Insert the rammer and push all the way down to finish

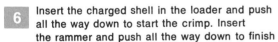

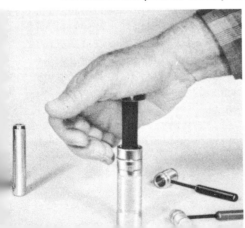

produce uniform loadings in both paper and plastic shells. The operation of such a kit is shown in the photos on this page.

The single stage reloading press is similar to a small arbor press. It has a stationary stage, or platen, on which a single shell is placed at several stations for depriming, repriming, etc. This type of loader usually comes with shot and powder containers, or hoppers, and is fitted with either a manually or automatically operated charging bar which measures and drops given amounts of powder and shot.

The semi-automatic reloading press automates many of the hand operations required with the two types just described, and is popular with gun clubs and many individuals who reload shotshells in quantity. Such a press requires close attention to the loading sequence as it has a carrier taking as many as six or more shells in progressive stages of loading from deprime to final crimp. On some loaders of this type the shell carrier is advanced automatically at each stroke of the actuating lever. On others it is operated manually. Usually the charging bar is automatically shifted and on some units the live primers are fed automatically from a magazine. Some units are fitted with powder and shot dispensing drums having interchangeable measuring sleeves or bushings.

reloading is safe

Reloading shotshells with modern equipment is a safe operation when carried out in accordance with accepted practices. Ignition and propellant components (live primers and powders) are quite stable. They withstand any ordinary handling and can be stored in suitable locations for comparatively long periods of time. There are, of course, precautions which should be observed. For example, never store live primers and powders where they can be reached by youngsters or found by those not acquainted with the possible hazards of careless handling. Always store them, even for short periods between loadings, in a relatively cool, dry place. Don't store components where they may be subjected to wide variations in temperature and humidity. Keep live primers in a sealed container except when in use. Keep powder containers tightly closed.

The paper shot shell is presently being displaced by the plastic shell having a conventional brass head. In time, all-plastic shells will probably be available. Also, conventional felt, fiber and cork filler wadding may in time be displaced by other developments in over-powder and filler waddings and separate shot sleeve or cups, or by recent innovations such as the one-piece plastic insert which combines the entire wad column and shot cup.

The primary function of the wad column in a shotgun shell is sealing in the gases produced by ignition of the powder, and cushioning the shock of the sudden expansion of the gases to prevent

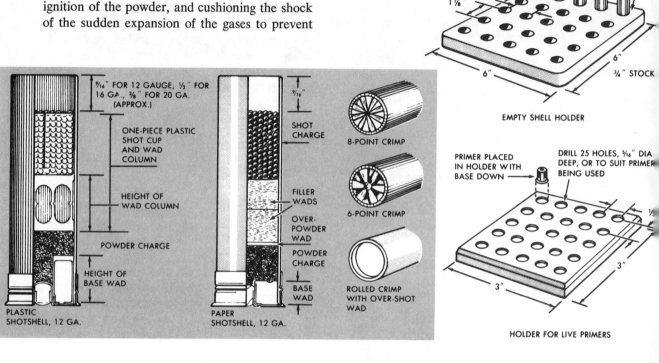

EMPTY SHELL HOLDER

HOLDER FOR LIVE PRIMERS

PLASTIC SHOTSHELL, 12 GA.

PAPER SHOTSHELL, 12 GA.

8-POINT CRIMP

6-POINT CRIMP

ROLLED CRIMP WITH OVER-SHOT WAD

A single stage reloading press performs the same basic steps as a hand loader but it is faster. The containers on top of the loader hold powder, shot

deformation of the shot pellets. The secondary function of the column, of equal importance to reloaders, is in determining the total height of the components in the shell to give the correct distance from the top, or mouth, of the shell to the top of the shot column for turning a folded crimp.

Detailed drawings which show cutaway views of loaded, uncrimped shells indicate the importance of wad-column height. The left-hand detail shows a plastic shell having a high base wad, the latter an integral part of the shell, loaded with the new one-piece plastic shot cup and wad column. Note that the shot charge is encased in the plastic cup (to prevent deformation of the shot) and that this loading allows the required $\frac{9}{16}$ in. (approx.) for turning either a 6- or 8-point star crimp on a 12-gauge shell of standard 2¾ in. overall length. The center detail shows an older type loading in a 2¾-in. paper shell having a low base wad. Here the conventional filler wads of felt or other materials are combined with an over-powder wad. An over-powder wad of plastic or other suitable material should always be used with this type of filler wadding. Note that the shot charge is not en-

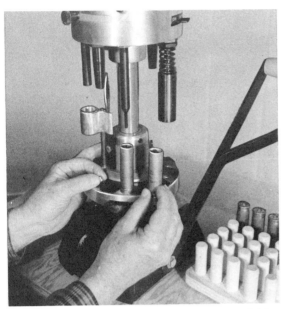

Semi-automatic loaders are the fastest type available to most shooters. The shells are moved in sequence through the various steps in the reloading process

cased in a plastic cup or other type of liner or container.

Some plastic shells require an 8-point star crimp as detailed. Some other plastics (also most paper shells) require a 6-point crimp. The older rolled crimp is no longer commonly used in the larger gauges except for some slug and magnum loadings.

When reloading plastic shells you will probably need a crimp starting die (6 or 8-point as required), since these shells do not always re-crimp readily without a starter. Most starting dies have an index mark or marks to aid in locating fired plastic shells in the loader for the crimp-starting stroke. The crimp starter will also be necessary when loading new plastic cases, but is not normally required for fired paper cases.

Before reloading, examine each fired shell for defects such as pinholes (in paper cases), frayed open ends, splits, tears or dented brass. Discard any cases that show these defects, also any that are unduly oversize, bulged, or otherwise damaged. And be sure to segregate shells having high and low base wads. Have everything in order and remove any small objects other than reloading components from the bench top.

You'll save a lot of time and possible miss-fires by arranging the loading components within easy reach of both hands. For this purpose, you'll find blocks like the ones detailed on page 78 are handy for holding empty shells, wads, primers and the like. All blocks can be made to

hold 50 or 100 components if desired. The empty block keeps the empty shells in order with heads up, preventing dust and small objects from dropping inside. The wad block holds separate wads conveniently stacked to column height, or the unitized plastic wad column-shot cup. The primer block holds live primers with bases down in the most convenient position for picking up one at a time and placing in the re-primer of any loader not equipped with automatic primer dispensers.

The actual reloading procedure merely requires following a few simple hand movements. Take it slowly at first to avoid missing any step, or performing any steps out of sequence. Follow implicitly the instructions furnished with your equipment. If the charging bar on your loader is manually operated, manipulate it properly, using a positive, fairly fast hand movement—not a quick, hard snap or a slow, jerky motion. Unduly slow shifting of the bar can result in slightly heavier than normal charges of both powder and shot; a quick snap may result in lighter, less uniform charging.

Always swing the actuating lever through the full stroke, all the way down and all the way back to the stops at both points. Don't release the lever at the end of the down stroke, then permit it to snap back to the up position. This can agitate the powder in the container excessively and may result in appreciably heavier charges being thrown by the loading bar.

If you accidentally spill or drop powder or shot when loading, some may find its way into the mechanism of press-type loaders. Stop everything and do a thorough clean-up, paying particular attention to any shot pellets that may have worked under the shell carrier or dropped into the reprimer. A shot pellet—or any other small, hard object—in the reprimer could fire a live primer. A remote possibility perhaps, but a precaution to be kept in mind. Another precaution in connection with primers: Never try to seat a live primer by any means other than that provided by the loader's reprimer. And don't for any reason punch out live primers with the loader deprimer, or with a nail, pin-punch or other tool. Don't for any reason insert your finger in the wad starter. You may have trouble removing the finger, may even suffer injury. And finally, *don't smoke while reloading.*

See also: antique guns; chronograph; marksmanship; pheasant hunting; shotguns; targets.

Blast away indoors with wax bullets

Target practice in the living room?
Yep, you can plink away with any
handgun if you load it with soft bullets

amperage, determining: see appliances

amplifier, guitar: see guitar amplifier

amplifier, transistor radio: see transistor radios

AM radio repair: see radio repair, AM

AM receiver: see electronics

■ PISTOL SHOOTING is a tough sport. To be good you've got to work at it. But how can you practice shooting when the local range is under 3 ft. of snow, or you get home from work late and don't have enough time to drive all the way to a distant range and back?

You don't have such problems, of course, if you shoot a .22 and local laws permit you to set up a basement range. But that solution wouldn't do you any good if you favor such center-fire calibers as the .38, .44 or .45.

Hopeless? Not at all.

Today you can shoot indoors—even with the bigger caliber pistols. You can even practice in your living room if you like!

How do you protect the walls, tone down the muzzle blast and stop bullets from ricocheting all over the neighborhood? Simple. Just use wax bullets, fired by primers only. Aside from being amenable to parlor practice, these bullets are gentle enough to be stopped by a sheet of plywood, and accurate enough to keep your shoot-

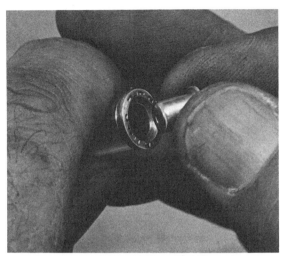

You can keep your shooting eye sharp by using homemade cartridges that are gentle enough to shoot in the living or family rooms. Use plywood and a bullet trap for a backstop

ing eye in good trim. They're also perfectly safe if used with ordinary care.

Loading wax bullets is quite simple, even if you don't own a loading tool. All you do is drill and countersink a set of empty cartridge cases— say a minimum of six—to accommodate shotgun primers. The primers can be inserted by hand. In fact, experience has shown that the rounds work best when the shotgun primers fit loosely enough to simply fall out after they are fired.

Since primers vary somewhat from one manufacturer to another, the cases should be drilled to take a particular brand of primer. The case shown on page 82 was first drilled with a $^{15}\!/_{64}$-in. drill, then countersunk with a $^{5}\!/_{16}$-in. drill.

The countersinking is really the only critical part of the bullet-making job. If you overdo it even slightly, the primers will seat too far away from the firing pin to insure ignition. If you don't drill deep enough, the primer rims will protrude from the cartridge cases and bind the revolver

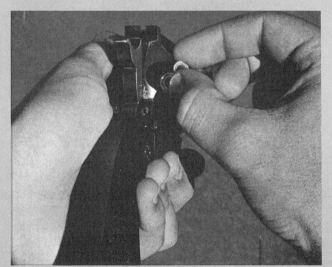

Put primers in the cartridges either before loading your pistol, as shown above, or after the cartridges have been inserted. The latter works best

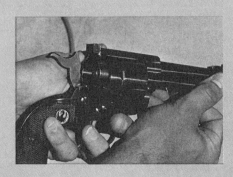

Generally the primer falls out when the cartridge is fired. If this doesn't happen, a push from the inside with a nail or scriber is all that's needed

Cut the bullets from a sheet of wax by pushing unprimed cartridge cases into the wax. Twist the case slightly, withdraw it—and there's your bullet inside

The basic component of an indoor target load is a spent cartridge case (left) drilled and countersunk for a shotgun primer (center). The bullet at the right was made of paraffin, but special bullet-making waxes are available. They are more expensive but safer and easier to use. They also provide cleaner shooting, which boosts accuracy

wax bullets, continued

cylinder. The wisest course is to proceed with the work slowly and, by trial and error, see to it that each primer rim sits exactly flush with the bottom of the cartridge case.

Making the bullets and loading them into the cartridge cases is accomplished simultaneously. The bullets illustrated on these pages were made with ordinary household paraffin or home canning wax. Your first step is to melt the wax in a flat-bottomed pan until there's about ⁵⁄₁₆ in. of wax in the pan. Don't worry about this measurement; it's not critical, since variations of ¹⁄₁₆-in. or so don't affect accuracy very much. Now, after cooling the wax to room temperature, take a cartridge case and push it into the wax as you would press a cookie cutter into dough. Finally, twist the case slightly and withdraw it from the wax. The cylinder of wax left in the case is your bullet.

an even easier way

If that's not simple enough, here's an even easier way: Sporting goods dealers stock wax that is specially formulated for making bullets and comes in sheets of the desired thickness. Since you don't have to melt it down, this wax is safer than paraffin. It also leaves less residue in the bore of the pistol, and the residue that does remain is much easier to clean out. Less than a buck will buy you enough of this product for 200 or so .38 slugs. (A pound of paraffin, by the way, should be sufficient for manufacturing more than 500 homemade bullets.)

Concerning the primers, you can handle these in either of two ways. First, of course, you can insert them in the cartridge cases just before loading the revolver. But since the primers fit rather loosely in position, a more advisable procedure would be to load the unprimed cart-

ridges into the pistol before inserting the primers. The primers should come out readily after firing, with little or no help from you. If for some reason they don't, just push them out with a long nail, a scriber or some similar object.

As you might expect, the accuracy of wax bullets is not as good as that of standard loads. There is more dispersion due to bullet variations and fouling of the bore. And velocity falls off quickly. This doesn't mean that you can't have some good shooting practice, though, because at ranges of around 20 ft.—and how many living rooms are much larger than that?—you can expect consistent groups of around 3 in. in diameter on the target if your hold is good.

loads can hurt you

One word of caution is in order. Don't be careless with these wax bullets. Although wax has little penetration, it can break glass and is capable of bruising a person badly. It might easily put out an eye. So practice the same safety rules when shooting wax loads as you do with standard loads. As for a backstop, a simple plywood bullet trap is all that is needed. Without the trap—that is, if you just shoot against a straight wooden or metal backstop—the wax bullets splatter badly and can spoil the appearance of a room or basement in a hurry.

As you blast merrily away with these tranquilized pistol loads, you'll begin to appreciate one of their most attractive features—low cost. It should cost only around $10 for about 500 rounds, which is a good deal less than full-power loads, even when you load your own. At that rate, a winter's pistol shooting won't run much above 30 bucks—a reasonable price, indeed.

And, best of all, you'll be able to practice right in your own home. By the time spring arrives, you can be in top shooting form.

Names and addresses cut from envelopes make excellent name tags for luggage and other personal gear.

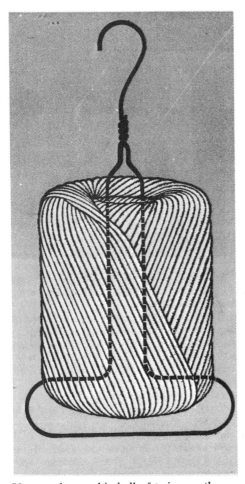

You can hang a big ball of twine on the wall if you bend a wire coat hanger so that the hook slips up through the opening in the center.

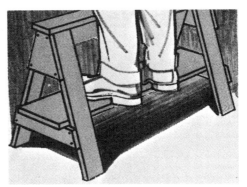

A simple one-step ladder can be made by adding brackets to the legs of your sawhorse.

A stiff rubber hose becomes easier to force over a tight connection after a hot bath.

83

Learn the ABCs of anchoring

BY GORDON P. MANNING

There's more to boating
than just wearing a yachting cap.
The smart skipper knows his anchors
and how to use them
in fair weather and foul

IF YOU'RE going fishing in a 9-ft. dinghy and want to take along a tried-and-true anchor, just tie a big rock to a line and toss it over the side when you want to stop. Such an anchor is difficult to stow and requires plenty of muscle, but it worked for the cavemen, and it still works if you don't get caught in a bad blow. However, for anything larger than a dink, you'll have to leave the Stone Age and use one of today's light-weight anchors.

Modern anchors rely almost entirely on efficient hooking action instead of weight. Some of the heavier types are simply improved versions of designs going back hundreds of years; others, like the ultra-light patent anchors, are entirely new, the result of applying modern science to the ancient problem of holding a boat in one place.

Yachtsman, or kedge, anchor is what most people think of when they hear the word "anchor." The basic design was developed almost 2000 years ago, and it's still one of the best for getting a quick grip in any kind of bottom. While a yachtsman is extremely heavy in proportion to its holding power in most bottoms, this extra weight can come in handy when anchoring in a rocky bottom where it's almost impossible to get a good grip. It breaks out readily and with a folding stock (a relatively recent innovation) can be stowed without too much difficulty. However, if the boat swings, the anchor line can become wound around the exposed fluke result-

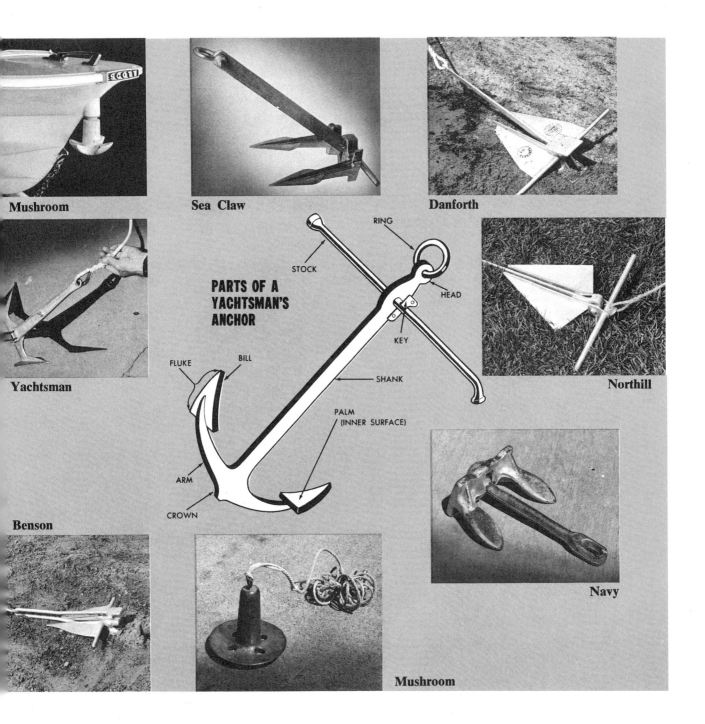

Mushroom

Sea Claw

Danforth

PARTS OF A YACHTSMAN'S ANCHOR

STOCK

RING

HEAD

KEY

SHANK

FLUKE

BILL

PALM
(INNER SURFACE)

ARM

CROWN

Yachtsman

Benson

Northill

Navy

Mushroom

ing in a pulled-out anchor. Also, it's heavy and ungainly to handle in a small boat.

Navy, or stockless, anchor has been around a long time, too. Consisting of a shank with arms and flukes, it's used on larger vessels because it requires almost no handling (the shank can be drawn right up into the hawse pipes). Once set, this type doesn't foul easily, but getting it set on a small boat is sometimes difficult. If the bottom's rough, the anchor may capsize before digging in, and when the boat swings from side to side, it has a tendency to dig itself out, as first one fluke comes free, then the other.

Sea Claw, an improved version of the Navy anchor, has sharper flukes to achieve faster, more certain penetration. Oddly enough, this variation on the "stockless" anchor includes an opposed stock in the crown to prevent tipping. While still somewhat heavy by present-day standards, and hard to clean as well, this type is quite popular on larger boats.

Mushroom anchor, also an old design, is now used almost entirely for permanent moorings. It's virtually foul-proof, but only useful in a bottom soft enough to allow the anchor to dig itself in deeply. A small streamlined version of

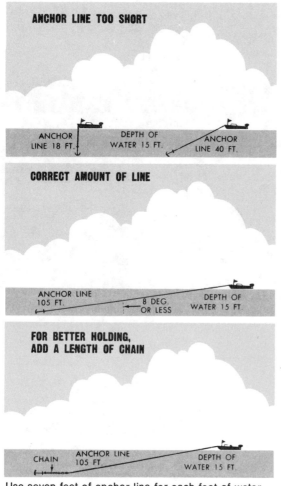

ANCHOR LINE TOO SHORT

ANCHOR LINE 18 FT.   DEPTH OF WATER 15 FT.   ANCHOR LINE 40 FT.

CORRECT AMOUNT OF LINE

ANCHOR LINE 105 FT.   8 DEG. OR LESS   DEPTH OF WATER 15 FT.

FOR BETTER HOLDING, ADD A LENGTH OF CHAIN

CHAIN   ANCHOR LINE 105 FT.   DEPTH OF WATER 15 FT.

Use seven feet of anchor line for each foot of water depth for normal anchoring. The addition of a length of chain will absorb shocks caused by waves acting on the hull, increasing holding power and making it possible to use a shallower angle of pull

Benson's snag-proof anchor has a split shank holding a sliding ring to which the line is attached. When the anchor is snagged (top photo) it can be freed simply by reversing the directon of pull so that the ring slides back to the crown (middle photo) and pulls the anchor out the same way it went in (bottom photo). When released by a change of wind or current, the Benson will flop over and reset itself within a short distance if the bottom is soft enough to make quick penetration possible

this design is quite popular with anglers who want a low-cost anchor which is particularly effective in soft mud bottoms.

Grapnel anchor (not shown) has four or five curved, sharp-pointed arms and holds by entangling itself in bottom growth. It's hard to stow, fouls cable easily and is seldom used except under special conditions.

Today's most popular anchors, the lightweight patent models, have all been developed within the last 30 years. They dig in quickly, hold like bulldogs and are easy to stow.

Danforth anchor, one of today's most popular designs, was used on thousands of W.W. II landing craft to kedge off the beaches. Its two long flukes dig in quickly under a heavy pull and it's one of the easiest to handle and stow.

This lightweight anchor has only one real disadvantage: when anchoring in a strong current an unweighted Danforth will sometimes "sail" down through the water at a flat angle, making digging-in more difficult. However, this can be corrected by adding a length of chain between anchor and line, a practice recommended for all anchors.

Northill looks a lot like an angular version of the yachtsman's anchor, except that the opposed

A trip line attached to the crown will often free a snagged anchor which won't loosen by reversing pull

A chain installation consists of 8 ft. of ¼-in. galvanized chain shackled to an 8-lb. anchor

stock is in the crown instead of the head. This, plus the angle and shape of the plowlike flukes, makes it dig in faster and hold better. However, it has the same disadvantage of holding by one fluke while the other is exposed, making it possible to foul the anchor line on this projecting arm. Northill's twin-fluke model resembles the Danforth, but features angled fins on both sides of each fluke.

Benson anchor has a divided shank holding a sliding ring to which the anchor line is attached. If the anchor snags under a rock, etc., you just reverse the direction of pull and the ring slides back toward the crown, allowing the anchor to come out the same way it went in. Danforth's Shearpin model accomplishes this by notching the foot and blocking this notch with a pin which will break under pressure.

There are literally dozens of other modern anchors which make use of these same principles, achieving greater holding power through the use of quick-penetrating flukes with large surface area. In addition, each design has a number of sizes.

Choosing the proper anchor for your boat is no simple task, because there are so many factors which must be taken into consideration. Have a talk with your marine dealer before deciding on a particular type. He'll be familiar with local conditions, and can inform you as to how different types have performed in your area.

Once you have decided on a particular type, you can use the manufacturer's table as a rough guide to finding the right size anchor and line for your boat. However, don't rely completely on manufacturer's recommendations since these are based on average anchoring conditions. You also have to consider anchorage exposure, type of bottom, shape of your hull, wind and many other things.

Since modern lightweight anchors get their holding power by digging into the bottom at a shallow angle, it follows that the direction of pull on the anchor line should be at the shallowest possible angle to the bottom. Double the angle and the holding power of the anchor drops by one half. Continue to increase the angle and the anchor will finally break out of the bottom alto-

Choosing an anchoring site

• If you're in a strange area, consult the chart before making any decisions.
• Choose a landlocked anchorage if possible, otherwise look for the best protection.
• Avoid the lee shore where unexpected squalls can blow your boat toward the beach.
• Give rocks, reefs and shoals a wide berth as the boat may swing full circle in the event of a sudden change of wind direction.
• Stay away from cable areas. These are indicated on the chart and also marked by large warning signs on the shore.

• Try to anchor over a bottom which will give the best possible bite. Soft mud and clay make for very good holding, so look for spots marked "sft" or "stk" on your chart.
• Steer clear of rocky bottom, hard sand and heavy bottom growth (eel grass, etc.) where the anchor might get fouled. If forced to anchor in such places, always use buoyed trip lines.
• Never anchor in channel or waterway, or near enough so your boat could swing into the traffic.
• Check the level of tide if any and make allowances when figuring scope.

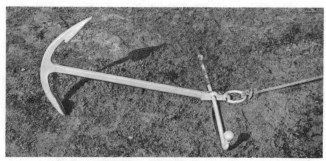

The opposed stock on the Yachtsman causes it to land on the bottom ready to dig in quickly

One bad feature of the Yachtsman is the projecting fluke, on which the anchor line often fouls

gether. This means that you'll have to put over plenty of anchor line, or "rode," to get the best grip on the bottom.

For average conditions, the "scope" (amount of line in use) should be about seven times the depth of the water; for a hard blow, increase this to ten or fifteen times the depth. However, you can cut down the length of line required without seriously affecting holding power by breaking the straight-line pull between boat and anchor. On larger boats, this is achieved by running a second anchor or weight part way down the line. On smaller boats the most common solution is to add a 6 to 10 ft. length of ½-in. or ¼-in. galvanized chain between the anchor and the end of the line. This will increase the holding power of your anchor under all conditions, and also cut down on anchor failure due to surge action from the boat. Many marine dealers offer a ground tackle package with anchor, chain and line in a single unit.

You can use your anchor as a lead to check the depth of the water if you mark the line at specific intervals. These markings will also come in handy in keeping track of the scope which you have paid out. Of the many marking methods in use, one of the most practical is a small dot or ring of colored paint. Mark the first 20 ft. at 2-ft. intervals, then mark the rest of the line at 5 or 10 ft. intervals. By varying the colors or number of rings, you can read the rode at a glance.

The actual process of anchoring a small boat seems to be one of the least understood operations in boating. However, assuming you have the proper ground tackle, it's actually quite simple. First, pick the exact spot where you want your boat to be when she's finally at anchor. Then head up into the wind or current, whichever is stronger, and go far enough *beyond* this spot to allow for the proper scope. Next, with the boat stopped, lower the anchor slowly over the side directly to the bottom, pay out a scope at least three or four times the water depth and make it fast temporarily. Finally, reverse the engine and idle slowly backward until the anchor digs into the bottom and stops the boat.

If you're just stopping for an hour or two in calm water and plan to stay around the boat, this scope of three or four times the depth will be sufficient. However, if you plan to leave the boat unattended for long, increase the scope.

Getting the anchor up is simply the reverse of anchoring. Just run slowly up over the anchor, give the line a tug and the anchor should break free. If it's dug in deeply, make a quick turn around the bitt when all slack is out and power ahead very slowly. If this doesn't work, run in a tight circle around the anchor, since pulling from another angle may free it.

See also: boat camping; boat equipment; boat handling; boat repair; boats, buying; boats, used; boats, rope; ladders, boat; propellers, boat.

Anchoring tips

● Never heave an anchor over upside down. The anchor may fail to bite, and the line will snag.
● In a real blow, let out every bit of line you have aboard, provided you have space enough to do so without danger.
● After setting the anchor, take a cross range on nearby shore objects and check after 15 min. to make sure you aren't dragging.
● Never attach a line to an anchor with a knot; use an eye splice with a thimble.
● Any pleasure craft over 25 ft. should carry two anchors—a service anchor for normal use and a storm anchor which can be put out to provide extra holding power in a big blow.
● Don't leave a releasing anchor (Benson, Danforth, Shearpin) unattended for long periods of time as a sudden change of current or wind can release it.

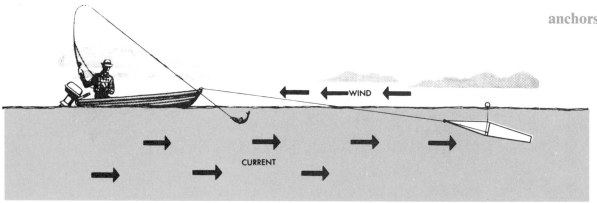

Drift sock for fishermen

■ THIS FISHERMAN'S VERSION of the old-fashioned sea anchor will be welcomed when wind and fast drift make it almost impossible to cast and cover weed beds and sand bars. Even when you aren't faced with the ideal current-wind situation illustrated above, the sock will cut your drift speed greatly and keep the bow heading into the wind with no side twisting.

The sock illustrated here is large enough for boats 14 to 16 ft. long. To make it you'll need: a ⅛ x ¾ x 56-in. aluminum bar; three ⅜-in. aluminum rivets or bolts; three ½-in. grommets; a 2-in. metal ring; plus canvas, heavy nylon thread and ¼-in. nylon rope.

Bend the aluminum bar to form a hoop, overlapping the ends 3 in. Drill three holes in this overlapped portion and rivet or bolt the ends together. After cutting the canvas, double-stitch a 1-in. seam to form a cut-off cone shape and turn the sock inside out so the seam doesn't show. Then slip the hoop over the front of the sock about 1¾-in. from the edge and fold the canvas back over it. Stitch it at least three times.

Install the three grommets in the double thickness of canvas behind the hoop and attach the three tie-ropes with bowline knots. Using the same knot, tie the ropes to the 2-in. ring that is attached to the pull rope. The pull rope should be at least twice as long as the boat. For shallow water, add a cork float to the sock.

angels: see Christmas decorations
animal cutouts: see gifts, Christmas
animal novelties: see whittling

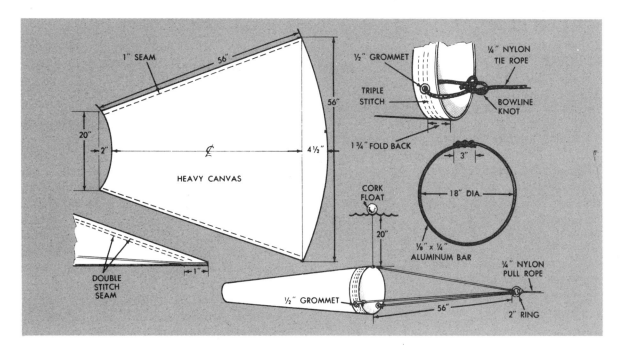

see page 191 for Project-a-plans

Hang them in the kid's room,
the rec room or the kitchen,
both to add a decorative touch
and to carry the family messages

Animal plaques

BY DAVE SWARTWOUT

NO REASON why bulletin boards can't be decorative while hanging around, and here are six good examples of how the lowly square board can take the shape of animal wall plaques to dress up various rooms of the house.

By making them from common ½-in. insulation board, you can stick a pin in them anywhere, and it's no trick at all to cut such soft material into fanciful shapes.

animated Christmas displays: see Christmas displays
animated Easter egg: see Easter decorations
annular-wing model airplane: see airplane models

You can enlarge the patterns which appear on this and the next page by using Project-a-plans, which make it as easy as showing colored slides. Turn to page 191, clip out the pattern of your choice, and coat it on both sides with clear nail polish or shellac.

After it dries, insert it into a standard 35-mm. slide mount. Then you can project it to any size you want, using the material from which you intend to cut the design as a screen. Trace the projected plan on insulation board, and you're ready to start sawing.

If you don't have a projector and can't borrow one, the cutouts are presented on a grid pattern so that you can enlarge them by the square-at-a-

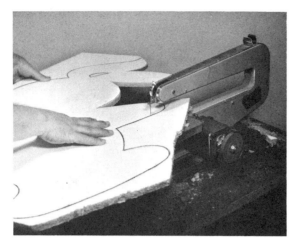

A fine-toothed blade in any type of saw
cuts insulation board best

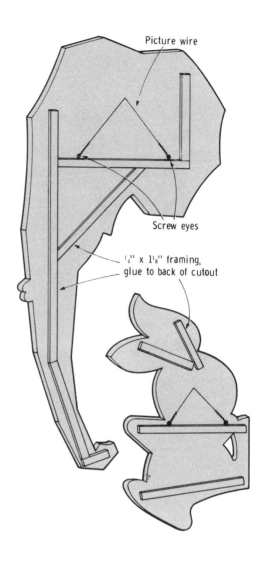

Picture wire

Screw eyes

¼" x 1⅛" framing,
glue to back of cutout

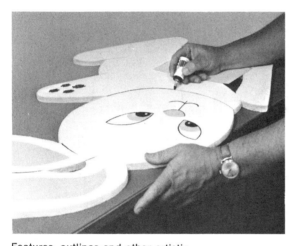

Features, outlines and other artistic
touches are added quickly to the
painted cutouts with felt-tipped markers

turn the page for patterns.

time method. It's a little slow, but with care
you can enlarge the pattern to any size.

Insulation board comes with a nice white
base finish which makes a pencil line show up
like tracks across snow. Of course, you can't
beat a sabre saw for sawing out such large cutouts since you can take the saw directly to the
work. But where it's necessary to saw them out
with a jigsaw, you'll first have to saw apart any
nested patterns to get the ungainly 4 x 8 ft. sheet
down to a workable size. Where there's an inside cutout, pierce the board with a sharp instrument so you can insert the saw blade. Sand the
edges slightly and treat them with two coats of
white waterbase paint. All surface painting can

be done with one coat of latex colors. For dark
outlines, felt-tip markers are faster than a brush,
and they come in a wide selection of colors.

Since it's easy to snap off a portion of a cutout due to the "brittleness" of insulation board,
you should handle it gingerly during and after
sawing. In fact, it's wise to add thin wood strips
(such as lath) to the backs of the cutouts to
strengthen them. These also provide a means of
attaching any type of wall hanger, from screw-
eyes to the new glue-on hooks. The drawings
above show how the wood strips can be ar-
ranged to brace the elephant's trunk and the
rabbit's ears.

See also: boys' projects; gifts, Christmas.

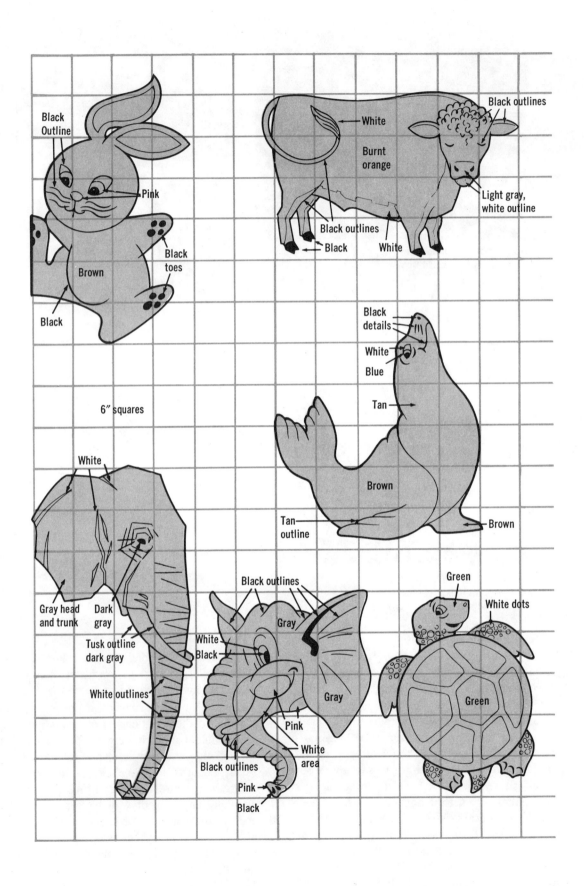

6" squares

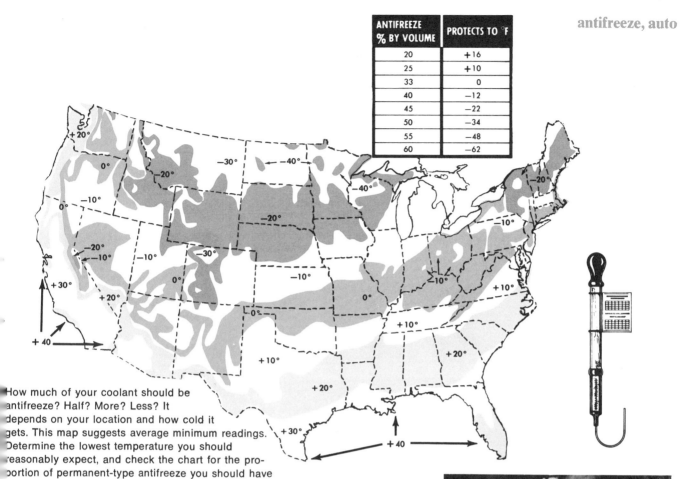

ANTIFREEZE % BY VOLUME	PROTECTS TO °F
20	+16
25	+10
33	0
40	−12
45	−22
50	−34
55	−48
60	−62

How much of your coolant should be antifreeze? Half? More? Less? It depends on your location and how cold it gets. This map suggests average minimum readings. Determine the lowest temperature you should reasonably expect, and check the chart for the proportion of permanent-type antifreeze you should have

Nothing lasts forever, including antifreeze. But just how safe are the kinds they tell you to leave in the year–round? Read the facts

How permanent is permanent antifreeze?

BY MORTON J. SCHULTZ

Frequent checks of the coolant level are vital with anything but permanent-type antifreeze, to avoid loss by "afterboil." And once you've had to add make-up water, use a hydrometer to be sure the antifreeze proportion is still enough to give the protection you need

■ IN AUTOMOTIVE AFFAIRS, as in politics, there's often more below the surface than comforting promises might suggest. Take the situation surrounding so-called permanent antifreeze.

There's nothing truly permanent about "permanent" antifreeze of course. It doesn't last forever. In the words of the U.S. Bureau of Standards: "From the standpoint of inhibitor service life and corrosion protection, the term 'permanent' as applied to antifreeze is a misnomer."

And right now there's an argument going on among antifreeze producers as to whether "permanent" antifreeze will maintain its protective

"antique" cobbler's bench: see cobbler's bench

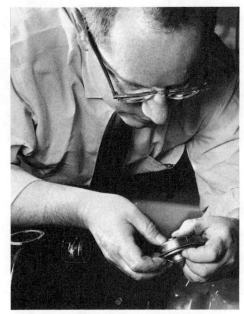

Your choice of antifreeze depends partly on the temperature rating of the car's thermostat —printed right on the unit. Add 20 deg. to this figure and check the boiling point table at right to see if non-permanent types are safe

TYPES OF ANTIFREEZE	BOILING POINTS OF SOLUTION RATED TO FREEZE AT:			
	+10°	0°	−10°	−20°
ETHYLENE GLYCOL	218°	220°	221°	223°
METHANOL	190°	185°	182°	179°
ETHANOL	187°	184°	182°	180°

The graph at the right shows that non-permanent methanol gives the most protection per unit volume. For 20 deg. below less than 40 percent of methanol would give as much protection as 50 percent of ethanol. But the table (above) shows ethylene glycol is least likely to boil off

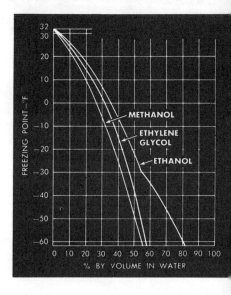

permanent antifreeze, continued

qualities for as long as *two years*. Some claim only *one season*. That's hardly "permanent"!

Everyone does admit, however, that "permanent" antifreeze does have a few qualities (the ability to withstand evaporation by boiling is one) that makes it *more* permanent than other types of antifreeze. Thus, the word is justifiably used in this context: It *is* an antifreeze that's meant to stay in your cooling system year 'round, in contrast to the old type you put in, come fall, and drain out next spring.

Of the two major types of antifreeze, the "permanent" one has a base of ethylene glycol; the alcohol type has a methanol or an ethanol base.

When put into a car's cooling system and mixed with water, the ethylene "permanent" glycol antifreeze provides indefinite protection against freezing. In other words, as long as the antifreeze is not further diluted, the freezing protection provided by a specific amount of antifreeze when mixed with a certain amount of water lasts indefinitely.

Why, then, is it necessary to drain out "permanent" antifreeze? Why can't you leave it in your car's cooling system until it's so weakly diluted by water that it must be replaced?

The answer to these questions lies in the dual functions antifreeze is supposed to perform. It's supposed to protect against freezing, of course, but it's also supposed to protect the car's cooling system against corrosion.

Most quality antifreezes, "permanent" or otherwise, have inhibitors added to their base to retard corrosion. These inhibitors are needed to offset the natural tendency of metal to return to its organic state. Iron, for example, tends to return to its state as iron oxide which, when it appears in an automotive cooling system, can clog the system. At first it appears black but as it absorbs more oxygen it turns a rusty brown.

Inhibitors used today take two general forms: One type of inhibitor is chemical in nature to counteract (or neutralize) the action of metal; the other type of inhibitor is the so-called polar film inhibitor designed to protect metal (aluminum in particular) by forming a film over it.

Various chemical inhibitors are added to antifreeze, then—each type designed to provide protection against a specific metallic corrosion problem. For many years, for example, the government specified sodium borate as the inhibitor for military vehicles equipped with cast-iron en-

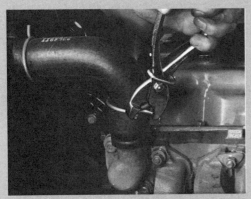

Check hose clamps to be sure they haven't lost tension and aren't cutting into the hose. The common spring type (above) can be squeezed off with a large pair of pliers

Check the hose itself by feeling it inside and out. A rough or flaking inside surface and either a spongy or extra hard exterior—as it's squeezed—indicate replacement time

gine and cooling system parts. But recently, chemists at the Aberdeen Proving Ground came up with an inhibitor designed for today's higher-horsepower engines, in which aluminum components are used in conjunction with other metals. It consists of borax, disodium phosphate and something called mercaptobenzothiazole—and it's mixed right in with your radiator's water and permanent-type antifreeze. If you're a determined do-it-yourselfer, you can get a copy of the Army's report by ordering AD 433 829 from the Office of Technical Services, U.S. Dept. of Commerce, Washington, D.C. 20230, enclosing 75¢. Of course, most commercial antifreezes already contain more than one type of chemical inhibitor—one to protect iron, another for aluminum, still another for brass. You don't mix these in yourself.

The polar film inhibitor is a synthetic organic compound designed specifically to protect aluminum parts. The compound is suspended in the system as the antifreeze is added, but then forms a protective film over aluminum. Polar film inhibitors are used in combination with several chemical inhibitors to protect *all* metals.

The one specific reason why "permanent" antifreeze is *not* truly permanent involves these inhibitors. *They wear out with use. How quickly* is the question around which the "one-year or two-year" advocates argue. Recommending "one year" usage are Union Carbide and Chrysler, Ford, General Motors, American Motors and some "permanent" antifreeze makers still recommend "two year" usage.

How quickly inhibitors wear out cannot be determined—if it could, there'd be no controversy. There are too many factors reacting against the inhibitors which make it impossible to reach a hard-and-fast rule for cars, straight across the board. Some of these factors are the mileage put on a car during a specific period, the temperature reached by the engine, the presence of an aeration condition, exhaust and fuel fumes that come into contact with the antifreeze, and the type of terrain over which the car is driven (mountainous, flat, near the ocean).

In other words, the inhibitors in antifreeze become exhausted when used under any set of conditions, but this life expectancy also depends on how and where the car is operated, and on the car's mechanical condition.

Both sides in the argument agree that as soon as "permanent" antifreeze solution loses its original color and becomes tinged with the slightest bit of rust, it should be dumped immediately, no matter what the time factor. This must be checked when the coolant has been circulated—that is, after the engine has been run a while.

The argument, basically then, is between a more conservative approach to time and a less conservative approach—a safer approach, if you will, and one that tries to extend the life of the solution so the customer can get maximum use from it. Both camps, naturally, have the interests of the customer in mind.

The most damaging piece of evidence against use of "permanent" antifreeze for more than one year was disclosed by Union Carbide Co.

Union Carbide made a spot check of 2155 various cars filled with two-year factory coolant. It found that cooling system malfunctions were reported in one out of every 20 cars within the first year of service. Furthermore, the coolant in about 15 percent of the cars had lost 50 percent of its inhibitor protection between 8000 and 16,000 miles—and this same amount of protec-

95

tion was lost in about 33 percent of the cars with over 16,000 on them.

Union Carbide makes these other points to back up their position as to why "permanent" antifreeze should be discarded annually: too many car owners take the word "permanent" too literally and do not examine the coolant and, even if they did, most would not be able to recognize a weakened solution.

By an annual change of coolant, Union Carbide states that it means the antifreeze should be drained after a winter's use and new solution added in the fall, except in airconditioned cars that send frigid air through the heater core. In these, antifreeze is required all year round to prevent freezing of coolant in the heater. Thus, airconditioned cars, says the Union Carbide theory, should have antifreeze changed twice a year: once in the fall, at the start of cold weather, and again in the spring when old antifreeze is dumped. (In non-airconditioned cars, it's assumed that a commercial inhibitor will be added to the radiator water for summer driving.)

Union Carbide, by the way, is so convinced of its stand that it refuses to designate as "permanent" its own antifreeze with an ethylene glycol base and polar film and chemical inhibitors.

watch the color

If you use ethylene glycol ("permanent") antifreeze you can play it safe either by adding new antifreeze in the fall and draining it in the spring, or by checking your antifreeze color as often as you check your oil. The slightest off-color change can be a sign the solution has weakened and may need changing.

If antifreeze does become exhausted and contaminated without you knowing it, the car's cooling system can be severely damaged. And repair of that damage will cost you a lot more than the few dollars needed to drain and replace antifreeze periodically.

What about using an alcohol-base antifreeze which costs about half what a "permanent" type will cost per quart? Will it do the job as well? Actually, the non-permanent alcohol-base antifreeze, methanol, provides *greater* freezing protection per unit volume than the "permanent" ethylene glycol type. But there's more to consider.

For example, today's engines run at high temperatures and every antifreeze solution has a boiling point—that is, a temperature level which, when reached, causes the antifreeze to boil and evaporate. In laboratory tests it's been proved that the "permanent" ethylene glycol type has

a higher boiling point than either the alcohol-base methanol or ethanol types. A chart on page 94 gives comparisons.

When boiling of ethylene glycol solution occurs, it's not the ethylene glycol that evaporates, unless that car reaches a temperature at which it's actually overheating. Instead, the water used in the solution evaporates. When this happens, you simply add water to bring the solution back to level, although to be safe you should always double-check the protection with a hydrometer.

When boiling occurs in cars equipped with a non-permanent alcohol-base antifreeze, the *antifreeze itself* evaporates. Thus, use of this type demands that you keep a constant eye on coolant level throughout the winter. If the level falls off and you have to add coolant, it must be in the form of new antifreeze to maintain protection against the low temperature. This additional antifreeze, then, could in the long run be more expensive for you than if you filled the cooling system with ethylene glycol to begin with.

check heater and thermostat

Another factor to mull over in your consideration of what antifreeze to use is the type of heater you have in the car. Most cars produced in the 1960's have forced air heaters. These usually require a 180 deg. or higher thermostat to operate efficiently. The addition of alcohol-type antifreezes to the cooling system demands lower temperature thermostats, usually those rated at 149 or 160 deg., to offset boiling.

In other words, the 180 deg. thermostat needed for efficient heater operation doesn't permit the antifreeze to circulate and cool until it reaches 180 deg., which is too close to the boiling points of methanol and ethanol. Thus, on the one hand (by switching to a lower-temperature thermostat), you compromise heat output. On the other hand (by keeping the 180 deg. thermostat), you maintain heat output but stand a good chance of boiling out the antifreeze.

In any case, a smooth-running, long-lived engine requires a clean cooling system. Putting clean antifreeze in a dirty system makes little sense. And corrosion deposits in the cylinder head, for example, act like insulation, preventing the coolant from doing its job properly.

You'll be money ahead if you check your antifreeze frequently, and replace it whenever it shows signs of "wearing out."

See also: batteries, auto; battery chargers; driving, snow; electrical system, auto; rust prevention; spark plugs, auto; starting, auto, cold weather.

Furniture refinishing—new to old

■ "NEW-OLD" LIFE to furniture that may have been stored in your attic for a generation or more; antique color and flavor to new pieces you may have built in your workshop; these are the intriguing possibilities with new antiquing finishes applied in simple A-B-C steps. The finish itself does most of the antiquing. There are no involved procedures to learn the hard way, no cranky tricks to follow through with beforehand; just paint the stuff on and wipe off a part of the glazing coat with a deft touch and a little play of imagination. And that's it—almost.

But if you plan to "reantique" an old piece,

take a hard, appraising look at it before you paint on the ground coat that comes with your antiquing kit. There are likely rough spots that need smoothing up and the thing will need washing with mild soapsuds to get off the embedded dust and grime of the years. And perhaps there's some little shelf-like affair or some other old "gingerbread" you decide you may want to remove. Then take off all the hardware and store in a marked container. Next wash, sand or steel-wool lightly, fill all nail holes, screw holes and the like and sand the filler flush so you don't end up with unsightly lumps under the new

Remove all the hardware first, being especially careful to preserve it without damage if not replaceable. Store it in a labeled container

antique finishes, continued

If the piece is old and has been stored in attic or basement, wash it thoroughly with mild soapsuds to remove accumulated grime and discolorations

Then sand or steel-wool lightly and wipe off *all* the dust. Apply ground coat and allow to dry. After applying the top coat, use any technique desired

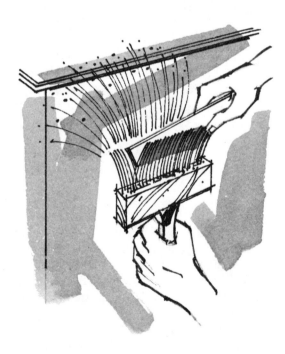

A light spatter applied as indicated gives that certain "distressed" effect so desirable on many pieces. Try spattering a waste piece first

Wiping the finish coat with an artificial sponge can give a realistic wood-grain effect. Apply ground and top coats to a waste piece and experiment first

finish. Make any necessary repairs, such as regluing loose legs and freeing drawers that stick. If the piece has been painted and there are paint drips along edges, sand these off smooth. Steel-wool the painted surfaces to form a "tooth" for the new finish.

But don't remove the old finish, either paint or varnish. If it is still in reasonably good condition and sticking tightly, all the better. If you suspect it has been waxed at some time or other, play it safe and rub down with turpentine or a wax remover; otherwise you're in trouble.

Now you're all set for the new finish. Give the piece a final, thorough wipe-up with the tack cloth you get with most kits. Or give it a thorough brushing—anything to get *all* the dust off the surfaces and out of the corners. A "pick-stick" made by sharpening the end of a small-diameter dowel is handy for loosening that stuff-and-things that tend to gather in corners and just won't be brushed or wiped out. Now give the ground coat a thorough stirring, making sure you loosen all the pigment that may have settled to the bottom of the can. Lay it on the larger surfaces with a

1½-in. brush in long, one-way strokes; no back-brushing. Be sure the strokes overlap just enough to give a uniform coating with no drips or sags. Watch closely the underside corners of tops, the bottom edges of doors and drawers to see that no unsightly drips form; watch any intricate moldings to see that the ground coat does not collect in a heavy coating. Such drips and sags will take days to thoroughly dry. Brush out these places, also corners, to a uniform film thickness matching that on the flat surfaces. Give the ground coat at least 24 hrs. to dry. In some instances you may require a second ground coat. Be sure the first is dry before applying a second.

wiping glaze coating

Comes now the "creative" fun of the whole procedure. Apply the color glaze as directed on the container in a relatively thin, uniform coating, being especially careful to hit all indentations, corners, molded edges and any other finer detail. Allow the glaze coat to dry 10 to 15 minutes or until it becomes somewhat tacky to the touch. There's no need to feel in a tearing hurry; the gel-like glaze coating takes time to set beyond the complete wipe-off stage. But in this step it is generally best to cover only relatively small areas such as the top only of an average-sized table or the front of a chest. With the latter it is usually best to take the drawers first; the top, sides and front rails last. So you begin by gingerly wiping a surface lightly with the cheese-cloth wiper that comes with the kit. If, after a few strokes, you like what you see you keep right on with the same technique. Or, if it is not just what you expected, you try some other wiper, such as a small sponge, or a brush cleaned in solvent and used "dry." Just about anything in wipers goes—if the results satisfy you. If you don't like the look of what you get with several experimental wipers, clean the whole glaze coat off with solvent and start all over again. If you're new at antiquing with the kits, you won't be long discovering that the glaze coat is amenable to almost any treatment.

Colors available? Almost anything you can dream up, either regular or intermixed, pastels, solids, wood colors in natural or stained, or grained in simulation of the natural graining of a wide range of wood varieties. Even marble can be simulated with rather amazing reality, so good you have to look hard to tell it from real.

See also: abrasives; finishes, furniture; finishes, removing; finishes, urethane; finishes, wood; floor finishing; staining, wood.

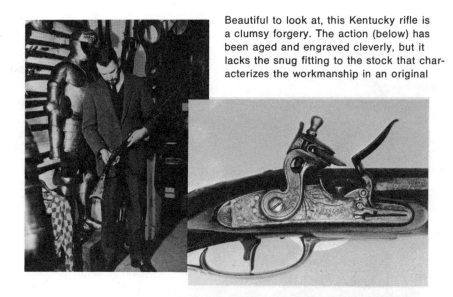

Beautiful to look at, this Kentucky rifle is a clumsy forgery. The action (below) has been aged and engraved cleverly, but it lacks the snug fitting to the stock that characterizes the workmanship in an original

Closeup (right) of Palmetto 1842 being examined (below, right) shows engraved palm tree with drooping leaves. On forgeries, tree's leaves do not match

That antique gun—
fortune or forgery?

Old firearms are worth big money, but beware of magnetic "brass," fake stamping and clever assembly jobs

BY MORTON J. GOLDING

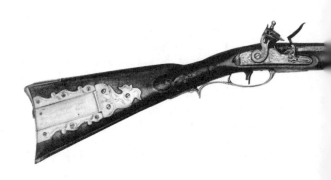

Common weapons are the most popular forgeries, but they also are the most easily detected. For example, the Palmetto 1842 can be judged during a cursory examination

■ A FEW YEARS AGO, a wealthy collector of antique firearms decided to specialize in pistols with solid brass barrels. Although these pieces are relatively scarce and hard to come by, a large number suddenly appeared on the market and

antique tools: see rust removal

ants: see carpenter ants; insect control

anvils: see stake plate

aphids: see insect control

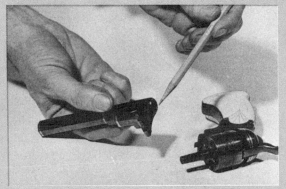

Colt pistols are best checked through their serial numbers. This genuine Paterson Colt has the number stamped on the inside base of the barrel, and its pedigree can always be obtained from the Colt Arms Company

the collector was able to buy just the ones he wanted.

One day, however, he invited a fellow collector with a suspicious nature to view his prize possessions. When the man examined the pistols, he took a magnet from his pocket and touched it to several of the barrels. Each time, the magnet held fast!

There could only be one of two explanations. Either the laws of nature had been suddenly and mysteriously suspended to allow brass to become magnetized—or the barrels were made of iron covered by a thin brass plating.

Actually, the guns were nothing more nor less than well-made forgeries. The collector was willing to pay large sums of money for old guns that were not readily available. And the gun fakers were making the most of the situation by having them brass plated locally.

A man who has been fighting the gun fakers for many years is Henry M. Stewart of Wynnewood, Pennsylvania, former president of the American Society of Arms Collectors. According to Mr. Stewart, about $200,000 a year changes hands in the buying and selling of forged antique firearms.

Although gun fakery has a long if inglorious history, its current rise parallels the tremendous growth of gun collecting as a hobby. Since 1940, the number of collectors in the United States has increased 25 times or more. And in the same period, the value of the average collector's item has risen more than 350 percent.

The first Colt Walker models once sold for as little as 50 cents. By 1911, the price had gone up to $500. To buy a Walker in really good condition nowadays, however, you'd have to shell out at least $5000—and many collectors would not let one go that cheaply!

Samuel Colt originally made 1100 of the heavy, long-barrelled Walkers. There are about 150 in existence today. Of that number, Henry M. Stewart estimates that some fifty are fakes in whole or in part.

How does a faker go about forging a Walker? He may begin by purchasing a genuine frame which costs $400 to $500. He can then pick up some Colt replacement parts which do not have serial numbers, but which can be stamped to agree with the number on the frame. By combining these with other parts which he can make himself, and attaching a lengthened barrel of a less-rare Colt Dragoon model, the forger can realize a quick profit.

Fakery was not always directed solely to antiques. The tiny, one-shot Deringer pistol was

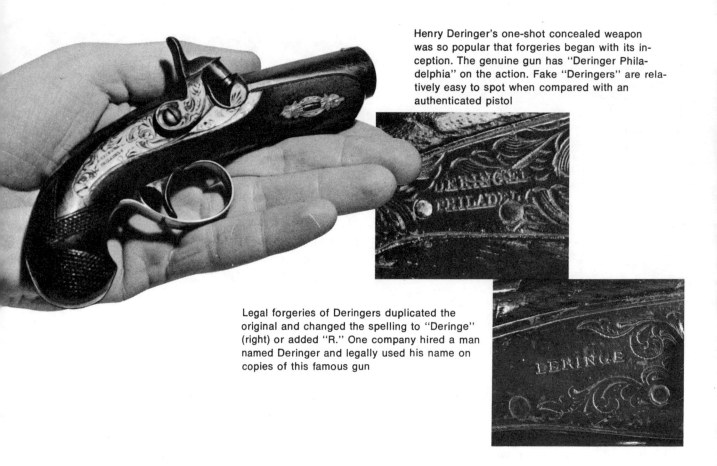

Henry Deringer's one-shot concealed weapon was so popular that forgeries began with its inception. The genuine gun has "Deringer Philadelphia" on the action. Fake "Deringers" are relatively easy to spot when compared with an authenticated pistol

Legal forgeries of Deringers duplicated the original and changed the spelling to "Deringe" (right) or added "R." One company hired a man named Deringer and legally used his name on copies of this famous gun

forged almost from the beginning in order to cash in on Henry Deringer's reputation. By now, however, many of these early forgeries have found their way into the antique market.

Some of the early Deringer fakes were produced by former workmen of his, and are extremely hard to detect. One company actually hired a Philadelphia tailor named Deringer so that they would have the legal right to use the name on their gun. Others used two "r's" in the name, and the "Derringer" forgeries have become proverbial among gun collectors.

Another famous group of forgeries were of the early 19th century Forsyth pistols. Though little known outside of gun collecting circles, the Reverend Alexander Forsyth ushered in the modern era of percussion weapons. Before Forsyth, gunpowder was exploded either through friction or by fire. In the modern method, a light blow is given to certain chemical powders known as fulminates. The fulminate explodes and sets off the gunpowder.

The Forsyth system was patented in England in 1807. The most famous of his detonators is known as a scent bottle because it roughly resembles one. These early pistols have been sought by collectors for many years. And in the

1920s, a British gunsmith decided to forge them.

His main difficulty was in making the scent bottles, but as a skilled metal worker he was able to solve the problem. He attached the forged scent bottles to later models both of the Forsyth and other pistols, and then proceeded to sell the fakes for high prices.

The real pistols almost always have the word, "Patent," as well as a scroll engraved on the scent bottle. Since England has strong laws against the false use of this word, it has been left off most of the forgeries. In addition, the Forsyth signature on the barrel was engraved in steel on the early models, while the later ones have the signature in gold inlay.

An extremely rare American pistol which has fallen prey to the forgers is the North and Cheney 1799 model. This is the first U.S. martial pistol to be made by private contract, and its design was greatly influenced by the French military model of 1777—a much less valuable gun.

Taking advantage of this, the forgers often doctor one of the French pistols to resemble the North and Cheney.

There are several tests by which collectors determine the real North and Cheneys. For one thing, the U.S. pistols were made without belt

In an effort to distinguish his authentic weapon from the dozens of copies, Deringer engraved the base of the barrel with a registered trademark, the letter "P" surrounded by a sunburst pattern

Most forgeries of the Deringer in circulation today are also engraved on the barrel (left), but the makers carefully avoid legal entanglement by omitting the registered "P" trademark

hooks. For another, their barrels are slightly longer than the French models. But the only sure test is a close comparison with a known, authentic North and Cheney. Without such a comparison, no matter how sharp your eye, it is possible to wind up with a French piece worth from $50 to $75 instead of a gun valued at from $2500 to $3000.

The Confederate field is one of the most lucrative markets for today's busy forger. One common trick is played with the Enfield rifle which was both imported from England and manufactured in the Confederacy. Since the homemade model is more valuable, forgers remove English markings from the British Enfields and replace them with phony Confederate markings.

Another class of rifle which many collectors are interested in is the old Kentucky long rifle. Mr. Tom Hall, curator of the Winchester Museum in New Haven, Connecticut, told me of one man who bought a long rifle which looked perfectly genuine. In the manner of these old guns, the barrel was not "blued" but "browned" —a process using controlled rusting. When the gun was cleaned, however, the collector found

that it was really made up of two barrels welded together to make one long one.

The value of a genuine Kentucky rifle depends partly on whether it is a flintlock or a percussion gun. Since the flintlocks are older, they are worth more than the percussion types.

Many original flintlocks were later turned into percussion guns by their owners, though, and these guns are not worth nearly as much today as they would have been if left alone. The faker's solution? Change them back into flintlocks again. Sometimes, also, original percussions are changed into flintlocks.

It takes a sharp eye to tell when this is done. The Winchester Museum, for instance, has a changed-back flintlock with the name "John Philip Beck" on the barrel. To a casual glance, the gun appears genuine enough. But a closer examination will show that the lock plate doesn't fit into the mortise as closely as one would normally expect, even though the piece is old.

Another interesting fake at the Winchester Museum is that of a cavalry wheel-lock pistol supposedly made in England or Germany in about 1650. It was actually built around a few

North and Cheney pistols originally were copied from the French military model 1777, and confusion between American ($3000) and the French ($50) can be costly. The French model (right) has a shorter barrel and ramrod

old pieces in about 1910. One way the gun proves itself a fake is by the inside of the barrel. Although the muzzle is for a large-caliber shell, the size is considerably reduced about halfway down. Also, the barrel is not bored all the way to the touchhole. The gun, in other words, could never have been fired!

Winchester's own "One of One Thousand" series of 1873 and "One of One Hundred" series of 1876 consist of guns that were selected at the factory for their shooting ability and then marked with the appropriate slogan. The forgers often take an ordinary 1873 or 1876 model and engrave "One of One Thousand" or "One of One Hundred" on the barrel. You can check these guns by sending the serial number to the factory where all of the genuine ones are on file.

Recently a pair of carbines marked "One of One Thousand" showed up with their serial numbers worn away. The people at Olin Mathieson, who now own Winchester, were able to bring the original numbers back with the aid of acid, and the guns turned out to be fakes.

Today's typical gun forger is likely to be a small-time operator who joins a local gun club and finds his victims there. Within a club, members show off their collections, trade and buy in an atmosphere of good fellowship. A man is most likely to be off his guard there, and can often be persuaded to ignore the usual safeguards.

One such recent victim was approached by a fellow club member and asked if he was interested in buying an 1848 Colt Dragoon pistol in first rate condition for $600. While not as costly as some other Colts, the Dragoon model will still fetch around $1000 on the open market. But the would-be seller said that he was in urgent need

of cash and would let his gun go at the lower price if he could have the check immediately.

This is the sort of offer which will bring a gleam into the eye of any collector. The victim did feel a small twinge of suspicion. But he was quickly soothed by being assured that the pistol had been looked at and admired by several experts whom the forger mentioned by name.

Investigation, however (including comparison with a genuine antique), showed that the gun was actually a modern replica which was legitimately sold as a copy but then was artificially aged by the forger.

In the aftermath of this affair, the forger was forced to return the victim's money and asked to leave the gun club.

Since the comparison method is the best way to detect fakes, probably the most difficult to catch are those of odd guns which may or may not have ever existed.

At the time that Sam Colt was turning out his pistols in Paterson, New Jersey, for example, many European makers were coming on the market with variations of the Colt. These "Colt types" had a similar relationship to real Colts that "Scotch type" whiskey has to the stuff actually made in Scotland. But they have picked up a certain value of their own as antiques.

A few years ago, a New York gun dealer was offered a pistol marked "Systeme le S. Colt" which was presumably made in Belgium about 1840. The dealer asked Henry M. Stewart to examine it for him and the gun turned out to be a recent English fake. Apparently trying to play it safe, the forger did not attempt to copy a Colt, but went after an old imitation which he knew would be harder to check.

On still another occasion, the same dealer asked Stewart to check a pair of martial Palmetto 1842 pistols. When the gun expert compared them to a pair of authentic Palmettos, he noticed a curious thing. The real pistols are stamped with small palmetto trees, the bottom branches of which curve out and back to form a sort of "O." On the ones that the dealer gave him, though, the bottom branches did not match. For this and other reasons, Stewart decided that they must be fakes and the money was returned.

Some forgers work by making relatively minor changes in genuine old guns in order to add to their value. It is they, for instance, who exchange English for American markings on Confederate Enfields.

Another example of a minor change meaning major money is sometimes worked on snaphance pistols. These early precursors of the flintlock are worth about $3000 each if made in America, but only about $1500 if Englishmade. To double the value of an English gun, then, a man need only file off the original name of the maker and add a presumed American one.

One probable snaphance fake now in the Winchester Museum is marked "J. Pim of Boston." It is likely that Mr. Pim never even existed.

easy tricks scorned

But the most enterprising fakers of all will scorn easy tricks. They will go to any lengths to recreate a gun.

A top-flight gunsmith has prepared roller dies of cylinder engravings and a machine to apply this engraving to a cylinder. The owner of a gun can buy this service for about $50. The value of the piece soars until the illegitimate reengraving is detected through small errors which can be found by comparison with authentic cylinders.

The engraver, incidentally, strongly denies that *he* is a forger. He merely makes the dies, he contends. What people do with the guns afterwards is no concern of his, as he sells only a service.

Then there was the man who decided to reproduce the rare, silver-mounted Frederick Zorger single-shot pistols that were made in Yorktowne, Pennsylvania, during the Revolutionary War. He created the guns from a pair of Irish Flintlock pistols, then went to the York–Lancaster area (formerly Yorktowne) and bought several old spoons with "touches" or proofs of early silversmiths. He removed the touches, silver-soldered them to the trigger guards, then silver-plated around them. Examination under gamma X rays detected the forgery.

Is it possible to protect yourself from the gun fakes? While there may be no sure-fire single method, there are certain safeguards you can and should use.

Whenever you can, make a point-by-point comparison of the gun you are interested in with a known authentic model of the same type. This is the first test to make and the most important. The majority of fakes can be caught right here.

In addition, you can take advantage of modern technology. Metallurgical labs, which are found in most major cities, will employ X rays and other tools in order to show up rewelding that is hidden to the naked eye.

If you do not feel you have the experience to detect a fake, yourself, you can have the gun authenticated for you. Some gun clubs have authenticating committees for their members.

It's a good idea to protect yourself by buying guns from reputable dealers as opposed to private swaps and deals. If the gun you buy should later prove to be a fake, a reputable dealer will return your money.

shun low prices

At all times, shy away from bargain-basement prices and sucker tricks. Don't buy a gun because of its romantic history, for example, unless it is *fully* documented. It is as easy for a gun faker to put the name of a man such as Jesse James on a pistol as it is for an innkeeper to put up a sign saying, "George Washington slept here."

But don't let the possibility of fakes scare you away from antique gun collecting. It is an absorbing, educational and potentially profitable pastime. If you get serious about antique gun collecting, you'll soon find yourself absorbing more American history than you ever learned in school.

You'll begin to meet some informed and good-to-talk-with people. Crawl off in a corner some evening with a real gun buff, and you'll soon find yourself forgetting what time it is.

If you're the mercenary type and have the good sense to avoid fakes, you can make a nice profit from any collectors' items you buy. The demand for antique guns is increasing and the supply—due to breakage and loss—is shrinking. According to the law of supply and demand, that means prices will continue upwards.

Good hunting!

See also: chronograph; gun cabinet; hobby workspace; marksmanship; shotguns; targets.

When you buy a new appliance...

■ THE TIME TO SAVE money in servicing a major appliance such as a dishwasher, washing machine or dryer is before you make the purchase. Apply these rules *before* you buy, and you'll minimize service problems *after* you buy.

1. Buy a reputable make from a reputable dealer.
2. Make sure end-of-model-run "closeouts" entitle you to the original warranty.
3. Buy only up to your needs. Extra gadgets bring extra problems.
4. Buy a size, on the other hand, to fit your maximum expected needs. Growing teens will put growing demands on a refrigerator.

"what you are entitled to"

Free service during the period of the warranty according to the terms of the sale. As a general rule, major appliances carry a full labor-and-service warranty for a year from the date of purchase or delivery (find out which). Small appliances carry similar warranties, though here they often call for return of the appliance to the factory and sometimes are replacement guarantees. Such items as TV, radio, and stereo sets usually carry a parts-and-labor warranty for 90 days, a parts-only deal for a year. (*Warranty* and *guarantee* are used synonymously.) These warranties in any case apply only for defects in the machine present when you purchased it or defects that develop during normal use. Make sure the bill-of-sale shows no notation that would change the maker's policy.

fair service

For this you must pay at the going rate. In the event you are not satisfied, and can show why you are not, by all means complain; the squeaking wheel gets the grease. However, shouting won't get you any further than a nice quiet purposeful letter

satisfaction

This applies to the machine, the workmanship, the treatment you get from everyone concerned. When appliance people say they "guarantee" some device, they generally mean they will keep it running, not that it is perfect. When the amount of inconvenience reaches the ridiculous stage, it is time to talk about exchanging the device, getting a major shop job for free, or whatever other action will stop the problem. Keep a record of what you asked for and what you got, with dates. Since in-warranty service is free, you usually don't get receipts. If, in the end, neither the dealer nor the distributor satisfies you, and your complaints are legitimate, write a careful letter, including dates and other pertinent facts, to the president of the manufacturing firm that made your appliance (your newspaper or library Thomas Register of Manufacturers or Standard Advertising Register will give you his name and address if you want it) and ask him to do something. Send it special delivery, but don't send it registered mail, as many firms have solid policies against accepting registered letters. (It's a favorite stunt of the amateur inventor and acceptance carries legal implications.) You will get action. Most such letters start a chain of events that wind up with the distributor having to report to the president just what action he has taken to satisfy you, the customer. It won't do any good to do this, however, before you have given the local people every opportunity to make things right.

There will be some service bills during the life of your appliance. A fair estimate for an automatic washer is $20–$30 a year after the warranty period. In other words, for a five-year life, you will spend perhaps $80–$100 over the price of the machine. If you are careful, it will be less. If you consistently overload the machine, it will be more. Service on such appliances as refrigerators, airconditioners, ordinary gas and electric ranges will cost less than this figure, of course. Dishwashers and dryers and elaborately automatic ranges will almost equal the washer.

There will be fewer big bills if you make a practice of getting your appliances checked out by a qualified man once or twice a year. You can do this at the minimum rate, and often can stop problems in advance. For example, a little rumble can be adjusted out of the drive and save bearings, a poorly-fitting door gasket puts a heavy extra strain on a refrigerator, certain clicks and buzzes and hesitations during a washer cycle can forecast timer trouble that can be saved with adjustment.

106

"what you can do to save money"

When an appliance won't start. First, double-check the power supply. Plugs work out of the wall, or kids pull them out, fuses blow, occasionally the door safety switch may hang up, and, in the case of a washer, an overload may cause the overload switch to cut out the current.

Next, in the case of a washer, check the water supply. Make sure the faucets are on—you can usually feel the water pressure or hear it.

Now, if there's power and water, things should happen. Go over your starting procedures again, and make sure no selector buttons or switches are part-way down or stuck. Almost always, when an appliance worked fine the last time you used it, but now won't start, something has changed. Try to figure out or remember what it is—a different wall receptacle, kids fooling around, disconnected parts from cleaning (such as oven elements in an electric range).

If the trouble seems to be in the machine itself, try the time-honored methods of clicking the switches several times, cycling the control dial all the way around, slamming the door. Chances are, in the absence of loud noises or burning smells, the problem is minor when a machine won't start.

If all else fails, read the instructions.

If you do get it started, but don't know why, go ahead and use it, but get the serviceman over to check it before the next use.

if an appliance quits

If it makes loud noises, bad smells, grinding sounds, anything alarming, just pull the plug out of the wall and call the serviceman.

If it just stops, quietly, stop and think before you fool with anything.

Chances are with a washer that either it is hung up on a sticking switch or it is not getting water. Note just where the machine is in its cycle so that, if necessary, you can give the serviceman some advance notice of the trouble.

Now, try and check the same things as when an appliance won't start. On a refrigerator, work the cold control back and forth and rock the unit gently. With a washer, make sure the load is balanced, then try the reset button if the unit has one; run the dial through the cycle again.

And double-check the instruction manual.

when you call for service

Have the model number (usually a short combination of letters and numbers) and the serial number (less important, usually a 6–8 digit number plus one or two letters) written down to be sure to get them right—so the service truck will have the right parts on it. These numbers are to be found, if your instruction manual doesn't show them, on a brass or aluminum plate either on the back of the machine, or behind the front service panel on the bottom.

Be able to answer the question "What seems to be the trouble?" That is, know when it stopped, what sort of noises or smells (hot wires, for example) it made, that it isn't a lack of power or water.

Make sure your name, address and phone number get taken down clearly. If there is a genuine emergency, such as gas leaking, or food spoiling, make this plain. Don't expect a washer-load of clothes to be treated as an emergency.

When the serviceman shows up, if he arrives in a private automobile, get some identification from him, unless you recognize him—and do it before he's in the house. If you've never dealt with the firm before, get as many of the financial details as possible in advance—that is, is there a service charge just to make the call, to what does this entitle you, will the serviceman accept a check, will he be sure to consult you before making extensive and expensive repairs?

shop jobs are rare

Fortunately, there are few sharpies operating in the home-appliance service business, but there are some. In any event, a serviceman who is warned against spending any large amount of your money without checking with you, and who is not allowed to get the machine out of the house, has very little chance to pull an expensive fast shuffle. Almost every instance of shady operation reported in appliance repair is connected with a shop job. Usually, the sharpie diagnoses linkage trouble, for instance, as a need for a rebuilt transmission, and jerks the machine out of the house before anybody who knows machinery has a look at it. Don't let the machine go until you're sure—only major repairs have to be done in the shop.

Your best safeguard is to deal with the man who sold you the machine—he wants to sell you another. Next best is your neighbors' or friends' advice. And the factory outlet—listed directly under the brand name in the classified directory —won't be a shady operation, though it will charge for every service performed.

See also: blenders, electric; clothes dryers, electric; coffeemakers, electrical wiring; floor polishers; guarantees; irons; mixers, food; testers, electrical; toasters.

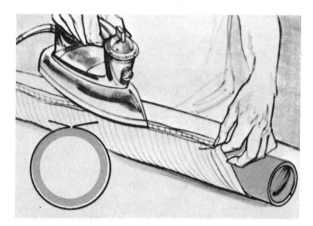

You can prevent creases when pressing seams if you insert a mailing tube inside the material.

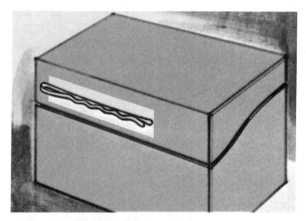

A bobby pin taped to your file box is an easy way to hold up a recipe.

Slip a pipe, with a cross-bolt, over an animal's tether stake. It's easier to drive the stake and protects the animal.

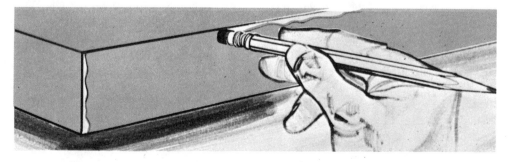

An easy way to remove excess contact cement is with a rubber eraser.

Ohm's law

The basic law of electricity in this chart form will help you to determine whether you can safely add more load to an existing circuit or whether it's time to add another circuit

■ EVER WONDER how much power flows through your TV, airconditioner or radial-arm saw? Or what the total power load might be if every appliance and light were turned on in your home at the same time?

You can find out by using the Ohm's Law chart above. In it, I stands for amps (Intensity), E for volts (Electromotive force), R for ohms (Resistance) and W for watts (Power). Thus it's easy to compute any of these four values by Ohm's Law if you know at least two of them. For example: you buy a new toaster rated at 1100 watts. You want to find out how much current it uses. Use the amperes section of the chart and pick out the formula that uses the two elements you know—wattage (1100) and voltage (115). Substituting in the formula $I = W/E$ you get $I = 1100/115$ or $I = 9.5$ amps. To find power, use the watts section of the chart and pick the two elements you know, $W = E \times I$.

Every electrical device has a clue to its rated power on it. It is given in watts, amperes or horsepower (1 hp = 746 watts). Use the appropriate formula and you can figure the electrical load at any point in your service.

In your home circuit, the voltage remains constant, usually 115 volts. Amperage draw will vary with the number of lights and appliances connected into each circuit. Stoves, hot-water heaters and air conditioners are usually on a separate, 220-volt circuit.

To figure the current load a standard circuit can safely carry, determine its wattage capacity by multiplying the voltage (115 volts) by the size of the fuse (usually 15 amps). Total the wattage of each item already in the circuit and subtract this from the wattage capacity. The remainder will tell you how much you can add safely.

Try "Scoot-About" if you
want a runabout that's different,
yet easy to make

Build a boat designed for fun

HERE'S A BOAT we think will appeal to almost everyone—fisherman, ski enthusiast and
the man who just likes something different in
boats. Designed by Albert Harrison, Ambler,
Pa., this 200-lb. powered aquaplane features a
removable control stand which can be lashed
flat on the deck for car-topping or trailering.

Ballast-type steering makes riding *Scoot-
About* a sport in itself. To turn, you simply shift
your weight in the direction you want the craft
to go—the more you lean, the sharper the turn.
Clamp a 15-hp. outboard on the motor board
and you can skim over the water at 30 m.p.h.

The motor is lashed in a straight-ahead position with shock-cord ties looped through the
steering bracket and fastened to the deck at each
side. This permits you to steer manually when
moving at speeds too slow for ballast steering.

Joints are fastened with plastic resin glue and
either silicon bronze annular-thread nails or
brass wood screws. Be sure to coat both mating
surfaces with glue and countersink all exterior

---

aqua sled: see water skiing

---

fastenings slightly so that they can be concealed
with wood putty. While fiberglassing the whole
boat will make maintenance easier, you may
want to skip this step. In such cases, we strongly
recommend that you cover all joints with fiberglass tape to protect the end grain.

Begin by assembling the bulkhead-type
frames. All of these have the same dimensions
except No. 4 which must be made ¾ in. higher
to allow for the necessary 12-deg. tilt and the
beveling of the upper and lower edges, Figs. 4
and 5. Don't add the ¾-in. reinforcing boards to
this bulkhead until you have assembled the hull
framing and installed the transom brace.

After cutting all bulkheads from ¼-in. plywood, attach 1 x 2 gluing strips flush with the
edges. Notch the corners of each to take chine
logs, sheer logs, deck stringers and bottom
stringers. The notches in No. 4 must be cut to
the same angle as the beveled edges.

You will note that the forward 3 ft. of the
chine logs and bottom stringers are laminated
from ¼-in. plywood strips, Fig. 7. This method
of forming is much easier and more practical
than bending solid 1 x 2s and will produce a
stronger frame. Make the forming block from

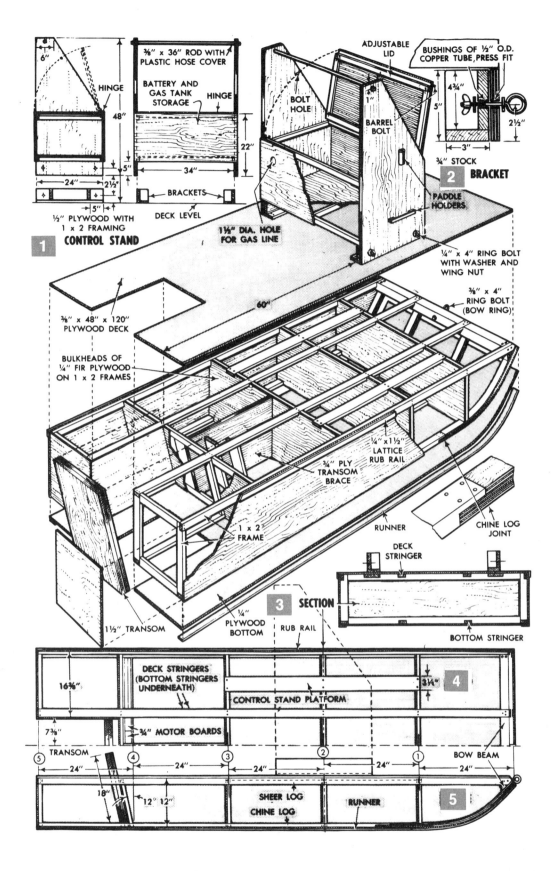

HINGE

6"

48"

24" **2½"**

5"

½" PLYWOOD WITH 1 x 2 FRAMING

1 **CONTROL STAND**

⅜" x 36" ROD WITH PLASTIC HOSE COVER

BATTERY AND GAS TANK STORAGE

HINGE

22"

5"

34"

BRACKETS

DECK LEVEL

ADJUSTABLE LID

BUSHINGS OF ½" O.D. COPPER TUBE, PRESS FIT

BOLT HOLE

1"

BARREL BOLT

4¾"

5"

3"

2½"

¾" STOCK

2 **BRACKET**

PADDLE HOLDERS

1½" DIA. HOLE FOR GAS LINE

60"

¼" x 4" RING BOLT WITH WASHER AND WING NUT

⅜" x 4" RING BOLT (BOW RING)

⅜" x 48" x 120" PLYWOOD DECK

BULKHEADS OF ¼" FIR PLYWOOD ON 1 x 2 FRAMES

¾" PLY TRANSOM BRACE

¼" x 1½" LATTICE RUB RAIL

1 x 2 FRAME

RUNNER

CHINE LOG JOINT

DECK STRINGER

1½" TRANSOM

¼" PLYWOOD BOTTOM

RUB RAIL

3 **SECTION**

BOTTOM STRINGER

16⅜"

DECK STRINGERS (BOTTOM STRINGERS UNDERNEATH)

CONTROL STAND PLATFORM

3¼"

4

7⅜"

¾" MOTOR BOARDS

TRANSOM

24"

24"

24"

24"

24"

BOW BEAM

5 **4** **3** **2** **1**

18"

12° 12"

SHEER LOG

CHINE LOG

RUNNER

5

scrap lumber and clamp the plywood laminae to the inner curve of the block. The bottom two laminae should extend 4 in. from the after end of the block, while the top lamina is flush with the end of the block. After the glue has cured, remove the laminated member from the block

and splice it to the solid member as shown.

Before assembling the frame, prepare the bow beam, Fig. 6. This is a 4-ft. length of 4 x 4 which must be beveled approximately 45 deg. and notched to accept deck stringers, bottom stringers, sheer logs and chine logs. Dowels inserted

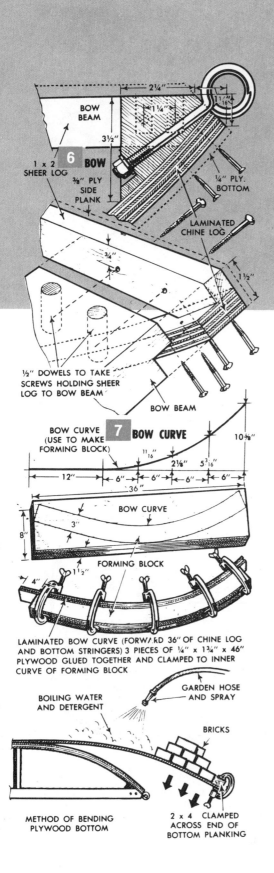

6 BOW

BOW BEAM

2¼"

1¼"

11/16"

3½"

1 x 2
SHEER LOG

⅜" PLY
SIDE
PLANK

¼" PLY.
BOTTOM

LAMINATED
CHINE LOG

¾"

1½"

½" DOWELS TO TAKE
SCREWS HOLDING SHEER
LOG TO BOW BEAM

7 BOW CURVE

BOW BEAM

BOW CURVE
(USE TO MAKE
FORMING BLOCK)

10⅜"

11/16"

2⅛" 5³/₁₆"

12" → 6" → 6" → 6" → 6"

36"

8"

BOW CURVE

3"

FORMING BLOCK

1½"

4"

LAMINATED BOW CURVE (FORWARD 36" OF CHINE LOG
AND BOTTOM STRINGERS) 3 PIECES OF ¼" x 1¾" x 46"
PLYWOOD GLUED TOGETHER AND CLAMPED TO INNER
CURVE OF FORMING BLOCK

GARDEN HOSE
AND SPRAY

BOILING WATER
AND DETERGENT

BRICKS

METHOD OF BENDING
PLYWOOD BOTTOM

2 x 4 CLAMPED
ACROSS END OF
BOTTOM PLANKING

Its shallow draft makes the "Scoot-About" a perfect
boat for fishermen who want to go after the
lunkers in out-of-the-way inlets and back waters

near the ends of the bow beam, Fig. 6, provide a
good grip for screws running into the end grain.

Use 1¼-in. boat nails and glue to assemble the
frame. Install the ¾-in. plywood transom brace
between bulkheads No. 3 and 4, then glue
and nail ¾-in. reinforcing boards to the center
section of bulkhead No. 4. To provide support for the control stand, two short 1 x 4 deck
stringers must be installed between bulkheads
No. 1 and 3, directly under the mounting locations of the stand brackets. Notch these three
bulkheads and install the stringers.

Glue and 1-in. boat nails are used to attach
the planking. To assure a perfect fit, you might
make a pattern for each piece from heavy paper,
allowing about ⅛ in. excess on all sides. This
excess can be trimmed off after the planking is
mounted on the frame. Plank the transom first,
then the motor well and sides. Before you plank
the deck, trim the upper edges of the side planking flush with the deck framing and fair this
framing to provide for perfect mating of planking and frame surfaces. Then install the deck
planking, and turn the hull over.

Fasten the bow ring to the bow beam before
planking the bottom. Begin nailing the bottom
planking at the transom and complete all nailing
and gluing up to bulkhead No. 1. Since the bow
curve is close to the critical bending radius for
¼-in. 3-ply fir plywood, soak the outer ply with
hot water for about 20 min. prior to bending and
wet the plywood often during the bending process. A boiling water and detergent solution will

112

The scow type of hull is very fast when planing. With a 15-hp. outboard motor, you can use "Scoot-About" for towing water skiers

Ballast steering adds new excitement to just plain boat riding. To steer, you lean in the direction of the turn. Manual steering is used at slow speeds

MATERIALS LIST

PLYWOOD (fir, exterior or marine, grade AB or AA)
2 pcs.—¼″ x 12″ x 10′—Side planking
2 pcs.—¼″ x 12″ x 16⅜″—Port and starboard transoms
2 pcs.—¼″ x 12″ x 24″—Motor-well sides
1 pc.—¼″ x 4′ x 12′—Bottom planking (trim after bending)
3 pcs.—¼″ x 12″ x 47½″—Bulkheads 1, 2 and 3
1 pc.—¼″ x 12¾″ x 47½″—Bulkhead 4
1 pc.—⅜″ x 4′ x 10′—Deck planking
2 pcs.—½″ x 24″ x 48″—Control-stand sides
2 pcs.—½″ x 24″ x 34″—Control-stand lid and bottom
2 pcs.—½″ x 17″ x 35″—Control-stand front and back
2 pcs.—¾″ x 14¼″ x 18″—Motor board
    (NOTE: Wherever possible, cut ⅛″ oversize on all sides and trim after plywood is mounted on framing. This will assure a perfect fit.)
LUMBER (white pine, spruce or fir)
12 pcs.—1 x 2, 10′ long—Framing
1 pc.—1 x 4, 12′ long—Stand stringers and backing boards for bulkhead 4
1 pc.—4 x 4, 4′ long—Bow beam
1 pc.—1 x 6, 5′ long—Control-stand brackets
1 pc.—1 x 4, 4′ long—Control-stand brackets
1 pc.—½″ dowel, 12″ long—Cross-grain anchor for fastenings in bow beam
2 pcs.—¼″ x 1½″—Rub rail
FASTENINGS
5 lb.—Plastic resin glue
5 lb.—1″ x .083″-dia. silicon bronze annular-ring nails (Stronghold, Anchorfast or similar)
3 lb.—1¼″ x .109″-dia. silicon bronze annular-ring nails (Stronghold, Anchorfast or similar)
2 doz.—2½″ No. 8 F.H. brass wood screws (mounting motor board)
3 doz.—2″ No. 8 F.H. brass wood screws (bow assembly)
FITTINGS, HARDWARE AND MISC.
1 pc.—½″ x ¾″ galv. steel pipe
1 pc.—⅜″ x 36″ tie bolt or threaded steel rod
1 pc.—⅝″ x 34″ plastic hose
1 pc.—1″ x 34″ continuous brass (piano) hinge
4 pcs.—5/16″ x 2″ eyebolts
1 pc.—½″ x 5″ eyebolt
2 pcs.—1½″ x 11′ aluminum stripping with screws (runners—mount on hull and trim off excess)
2 pcs.—barrel bolts

have greater penetration than plain water and can be applied with a garden spray, if one is available. If not, you might run a hose from the hot water faucet of your laundry tub and simply spray the plywood with hot water. Clamp a 2 x 4 across the extended end of the planking and pile bricks behind this, one at a time, until the weight pulls the plywood down to fit the bow curve. Then nail the planking in place, fiberglass all joints and mount the rub rails and aluminum runners. (These protect the plywood bottom during launching.)

Assemble the control stand, Fig. 1, and mount the stand brackets on the deck. Attach barrel bolts to the upper surface of the lid on each side and drill sockets in the side panels so that the lid can be locked in a raised position as a wind or spray shield. The grip bar at the top is simply a length of steel pipe covered with a piece of plastic hose and held in place by a tie bolt running through the pipe. Make the upper part of the two-piece paddle holder from a short length of radiator hose split down one side.

Four eye bolts running through copper bushings hold the removable control stand to the deck brackets. The brackets illustrated here are high enough to provide clearance for water skis. If you don't plan to use *Scoot-About* as a ski boat, these brackets can be made of 1 x 4s and the bottom of the box lowered accordingly.

See also: bicycle boat; canoes; catamaran; games; boating; hydroplanes; kayaks; paddleboat; pontoon boat; sailboard; sailboat; water skiing.

Bag it with a bow

BY FRED BEAR

For real thrills and the most exciting trophies,
I hunt the way the Indians did, with bow and arrow

■ THIS WAS THE SUPREME MOMENT. You can hunt all your life with a bow and arrow, but you're never really prepared to face the greatest of all wild game. I had come all the way from Grayling, Mich., to Mozambique in Portuguese East Africa and I was finally nocking the arrow for the big one.

Four tons of bull elephant started moving out across the clearing about 40 yards away. I stepped from behind my cover; the bull turned to look at me. I sighted and let fly. It was a killing shot, but the elephant ran. For a moment I thought I might have misjudged the power of the bow, and we would have to track the wounded elephant with rifles. But then, before he was out of sight, he dropped to his knees, then crashed to the ground.

A perfect trophy with a single arrow. I was proud of that shot because I had proven once again that no matter the size of the game, without question you can bag it with a bow.

I had always dreamed of going after big game and I had been lucky enough to sight an arrow on record-size grizzly, tiger and wild boar. But after hunting all over the world, I've learned that the most challenging game for the bow hunter is

right at home — it's the elusive whitetail deer.

If you can stalk and bring down an old buck, you can hunt anything with skill. It takes dedication to develop skill as a bow hunter, but if you're willing to practice you'll learn—and enjoy a satisfying, exciting sport at the same time.

Select a bow you can handle easily. For the novice, the best guide is to buy a bow that you can hold at full draw for 10 seconds. Archery muscles develop quickly so a slight tremor is all right. If you shake, however, the bow is too heavy. Practice a half hour a day for about two weeks and you'll be able to handle it with ease. A bow weight of about 35 pounds draw weight is about right for the average man.

Match your arrow to your bow weight. If properly matched, the arrow snakes around the bow when it is shot. Stiffness or spine is a factor in this fitting. Arrows are graded as to the size of bow.

To determine your proper arrow length, place a yardstick against your chest between your arms. Extend the arms horizontally along the yardstick and note the distance to the ends of your fingers. This is your correct arrow length.

As you become more proficient, the hunting

114

instinct will come to the fore. This usually means selecting a heavier bow. Men should use at least a 45-pound bow for hunting big game. This means extra practice, but the physique to handle this weight can be developed easily. You can shoot a 40-pound bow for years and not be able to handle a 50-pounder. The muscles must be developed by shooting a heavier bow.

Once you have a bow of the proper hunting weight, begin practicing each day. Shoot until you can hold the bow at full draw no longer. Each day you practice, note that you will be able to shoot a few more arrows. Keep at it.

Perseverance will enable you to easily handle this heavier bow. You may then want to develop your muscles to still heavier bows. The average hunting bow is 50 to 55 pounds draw weight. This is the weight that should be used for game the size of deer. For larger game such as moose, a weight of 60 to 65 pounds is recommended.

In building your muscles to heavier bow weights, care must be taken to avoid becoming a "snapshooter." This affliction is one that creeps upon you when shooting heavier bows. Muscles are built up by breaking them down. This is the progressive weight-lifting process.

Shoot only until your muscles are tired and then do not shoot again for 24 hours. If you continue to try to shoot beyond this tiring period you will find yourself not coming to full draw and well on your way to becoming this snapshooter. A snapshooter is one who cannot come to full draw. He loses the arrow before drawing it to full length. It is not likely that he will ever become a good shot.

stalking your quarry

Stalking is an art many of our younger hunters know little about. With the scope-sighted rifles, the hunter doesn't have to get as close as he previously did. Modern day archers, many of whom once carried a rifle, have to re-educate themselves in the ways of hunting. For the average bow-hunter, 35 yards is about the limit for accurate shooting. It boils down to this—if the archer wishes to be consistently successful, he must either sit on his duff in a blind and wait 'em out, or he must learn how to stalk.

Almost every animal has some defect in his makeup which may be turned to the hunter's advantage. I have learned that anyone who can successfully stalk whitetail deer can be successful on any other big game animal. So further observations will be more-or-less directed toward outwitting this clever species.

The object of stalking is to get as close to the animal as possible before shooting. You've got to think like a deer in order to get close to him. A whitetail is trained from birth to hide, camouflage, and creep away from noise and scent. Yet he has courage enough to lie motionless and let a hunter pass by him if he thinks he can escape detection. Deer have three principal faculties for detecting the presence of their enemies—nose, eyes and ears. The sense of smell is by far the most important to the bowhunter. Second is the amazing visual faculty for detecting objects in motion. These two, combined with a well developed sense of hearing, establish a protective screen about deer that extends well beyond the reasonable range and is difficult to penetrate.

The author demonstrates a uniform pull. One finger touches the corner of his mouth to insure that each arrow is released with the same power

The bow and arrow as a hunting weapon has three weaknesses. Most important is the short range of the weapon which makes it necessary to approach well within the protective screen of the deer to obtain a reasonable shot. Second is the exposed position necessary to make a successful shot plus the fact that it is necessary to create considerable motion in shooting. Finally, the "twang" of the bowstring travels faster than the arrow and affords the deer time to move if he recognizes danger in the sound.

In stalking deer with the bow, the natural instincts of the deer and the inherent weaknesses of the bow create a chain of never-ending problems. The still hunter or stalker must locate un-

Stalk big game against the wind at all times. In the morning and evening, cool air moves down the slopes, so you should stalk from the heights, quartering the wind and moving carefully behind and around any cover until you are close enough to your quarry to shoot

disturbed deer, penetrate their natural instinctive barriers and, at close range and sometimes in plain view, make considerable movement without being seen or heard. Impossible? No, it can be done by those who will take the time to learn the ancient art of stalking.

A smart hunter begins planning his hunt before the season opens. He visits the intended hunting area, looking for deer trails linking feeding areas, drinking places, shelter areas and bedding spots. Research on the favorite foods and cover is also a prerequisite.

Go into your hunting grounds against the wind if you can. Remember that air flows up the slopes when it is warm and into the low places during the cool hours. Since the best times for stalking are in early mornings and late afternoons (when the game itself is on the move) stick to high ground most of the time. Always move against or quartering into the wind. Rarely can deer be approached downwind to within arrow range.

These important rules used by successful stalkers stand out: (1) Never step on anything you can step over, (2) Take three steps and stop, and (3) Train your eyes to see detail. The first rule will aid in noiseless approach. The second gives you the advantage of seeing the animal before it sees you. The third allows you to spot the animal even in dense cover. Consistent success in stalking is absolutely dependent upon seeing the game before it sees you.

Don't look in open spots for deer. Look at small openings between trees and through brush. Try to single out a part of the animal; maybe his ears, his head, legs or rump and don't make the mistake of only watching ahead. Allow your eyes to rove back and forth, over every bit of cover. And don't just look—SEE what you are looking at. Look for patches of color out of place in their surroundings and be alert to any movements, no matter how small. A flick of an ear or a movement of the tail may focus your attention on a spot and suddenly the entire outline of the animal will take shape. Look back once in a while. Deer are crafty and sometimes hide as you walk by then sneak out behind you.

Thick brush may cause a stalker to make a wide detour or to give up the stalk entirely. Dry leaves, dry limbs or twigs, and gravel are murder. There are no shortcuts to a successful stalk. Once you lose sight of your quarry as you begin to stalk, you must always assume the animal is still there. The temptation to hurry must be curbed. Use the same timing as a feeding animal. If you move with a steady gait, any animal hearing you will at once become suspicious and alert. Seldom cover more than a mile in an hour, and a half mile is better. Never relax vigilance for a moment. Get down on hands and knees so you can see under tree limbs and take advantage of shorter and usually denser cover. A bowhunter, like a bobcat, should use every suitable particle of cover, no matter how scant. It helps break up that telltale silhouette.

Placement of the foot is one of the most important details in stalking. Short steps are favored. Long steps can cause loss of balance if you have to "freeze" while taking a step. Moccasins or tennis shoes in dry weather and rubber-bottomed, leather-topped "swampers" for damp going are ideal for stalking. Trousers must be of soft material that will not rustle. Loose objects allowed to jingle in pockets are out. Extra equipment should be securely strapped to your body. A soft arrow plate on your bow and silencers on the bowstring are "musts." A camouflage suit, or clothing of dull, neutral colors is a big help.

Don't stay in camp during wet or stormy weather. Deer may often be seen calmly feeding during a downpour. Such days provide excellent opportunities for a silent approach because the deer has to rely chiefly on sight for protection and this is sometimes dimmed by raindrops on

To determine the correct arrow length for you, hold a yardstick against your chest as shown, and extend your arms straight out in front of you. The reading where the fingers meet is the proper arrow length

its eyelashes. I'll never forget the rainy Sunday morning, when the water dripping off the trees into the leaves covered any slight noise of my progress, that I worked close enough to a slowly feeding deer to slap her on the rump with the end of my bow. Other stalks have culminated with kills but none gave me the pleasure that I felt that morning.

I have found the hour after dawn to be the best time of all for stalking deer. After feeding undisturbed most of the night, they are less wary and are on the move toward bedding grounds, feeding slowly as they go, keeping their heads down more than usual. Another trick to remember is that a feeding deer usually switches his tail before raising his head. So, if you are trying to close the gap on a feeding deer, watch his tail and "freeze" when it moves. Once a stalk is begun, always keep a close watch for other deer that might be standing unnoticed in the vicinity. I've lost several chances at deer because one I didn't see warned the one I was after. If a deer has already discovered you before you are ready —but is within range for a shot—slowly and with as nearly imperceptible movements as possible, work yourself into a shooting position, draw and shoot. If you don't, it is most probable that you won't get a shot at that particular deer.

If you think that stalking sounds like tough work, you're absolutely right. It is tough, both mentally and physically, and takes a different attitude than is usually brought to hunting. You will develop patience. You will use muscles you didn't know existed. Your mouth will become dry. You will sweat and silently curse, but you can never relax.

Yet, when at last you've made a stalk pay off, you will know beyond doubt why this is called hunting's greatest thrill. To best a big game animal in its own habitat, using the means which are inborn in the animal, yet have to be learned by man, is beyond compare in the world of sport.

where to aim

Usually, in the excitement of being close to game, there is an impulsive urge to just shoot at the animal. This will not put meat in the pot. A definite aiming spot must be picked. This is very hard to do. It takes considerable will power and usually some experience to curb this desire to shoot quickly at the whole animal. Pick one tiny spot on the animal and concentrate on that spot, then let fly. Make your first shot count . . . you don't usually get a second.

A shot entering through the ribs close to the shoulder will hit the heart or the lungs. Hits from the rear that enter behind the ribs and go forward through the diaphragm and into the chest cavity are deadly. Also effective are the hits through the rear quarters from either side or back. Try to hit low rather than high on the animal.

Whether hunting for birds, rabbit, deer, or big bear, the thrill of bowhunting is a unique one. You tend to meet the animal more nearly on his own ground. Your effective kill range is much shorter, so you must get nearer the target. There is no thrill as great as effectively stalking an animal in his own environment and winning the contest with a good clean shot.

In six hours
of easy practice
you can master . . .

Arc welding basics

BY ART YOUNGQUIST

■ IF YOU'VE ALWAYS shied away from "down-hand" arc welding as a skill beyond your abilities, you may doubt the claim that you can learn it in six short hours. Perhaps—somewhere in the distant past—you've tried to strike an arc, without notable success.

No reason to be discouraged. Ironically, this very first step in learning arc welding is the toughest hurdle of all. Though the arc principle, as sketched on the next page, is quite simple, it takes practice to strike one because the welding rod has a tendency to stick (or "freeze") to the work. It's no great problem, since you can free it by quickly wobbling it from side to side, but until you can strike an arc *without* freezing, you can't lay a bead. With a few tips, you can master the first step in about 10 minutes. From then on, it's simply a matter of controlling the rate of feed to maintain the correct arc length as the welding rod melts off, then synchronizing this movement with the rate of travel required for a uniform bead. (See sketch.)

It is not intended to suggest, of course, that you can become a professional all-position welder in six hours. But you'll be able to lay a good weld in the horizontal position ("down-hand")—and 98 percent of all the welding jobs you're likely to face can be done in this position.

First of all, you'll need a welder. You can buy a new 180-amp. size for around $100—not expensive as large shop tools go. This size will handle all garage and farm welding jobs. If you intend to do only hobby welding, a 100-amp. machine is big enough, and costs a few dollars less. Set your welder within reach of your workbench, as shown at left, so you can experiment with various amperage settings.

To protect a wooden bench from scorching, place a fairly large scrap of sheet steel on top of it. Clamp the end of the ground cable to this scrap. Then place the smaller scrap that you'll use for practice on top of the grounded piece; this automatically grounds the work-piece to the welding circuit. The work-piece should be at least ⅛-in. thick and free of rust or paint.

Now, grip the bared end of a ³⁄₃₂-in.-dia. welding rod or electrode in the jaws of the rod holder. The rod must be one made for welding mild steel with an AC welder (see the chart on page 123). Fleetweld 37 is a good choice for the beginner. Adjust the current setting on the welding machine to 70-75 amps. Then lower the welding hood over your face (or don your safety goggles) and gently touch the practice piece with the tip of the welding rod, using a scratching motion as if you were striking a match. This will cause the tip of the rod to spark and sputter like a short-circuited wire about to blow a fuse. As soon as the sparks occur, raise the rod slightly making at least an ⅛-in. gap be-

armature: see drill presses

arm exerciser: see exercise equipment

arrows: see archery

artificial respiration: see lifesaving

artist's easels: see easels, artist's

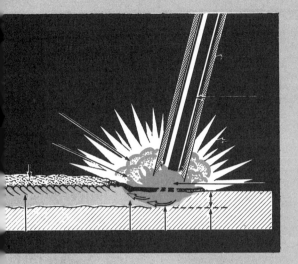

WHAT GOES ON INSIDE THE ARC

Immediately after you strike an arc, the intense heat generated melts the steel under the welding rod, forming a small pool of molten metal. The heat of the arc also melts the tip of the rod, and this molten rod metal is carried across the arc and deposited in the molten pool beneath. The blast of the arc forms a crater in the center of the pool and forces some of the weld metal out; this becomes the weld bead. The depth of this pool is the depth the weld has penetrated.

At the same time the rod-tip and the metal to be welded melt, some of the rod's coating burns to form an envelope of protective smoky gases around the arc and molten pool. This smoke screen shields the molten weld metal from harmful absorption of the oxygen and nitrogen in the air.

The rest of the rod coating melts to form a liquid flux that mixes with the molten metal and the impurities in the metal. The resulting slag floats to the top of the weld metal and forms a coating which covers the weld bead, sealing it off from the atmosphere.

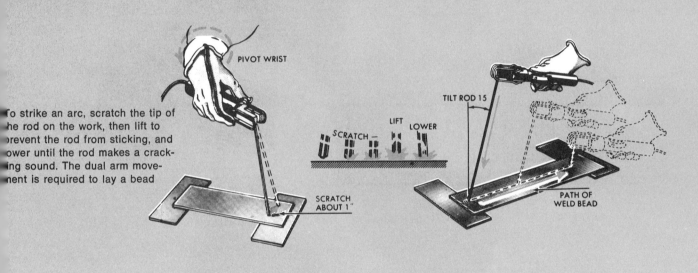

To strike an arc, scratch the tip of the rod on the work, then lift to prevent the rod from sticking, and lower until the rod makes a cracking sound. The dual arm movement is required to lay a bead

tween the tip of the rod and the practice piece. If your lift isn't quick, the molten tip won't have a chance to drop off and will actually weld the rod to the workpiece. The thing that's so frustrating for the beginner is that this takes place in a split second and the rod must be worked free at once.

Don't let a sticking rod discourage you because it happens to experienced welders too, and sometimes it's necessary to free a rod several times before starting to weld. But remember: you must free a stuck rod right away because it creates a direct short across the welding circuit that will heat up the rod and burn off the coating, rendering the rod useless. If you cannot free the rod by bending it from side to side, depress the rod-holder's thumb-lever grip and free

the rod from the holder jaws. Use this method only as a last resort, though—it causes arcing at the holder jaws that would eventually ruin them.

If, after eight or ten starts, the rod persists in sticking, increase the welding current to the next highest amperage setting. Line loads vary in different localities and it could be that you're not getting enough current to maintain an arc. If this doesn't help, don't give up—there's still another way you can learn to strike an arc: switch from steel to brass. A small piece at least ¼-in. thick will do the trick. Place the brass on the metal table top, as you did the steel scrap, and try striking an arc on it. You will notice that you can practically bury the arc in the brass before it sticks. This, of course, is a "crutch" and shouldn't be used any longer than it takes you to

DIMENSION TOP TO MATCH BASE OF DRILL PRESS

⅛ x 1½ x 1½" ANGLE IRON

MOUNTING HOLES

WELD

4½"

¾" PIPE

38"

¾" PIPE

WELD

9"

6"

16"

FLOOR STAND
FOR BENCH DRILL PRESS

OFF-THE-SIDE
DRILL PRESS VISE

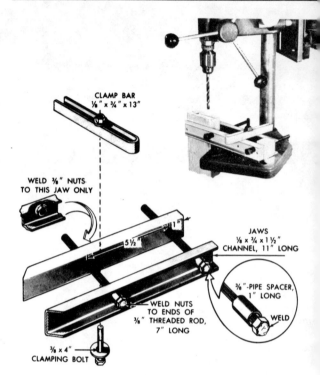

CLAMP BAR ⅛" x ¾" x 13"

WELD ⅜" NUTS TO THIS JAW ONLY

5½"

JAWS ⅛ x ¾ x 1½" CHANNEL, 11" LONG

⅜"-PIPE SPACER, 1" LONG

WELD

WELD NUTS TO ENDS OF ¾" THREADED ROD, 7" LONG

⅜ x 4" CLAMPING BOLT

welding basics, continued

develop skill in striking and maintaining an arc.

Don't attempt to run a weld bead at this time. Keep practicing the art of striking an arc and maintaining it for a few seconds' duration over and over again. To stop or break the arc, rapidly pull the rod away from the work, then switch off the welder if you're through.

If you can't even arouse a spark when attempting to strike an arc, inspect the tip of the rod. Sometimes the rod burns off faster than the coating, and the coating prevents the rod tip from touching the practice piece. When this occurs, vigorous scraping or striking the rod tip against the work usually breaks away the coating at the tip. A loose ground-cable clamp could also be the trouble. Check the clamp and fasten it directly to the practice piece if necessary.

Once you've mastered the technique of striking and holding an arc for a few seconds, you're ready to practice the dual arm movement. The

big trick here is maintaining correct arc length by feeding the rod downward. You can't judge an arc gap by *looking* at it (though an experienced welder can look at the puddle of molten weld metal and tell if the arc length is right). The best way for a beginner to judge the correct length is to listen to the noise of the arc. When an arc gap is too long, it makes a hissing or singing noise. A correct arc gap makes a uniform crackling noise—rather like eggs frying in a pan that's too hot. Too short an arc gap also makes a crackling noise, but it's not uniform because the molten metal dropping from the red momentarily shorts the circuit, during which time the crackling is smothered into silence. Practice holding a large arc and a short arc to familiarize yourself with the sounds.

Lay the bead from left to right (right to left if you're left-handed). Tilt the rod slightly toward the direction the weld is to be laid. This enables you to see the molten weld pool or pud-

ADJUSTABLE
SHOP STAND

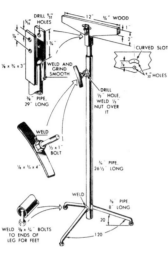

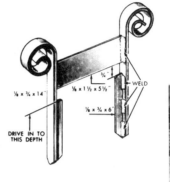

FOOT
SCRAPER

dle as you work, and observing this puddle is an all-important step in learning to weld.

Now, again strike an arc—only this time continue to maintain it while slowly moving the rod in a path from left to right for a distance of about 4 in. Be sure to feed the rod downward to maintain the crackling sound of a correct arc length. Then stop welding and, after allowing the weld to cool for a few seconds, chip away the slag covering with a cold chisel tilted away from you. Keep your hood down to guard against hot flying particles—unless you normally wear glasses which will serve the same purpose. After removing the slag, wire brush the weld bead until it is bright and clean so that you can inspect the results and find out just what, if anything, you are doing wrong. A good weld should have very slight uniform ripples on the surface that are curved to the radius of the weld puddle. Most beginners tend to travel too fast and hold too long an arc.

Compare your welds with the welds in the photochart on page 122 and decide what correction you should strive for. Repeat this check for each weld bead you lay until you have developed enough skill to make a good weld every time. It's also helpful to practice laying poor beads, so you can observe the weld puddle and thus recognize how a wrong condition looks during the welding process.

Lay your practice welds about 1 in. apart. If the scrap you're using is small, it may become hot enough, after a number of welds, to alter the conditions. This could be very confusing to a beginner, since proportionally less current is needed to weld steel as it heats up. So, alternate your practice welds on several pieces of scrap, if they're small.

We don't recommend that you cram the six hours of practice into one session. You'll learn faster working an hour at a time, spreading it out over a week or two. Meanwhile, the plans

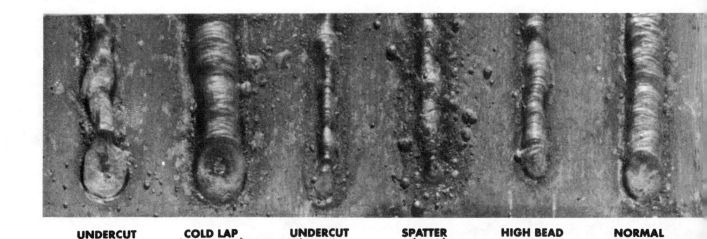

UNDERCUT	COLD LAP	UNDERCUT	SPATTER	HIGH BEAD	NORMAL
CURRENT TOO HIGH	TRAVEL TOO SLOW	TRAVEL TOO FAST	ARC TOO HIGH	CURRENT TOO LOW	CORRECT CONDITIONS
Arc makes hissing sound; long and pointed crater. Rod melts off fast, becomes red before being used up. Wide crater leaves the bead undercut	Excess weld metal piles up, overflows crater to cause cold laps. Molten slag flowing in front of crater could cause gas pockets, slag inclusions	Crater hasn't had time enough to penetrate the metal; small bead does not fill even this shallow crater in all spots, resulting in undercutting	Globules of molten metal from rod appear to be sprayed against steel, resulting in spatter. As with excess current, the arc makes hissing sound	Arc is hard to strike and hold; weld metal merely lays on steel, with little or no penetration. Crater is too narrow, much too shallow	Arc makes a crackling sound, indicating correct arc length; weld metal fills crater from edge to edge as rod is moved along at a uniform pace

Too long an arc gives off very bright white light and makes a hissing sound. Globules of molten weld metal can be seen dropping from rod. Spatter surrounds the puddle

Arc of correct length gives off less white light than long arc, makes a steady crackling sound. No globules of molten metal can be seen; puddle appears to be boiling quietly

Rate of travel should be fast enough to prevent slag from flowing in front of puddle, causing gas pockets, slag inclusions. Slag coat behind is chipped away with cold chisel

To avoid hump in bead when starting new rod, strike arc at front of puddle (A), quickly move rod to back of puddle (B), then to center of crater to resume former rate of travel

presented here are only for eager beavers—or for beginners with an experienced helper.

Once you're satisfied you can lay a good practice bead, you're ready for the advanced "course"— welding two or more pieces together. The first step to master in making a joint is tack-welding.

Tack welds are used to hold two or more pieces of steel together during assembly and prior to running the finish welds. Make all tack welds at least ½ in. long, spaced about 3 in. apart. Fill the craters before breaking the arc to avoid starting a weld crack at this point. Now, let's consider the types of finish welding.

Butt welding is simply the laying of a bead along the seam of two plates, placed edge to edge. Use ⅛-in. thick scraps. You'll notice, as you're laying this bead, that the weld puddle seems to sink deeper into the metal than it did when you laid a practice bead down the center of a plate. This is called weld penetration and the resulting depth of penetration determines the strength of the weld. Make the weld about 4 in. long. Then grip the welded piece in a vise with the top of the jaws just below the weld line, and break the joint to inspect the quality of your weld. Do this by striking the top plate with a hammer to bend it toward the welded

ELECTRODE TYPES	SIZES (ROD DIA.)	CURRENT RANGE (AMPS.)	SPOT COLOR IDENTIFICATION	USE AND WELDING CHARACTERISTICS
Fleetweld 37*	5/64 3/32 1/8 5/32	40– 75 65–100 90–140 120–180	Brown	For general-purpose welding of mild steel in all positions. Widely used on sheet metal lap and fillet welds where appearance and ease of operation are more important than speed
Fleetweld 180	3/32 1/8 5/32	40– 90 60–120 115–150	Blue	Best all-round electrode for repair of mild steel, particularly if work is dirty and rusty. Can be used in all positions. Has fast freeze characteristics with deep penetration and light slag. Good for welding galvanized steel
Jetweld 1 for AC	3/32 1/8	80–110 130–180	Yellow	For high speed welding of mild steel in down-hand position only. Arc is soft and spatter-free. Thick, dense slag, which is easily removed, produces exceptionally smooth-appearing weld bead
Jetweld LH-70	3/32 1/8	80–120 115–165	Orange	An all-position electrode for welding high carbon or sulphur steels and low-alloy, high-tensile steels which cannot be preheated
Ferroweld	1/8	80–100	No spot color. End of rod orange	For making all types of cast iron repairs where machining of weld is not required
Softweld	1/8	65–120	End of rod orange. Spot color blue	For welding cast iron which must be machined after welding
Abrasoweld	1/8	40–150	No color code	For hard-surfacing steel that is subjected to abrasive wear of sand, stone and other gritty materials
Stainweld A7	5/64 3/32 1/8 5/32	20– 45 30– 60 55– 95 80–135	No spot color. End of rod yellow	An all-position electrode for welding stainless steel and hard-to-weld steels

*All welds in photo made with this electrode

side. The fractured weld should show that it has penetrated $\frac{1}{16}$ in. or half the thickness of the scraps. The weld should be about $\frac{3}{32}$-in. thick, uniform along its full length, and free of gas pockets or slag inclusions.

Now, place two more practice pieces side by side, but this time leave about $\frac{1}{16}$-in. gap between them. While welding this seam, you'll notice that the puddle sinks even deeper than before, so you must reduce the rate of travel to fill the crater with a $\frac{1}{32}$-in. reinforcement.

With $\frac{1}{8}$-in. or thinner scraps and a gap of over $\frac{1}{16}$ in., you may find the weld puddle burns completely through, letting molten metal run out beneath. Burn-through is due to poor fit-up— a condition you'll meet often while welding, particularly with 12-ga. and thinner metal.

To prevent burn-through, quickly move the rod out of the weld puddle in the direction of travel and, once the puddle solidifies and starts to sink, move the rod back of it. This quick back-and-forth movement, while maintaining the arc, will not only give the puddle a chance to set but also deposits small globules of metal to bridge the gap ahead of the puddle, prevent-

ing further burn-through. However, if burn-through persists even where the fit-up is fairly good, you're using too high a current. Reset the welder to the next lower amperage.

After welding, flip the work to inspect the underside. The weld should have completely penetrated the $\frac{1}{8}$-in. metal, forming a small bead along the seam. Where the edges of the gap show, penetration is insufficient. When you try to break this piece as you did the first one, the weld should be ductile enough to bend but not break. Bending it back and forth will, of course, break it so you can inspect it for density.

These two practice butt welds (tight fit-up and gap fit-up) illustrate that: (1) you can achieve 100-percent weld penetration on $\frac{1}{8}$-in.-thick metal with tight fit-up by welding it on both sides, and (2) that the metal must be spaced so that a gap exists between the pieces to achieve 100-percent penetration when the piece can only be welded from one side.

When welding $\frac{3}{16}$ or $\frac{1}{4}$-in.-thick steel, leave a gap and use a $\frac{1}{8}$ or $\frac{5}{32}$-in. electrode with the highest amperage setting you can handle. The second (underside) weld can be laid with a still

Butt welding

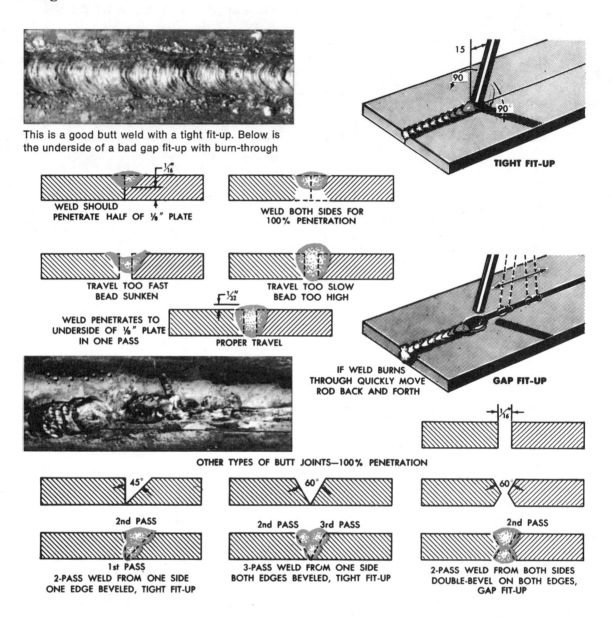

This is a good butt weld with a tight fit-up. Below is the underside of a bad gap fit-up with burn-through

TIGHT FIT-UP

WELD SHOULD PENETRATE HALF OF ⅛" PLATE

WELD BOTH SIDES FOR 100% PENETRATION

TRAVEL TOO FAST BEAD SUNKEN

TRAVEL TOO SLOW BEAD TOO HIGH

WELD PENETRATES TO UNDERSIDE OF ⅛" PLATE IN ONE PASS

PROPER TRAVEL

IF WELD BURNS THROUGH QUICKLY MOVE ROD BACK AND FORTH

GAP FIT-UP

OTHER TYPES OF BUTT JOINTS—100% PENETRATION

2nd PASS
1st PASS
2-PASS WELD FROM ONE SIDE ONE EDGE BEVELED, TIGHT FIT-UP

2nd PASS   3rd PASS
3-PASS WELD FROM ONE SIDE BOTH EDGES BEVELED, TIGHT FIT-UP

2nd PASS
2-PASS WELD FROM BOTH SIDES DOUBLE-BEVEL ON BOTH EDGES, GAP FIT-UP

higher amperage setting to assure complete penetration, with no danger of burn-through.

Multiple-pass welding. When 3/16 or 1/4-in. steel cannot be welded from both sides, grind a bevel along the edges to be welded and run both welds from the same side—one on top the other. Be sure to chip the slag off the first pass and brighten it with a wire brush before laying the second pass. Theoretically, beveling the edges and laying pass upon pass makes it possible to weld steel of any thickness with 100-percent penetration, using a 180-amp. a. c. welder. The beveled edges may be on one or both sides of the pieces

to be welded, as shown in the sketches on page 122. The number of passes needed to fill the beveled space between the pieces will depend upon the thickness of the steel and the size of the electrode used.

Always use the largest electrode possible to reduce the number of passes needed and save welding time. Also, always try to arrange the work so that the joint can be welded from *both* sides, because this will reduce the size of the weld you need (you'll save both time and rod). It will also equalize weld shrinkage stresses which cause distortion and warping. You prob-

Horizontal fillet welding

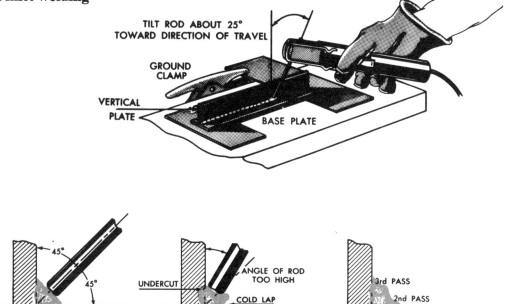

TILT ROD ABOUT 25°
TOWARD DIRECTION OF TRAVEL

GROUND CLAMP

VERTICAL PLATE

BASE PLATE

45°
45°
RIGHT-SHAPE WELD

UNDERCUT
ANGLE OF ROD TOO HIGH
COLD LAP
POOR WELD

3rd PASS
2nd PASS
3-PASS WELD

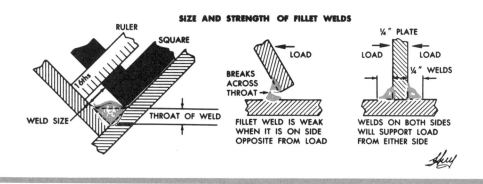

SIZE AND STRENGTH OF FILLET WELDS

RULER
SQUARE
16ths
WELD SIZE
THROAT OF WELD

LOAD
BREAKS ACROSS THROAT
FILLET WELD IS WEAK WHEN IT IS ON SIDE OPPOSITE FROM LOAD

¼" PLATE
LOAD
LOAD
¼" WELDS
WELDS ON BOTH SIDES WILL SUPPORT LOAD FROM EITHER SIDE

ably noticed, after completing a number of weld beads on a practice piece, that the ends lifted, as in the third sketch at right. This distortion is caused by shrinkage of the weld as it solidifies.

Butt welding thin sheet metal—1/16-in. thick (16-ga.) or less—requires considerable welding skill, so don't use it for practice work, unless you intend to do quite a bit of sheet-metal welding. In that case use 5/64-in. electrodes at 40 to 60 amps. and move the rod as fast as possible to avoid burn-through. For short-length seams, a copper back-up bar clamped directly beneath the seam will help draw the heat of the arc out of the sheet metal and prevent burn-through. If not objectionable, a strip of 16-ga. steel, tack welded or clamped to the underside of the seam,

can be used. The strip then becomes a part of the job and is left in place after welding.

Fillet welding is used to fasten two pieces of steel at right angles to one another, as shown at the top of page 125. The easiest way for a beginner to lay a fillet weld is to tilt the work at a 45-deg. angle (as in the photo on page 126), so that the sides form a trough like a beveled butt weld. Since it is not always possible to tilt the work, horizontal fillet welding, where one piece stands vertical and the other lies flat, should also be practiced. Both are down-hand welding.

Practice positioned fillet welding first, after studying the sketches at the top of page 127. Tack weld two 1/8-in. or thicker pieces of steel together in the shape of a T and block them up

Positioned fillet welding

with a piece of angle iron so that the sides are at a 45-deg. angle to the bench top. Use a ³⁄₃₂ or ⅛-in. rod and, after striking an arc, move the rod at a steady pace as you did when making a beveled butt weld. Be sure to center the rod over the corner of the joint. If the rod is held off the center so as to be closer to one side than the other, the arc will melt one piece more than the other and cause undercutting on the hot side and a cold lap on the other.

The size of a fillet weld is determined to a certain extent by the rate of travel. If the travel is too fast, a thin fillet weld with undercutting at the edges will result. Watch the weld puddle and move the rod just fast enough to keep the molten slag from running in front of the puddle. Chip and clean the slag from each fillet weld you run and compare the surface of the weld with those in the photo chart on page 122. A good fillet weld should have a slight convex curvature and be

126

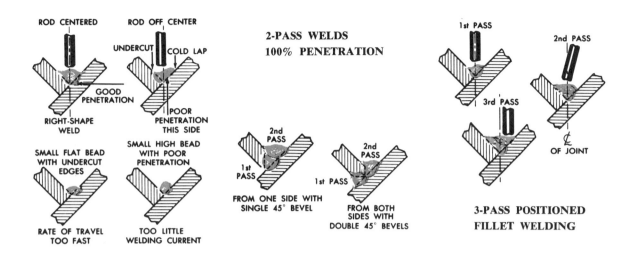

ROD CENTERED · ROD OFF CENTER · 2-PASS WELDS 100% PENETRATION · 1st PASS · 2nd PASS

UNDERCUT · COLD LAP

GOOD PENETRATION

RIGHT-SHAPE WELD · POOR PENETRATION THIS SIDE · 3rd PASS

SMALL FLAT BEAD WITH UNDERCUT EDGES · SMALL HIGH BEAD WITH POOR PENETRATION

2nd PASS · 2nd PASS · ℄ OF JOINT

1st PASS · 1st PASS

RATE OF TRAVEL TOO FAST · TOO LITTLE WELDING CURRENT · FROM ONE SIDE WITH SINGLE 45° BEVEL · FROM BOTH SIDES WITH DOUBLE 45° BEVELS · 3-PASS POSITIONED FILLET WELDING

"washed up" along the edges, forming a small concave cove.

Before laying a fillet weld on the other side of the T-shaped practice piece, break the weld apart by hammering the vertical member toward the weld. Inspect the fractured weld for penetration and soundness. The penetration should extend beyond the corner of the pieces.

If you need a fillet weld larger than you can make in one pass using the biggest rod your welding machine will handle, use one of the multiple-pass methods shown in the sketches on page 127.

Horizontal fillet welding. Tack weld two pieces together to form a T-joint as before, only this time place the base piece flat on the bench top instead of tilting it. Point the electrode into the corner of the joint at a 45-deg. angle. Hold a short arc as though you were almost "dragging" the rod along, with the rod coating scraping against the corner of the joint. Do not expect to lay as large a fillet with a given rod size as you did in the tilted position. If, after cleaning off the slag, you find that the weld bead is uneven with more of it on the base plate and evidence of undercutting on the vertical plate, it indicates you are holding the rod at too high an angle or too close to the vertical plate. Lower the rod the next time as though you were directing more of the arc stream against the vertical plate. (Too slow a rate of travel will also deposit excess metal on the base plate, resulting in a cold lap.)

Size and strength of fillet welds. The size of a fillet weld is equal to the length of one of the small sides of the largest isosceles right triangle that can be drawn within the cross sectional area of the weld (see sketch on page 125). Fillet-weld gauges are available for measuring welds of various sizes. For practice work, however, you can measure the welds with a square and ruler as shown.

The strength of a fillet weld is determined by the throat dimension multiplied by the length of the weld. For example, if the throat measures ⅛ in. and the weld is 4 in. long, ⅛ x 4 = ½ sq. in. Using a safe design strength of 15,000 psi. (pounds per square inch) the weld will support 7500 lbs. or 3¾ tons in tension.

Fillet welds should never be less than five to six times their size in length. For example, a ³⁄₁₆-in. fillet weld should be at least 1 in. long not counting the crater—unless of course, the weld is intended as a tack weld for assembly only.

To gain full strength from fillet welds on lap and T-joints, both sides should be welded. This was apparent when you broke the practice fillet welds run on one side only. If you had welded fillets on both sides before attempting to break it for inspection, you would have found it very difficult, if not impossible.

The size of the fillet welds need not be any larger than the thickness of the vertical plate as shown in the final sketch on page 125. This will produce a welded joint as strong as the plate itself. Welds larger than the plate itself would only be wasteful of welding electrodes and time. If it is not possible to weld both sides of a T-joint,

127

Cause and control of distortion

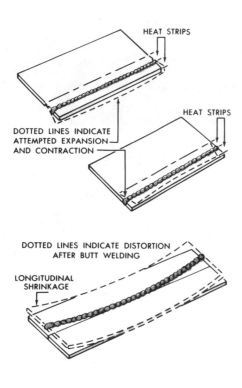

HEAT STRIPS

DOTTED LINES INDICATE
ATTEMPTED EXPANSION
AND CONTRACTION

HEAT STRIPS

DOTTED LINES INDICATE DISTORTION
AFTER BUTT WELDING

LONGITUDINAL
SHRINKAGE

SHRINKAGE ACROSS WELD

START 1st
WELD HERE

2nd 3rd 4th 5th

RUN EACH WELD
IN SAME DIRECTION

BACK-STEP WELDING

TACK WELD
TO START

5th

4th

3rd

2nd

1st

TEMPORARY BRACES
PREVENT DISTORTION
INDICATED BY DOTTED LINES

INTERMITTENT
WELDS—STAGGERED

the edge of the vertical plate should be beveled at 45 deg. so that 100 percent penetration can be achieved in two passes.

Distortion control. There are four steps to keep in mind when welding a job to prevent it from warping and twisting out of shape. (1) Tack weld as many of the pieces together as possible before running any continuous welds; (2) use the minimum amount of welding consistent with making the joint strong enough to support the load; (3) skip-weld around the job so that the heat at each spot will be kept to a minimum and the shrinkage of one weld will counteract shrinkage of another; and (4) reinforce the job where necessary with bars and clamps to prevent warping.

Distortion is caused by the heat of the arc expanding, or rather trying to expand, a strip of metal on each side of the weld. Since expansion of these heated strips is restrained by the adjacent cooler metal, the strips are stressed beyond their yield point and plastic flow or permanent deformation of the metal in the strips takes place. When the weld is completed and the metal cools, it contracts. The surrounding metal, which was not stressed beyond its yield point, contracts to its original size. But, the re-strained metal tries to contract to its deformed length which is slightly shorter than its original length. These opposing forces create a highly stressed area between the strips and the adjacent metal which—unless the metal is thick enough to resist these forces—causes bending and twisting along the weld.

This type of distortion is further aggravated by shrinkage of the molten weld metal as it solidifies and cools. This was noticeable when you ran practice beads on ⅛-in.-thick steel, causing the ends to lift. Or when shrinkage across the weld caused the T-joint piece to pull toward the weld.

To control shrinkage across the weld when tack welding a job together, alternate the tack welds from one side to the other so that the shrinkage of the tack welds will counteract each other. Also tack weld all pieces to each other.

On long butt welds the back-step method shown on this page will help keep the job straight. On long fillet welds, distortion can be reduced by staggering intermittent welds.

Temporarily bracing parts that are free to move or bend will hold them in place until all welding is completed. The braces can then be removed and the tack welds ground off.

See also: bandsaws, blades; soldering; welders; welding.

To renew the lip on worn sockets, grind off ⅛ in. to 3⁄16 in. from the end of the socket.

Choosing the right drill for a bolt is no problem if you use the nut to test the bits for size.

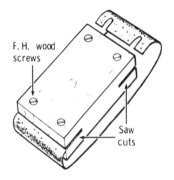

A palm-size sanding block can be made by cutting slits in the end of a 3½-in. piece of 1 x 2 stock. Use No. 6 screws to clamp the sandpaper.

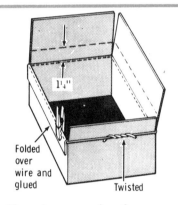

To make a scrap box from a cardboard carton, trim the flaps and glue them over a length of heavy wire.

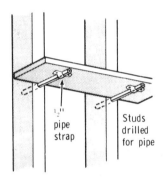

Shelves for your garage can be made by boring holes in the studs for ½-in. pipe. Fasten the shelves with pipe straps.

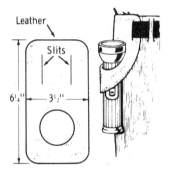

This leather holster hangs from your belt and keeps your flashlight handy.

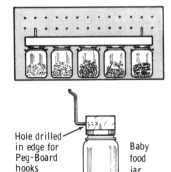

Jars can be hung on perforated hardboard paneling if the lids are screwed to a 1 x 2 as shown.

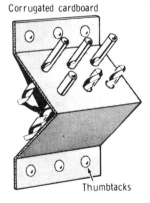

An improvised drill rack can be made from cardboard and thumbtacked to the wall.

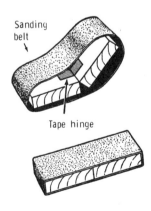

A spare sanding belt doubles as a sanding block if you slip it over a pair of blocks, hinged with tape, to fit inside.

Studio bedroom in the attic

BY ELEANOR EARLY

Make unused space blossom into
the most striking room in your home

audio oscillator: see oscillator, audio
auger bits: see honing

■ ONE IMAGINATIVE HOMEOWNER recently turned an unfortunate experience into a beautiful attic room when a tree toppled through part of his roof. He decided to do more than just patch the damage. He installed a skylight, then proceeded to create a studio guest room with a character all its own. Some of his ideas, as detailed on the next page, may be adaptable to the waste attic space in *your* home.

To utilize as much floor space as possible, this handyman pushed the boundary of the room back to a 4-ft. "knee" wall, and then even put to work the wedge of space between this wall and the eaves—by designing an ingenious unit that rolls part-way into that niche. It changes from a comfortable couch to a full double bed. The homeowner made use of an old flat spring already mounted on casters, but you can buy a rolling angle-iron frame from any bed dealer. Just box in the frame and springs, set a standard mattress in place, and construct the built-ins around it. In the design shown, the plywood ledge-seat (at right angles to the couch) provides a face-panel to which the bed-box can be attached for controlled movement. The cross section detail shows how you screw on the locking strip after you've fitted the frame's slot over the waxed slide-cleat. For smooth operation, the casters should be the non-swiveling ball type.

The space above the "bed slot" is enclosed and provided with a plywood door, to create ample space for bed linen, pillows and blankets. The rest of the bed corner is designed to create shelves and storage. (You can hinge that ledge-seat lid, if you wish.) The bed is flanked by built-in stacks of drawers and a shutter-door wardrobe for your guest's use, and for storing the family's out-of-season clothing.

Bamboo was used as a decorative motif. Long poles screen the stair well, and short lengths are fastened to the drawer fronts as pulls. But the most strikingly original feature is the ceiling. The exposed rafters and beams were covered with pressed-fiber trays designed for packing apples. Since the trays, as they came from the manufacturer, were dark purple and porous, it was necessary to spray them with shellac, then with

copper-bronze paint, before stapling them to the ceiling. A little touch-up spraying along the joints where the plasterboard peeked through, created a ceiling of uniform color—with a reflective quality that distributes the light well, day or night. (The skylight is just off the top of the page in the picture at the left.)

But before you apply so elaborate a ceiling—or even tuck insulation between the rafters—make certain your roof doesn't leak!

See also: building; dormers, framing; insulation; remodeling; roofs.

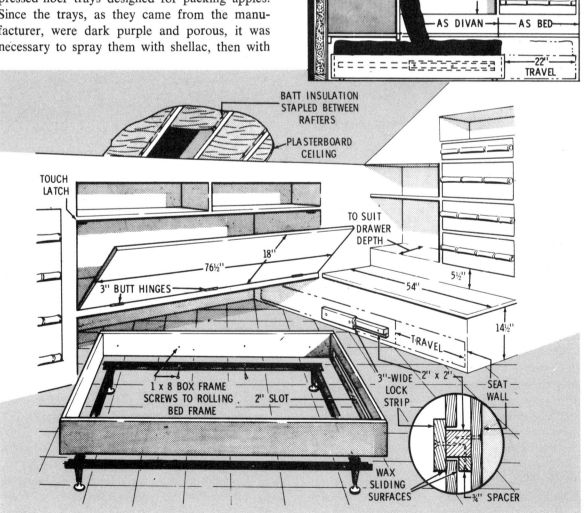

Eight common car problems— and their solutions

BY MORTON J. SCHULTZ

This collection of little-understood engine problems can be recognized and taken care of by the home mechanic. You won't need complex tools, once you understand the problems

EIGHT OF THE MOST common engine malfunctions won't be fixed by points-and-plugs tune-up—and their symptoms can often be confused as indicating a need for complicated, costly work. But all eight of these can be handled without much difficulty by the ordinary home mechanic—*if* he understands the symptoms.

And that's the purpose of this article—to help you understand the symptoms.

One warning, however. You can interpret troublesome symptoms according to these suggestions *only* if you know the car is in proper tune in the first place.

These engine gremlins are the sort that often show up after a tune-up. Or they're the sort that a normal tune-up often doesn't cure.

rough engine idle

Sometimes, no amount of adjusting of the carburetor-mixture adjusting screws will smooth down rough engine idle. While this might mean the carburetor has an internal malfunction, don't rush to tear it down. You might spend hours doing what 20 seconds worth of work would have accomplished just as easily.

The whole trouble may be a simple little air leak into the carburetor that's upsetting the critical fuel-air balance. Tighten each of the carburetor hold-down bolts. When these bolts are loose, air can get past the carburetor gasket and into the engine's induction system. When this happens, the engine starts running with a leaner-than-normal fuel mixture, and it can't be corrected by attempts at engine-idle adjustment.

Also, air leaking into the carburetor through the base can speed up engine wear. This air isn't filtered and could be carrying abrasive contaminants directly to the engine.

fouled sparkplugs

Examining all the sparkplugs in relation to each other and to their cylinder positions can tip you off to a number of internal engine malfunctions. This type of positive analysis is done by "racking" the plugs as you remove them.

Depending on whether yours is a six or eight-cylinder car, drill six or eight "plug-testing" holes in a scrapboard rack measuring about 10 x 18 in. These holes, large enough to take the threaded end of a sparkplug, represent the position of the plugs in the engine. As each plug is removed,

Periodically tighten the carburetor mounting bolts to guard against air leaks into the induction system

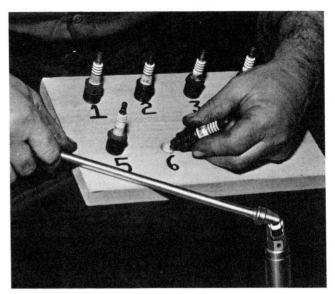

Positive sparkplug analysis is lots easier with a rack made of wood scrap and numbered as illustrated

insert it in its corresponding socket in the rack. Now you're ready to check them out. Six types of sparkplug malfunctions are illustrated in the chart and described in the next six paragraphs:

—If two adjacent plugs are fouled, look for a blown head gasket.

—Two fouled center plugs can cause raw fuel to "boil" out of the carburetor and into the intake manifold after the engine is shut off. This "boiling" can often be relieved by adjusting the float level, so long as the needle and seat seal are in good condition. In some cases, installation of a fiber-gasket block spacer between carburetor flange and intake manifold will help. Fouled center plugs may also point to a blown head gasket.

—If four plugs are fouled with carbon, check for an unbalanced carburetor (in a multicarburetor setup). With the right-side barrel running rich, the four plugs noted would foul while the other four would operate normally.

—Four overheated plugs in the back four cylinder holes indicate a cooling-system problem; coolant is not circulating to the rear of the engine. A good flushing of the system should cure this problem.

—If just one plug has overheated, check the firing order of the engine. When the burned plug is the second of two adjacent, consecutive-firing plugs (in this case 5-7), the trouble is probably due to crossfire. Separating the lead going to these two plugs often corrects the trouble.

—If excessive sludge has plugged up the rear oil-drain holes in the cylinder head, oil can be

pulled in around the intake-valve stems and foul the two rear plugs, especially in larger V8 engines. This condition usually leads to a smoky exhaust, and high oil consumption as well.

incorrect rotor gap

Rotor gap is the distance between the tip of the rotor and the distributor, and it is critical to engine performance. If this gap is too wide, there will be a buildup of resistance in the secondary circuit of the ignition system. When this happens, no amount of engine tuneup will eliminate short sparkplug life. Also, you won't get any clue to this problem by removing the distributor cap and rotor for a close inspection. Both will probably look okay. But think back—didn't you recently replace the rotor? You may have created the problem yourself by getting the wrong rotor for your particular car.

Keep in mind that all rotors are not the same, although several different ones might fit perfectly atop the distributor shaft. One mechanic ran across this problem and, in checking, found that a mismatched rotor left a 3/16-in. gap between rotor tip and cap segments.

How can the wrong rotor affect plug life? Well, new plugs require a minimum of firing voltage, but as they wear their voltage requirements increase. If there is excessive rotor gap because of the wrong rotor, a point is quickly reached where the ignition system can't supply enough voltage to overcome both the mismatched rotor gap and the wearing sparkplug electrode gap.

There's a moral to this tale: Whenever you replace a part—any part—with a new part, make sure it's the one specified for your car.

The diagrams below illustrate various spark-plug ailments. The malfunction in each case is described under each diagram. Use a "racking board" like that shown on which to arrange the plugs with the proper relationship

Two adjacent fouled plugs suggest a blown head gasket. Check compression

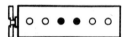

If a center pair of plugs is fouled, you should check gasket and carb float

Unbalanced carburetors (in a dual- or triple-carb setup) create special pattern

If the back four plugs overheat, flush the cooling system. That can be your trouble

A single plug overheats? Check the firing order and separate leads

A fouled rear pair suggests sludge plugging oil drain holes in cylinder head

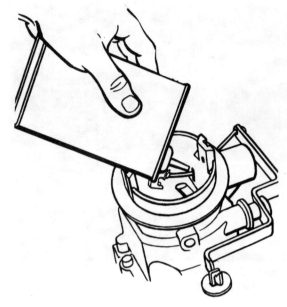

Keep the choke piston operating freely by occasionally squirting carb cleaner in the piston linkage hole

poorly lubed cam

The distributor cam should be lubricated at each tuneup to prevent rapid wear of the cam follower. Most instructions tell you to apply a "light film" of lubricant. That's okay, because excessive lubricating would lead to splattering of the lube around the inside of the distributor and contamination of the distributor breaker points. But just how much is a "light film"?

Researchers at the Champion Spark Plug Co. tested different types of distributors and found the correct amount of cam lube is about equal in size to a kitchen match head.

balky choke

What's the first part to check when your car's hard to start? Probably the automatic choke.

The choke unloader piston is often overlooked. If it sticks in its bore because of accumulated gum and dirt, the choke butterfly will stick wide open and the engine will be hard to start, especially in cold weather. (Not all cars have this type of choke setup.)

So, next time you tune up the car, squirt carburetor cleaner into the air horn opening through which the piston link passes. Operate the choke valve a few times as you apply the cleaner.

Lubricate the distributor cam with a dab about the size of a match head to avoid fouling the points

All replacements must be of the size specified. Match the original and replacement part numbers carefully

faulty multiple connectors

Today's cars are using an increasing number of quick-disconnect electrical connectors. These are multiple in nature and hook several individual wires or circuits together at a specific point. Watch 'em—they can be troublesome. A bent connector terminal in one of these units can stop your car dead in its tracks.

Most of these connectors are found on the engine side of the firewall bulkhead. When an odd electrical problem pops up—one that defies analysis—check multiple-connector alignment. Check this during tuneup too.

bad breaker-point adjustment

We all know that the degree-for-degree relationship between distributor breaker-point dwell and ignition timing is critical. As little as a 1-deg. variance of breaker-point adjustment changes initial timing by the same amount. If it's off by several degrees, engine performance will deteriorate noticeably.

The best way to adjust point gap to manufacturer's specifications is with a dwell meter. However, if you have only a feeler gauge to work with, set the breaker point rubbing block on a high point of the distributor cam and adjust point gap until a *light* drag is felt on the feeler gauge.

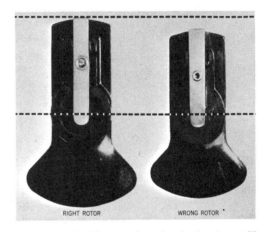

RIGHT ROTOR   WRONG ROTOR

They are clearly different sizes, but both rotors will fit the same distributor. Watch out for parts mixups

Lock the point assembly in this position.

If the point-gap specification for your car is given as a range setting—such as .014 in. to .019 in.—use the *higher* specification (.019 in.) for setting *new* breaker points. Research has shown that setting to the high side of the specification keeps point adjustment within the recommended range as the rubbing block wears.

If you set breaker-point spacing by means of a dwell meter, you'll find that specifications are usually given in degree ranges—for example, 28 deg. to 32 deg. The recommendation here is that you split the difference and set points midway between the two, which, for the range cited, would be 30 deg. It's been found that this method

135

keeps breaker-point spacing within the recommended range over the longest time.

In setting points, the right way is the only way. Points set too close will burn. Points set too wide apart will reduce coil output, at high speeds.

frozen distributor

Saturday mechanics often find a distributor so firmly stuck in the block that they can't budge it

eight car problems, continued

Some hard-to-reach even hard-to-locate multiple connectors are low on the engine side of the firewall

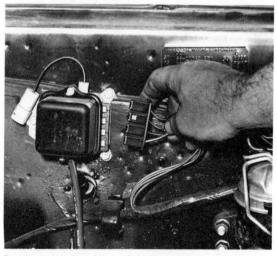

One bent terminal in a quick-disconnect multiple connector can put you out of action. Better check them

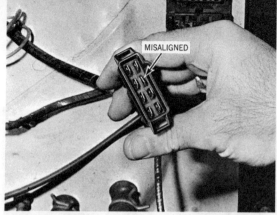

You can recognize the misaligned terminal by comparing it with others in connector. Bend it straight

Loosen the "frozen" distributor with a blast from a CO_2 extinguisher. CO_2 shrinks the distributor

to set timing. To loosen it, a hammer's *verboten* —but a CO_2 fire extinguisher isn't.

Aim the extinguisher's nozzle at the distributor beneath the bowl, then fire a few brief blasts at it. These frigid blasts of CO_2 should cause the distributor to contract so that it can be removed. If it still sticks, spray some heat-riser solvent right on top of the CO_2 adhering to the distributor. These solvents usually come in aerosol cans for easy application. Allow it to penetrate for a few minutes, then again try removing the distributor. If it still sticks, give it a couple of light taps with a mallet. That should allow the distributor to be removed with a twist of the wrist.

So there you have eight "popular" automotive ailments that can sink a financial 8-ball into any car-owner's side pocket. But you've also been given their symptoms and their cures—the "cues" that'll keep you ahead in this game, both financially and mechanically—and out from behind that 8-ball!

See also: brakes, auto; carburetors, auto; chassis, auto; chokes, auto; cleaning, auto; cooling system, auto; idling, auto; ignition system, auto; rust prevention; spark plugs, auto; used car reconditioning.

Stalled?
Here's how to get rolling again

BY MORTON J. SCHULTZ

With an understanding of the two basic engine symptoms— fuel and ignition—a systematic

approach to diagnosis can often get you under way again

THIS COULD HAPPEN to you! You're on a summer vacation trip. You just left a town 10 miles back and are driving through a region that, if it weren't for the strip of blacktop you're on, you'd swear no man had ever crossed before.

Suddenly the engine sputters. You shove the accelerator pedal down. The car gives a last gasp and slowly coasts to a stop.

You try to start it. It revs, but that's all.

Panic grips you. You open the hood, look at the engine for a long minute (because that's what one's supposed to do, isn't it?). Nothing's so wrong it *shows,* so you peer down the long, empty road, and begin to have grim memories of those basic-training hikes they always managed to schedule for just such a sweltering day.

What are your chances of getting *yourself* started? That's hard to say, because it depends on two factors: how lucky you are and how well equipped for on-the-road stalls.

Modern cars are engineered to minimize the chances of such a stall. But it could happen. And when it does, that modern engineering is the very thing that might prevent restarting.

In older cars, the common "bugs" that often led to a road stall were of a type that made troubleshooting easy.

Take the distributor, for example. In the old cars, all you had to do to check out a distributor was to short out an externally accessible wire attached to the distributor. If you saw that current was getting through that wire and, thus, that your trouble lay in the distributor itself, you just opened the cap, lifted off the rotor and

everything was plainly visible. You could quickly file the points and, if that was your trouble, you were perking again before Junior got out of calling range.

But modern design has set in. Now, what do you have to do? In many cases, the external wire once attached to the distributor cap on the outside is no longer there. You have to take off the cap to reach it. You no longer can just lift off the rotor—you have to unscrew it. You no longer have easy access to the points: they're hidden beneath a large rotor breaker plate. To get at them—if only to file them down—you have to remove the points as an entire assembly. If you go this far, you might just as well be carrying a spare set to replace the old ones.

Does this mean that you shouldn't troubleshoot the car in the hopes of getting it started and perhaps save yourself a lot of shoe leather? Of course not. But be aware of one important fact: as refinements were built into cars over the years to diminish the chances of an on-road stall, these same refinements also diminished your chances of getting started again.

Troubleshooting an on-road stall is a two-part job: First, you *diagnose* the problem, probing in a logical manner until you isolate the trouble area. This is the easy part, as you'll soon see. Then, you *repair* the trouble, using whatever means you have on hand. You're not necessarily concerned with a permanent or perfect repair. Your only interest is to get rolling long enough to get you within hailing distance of civilization.

The one important fact that simplifies diagno-

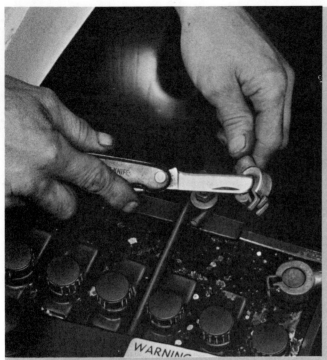

If the choke won't stay open, loosen the screws holding the control cover and twist to lean side

The powerful batteries in today's cars often surge acid through vent caps. If corrosion then gets between terminals and posts, it destroys the electrical contact. Cleaning (as above) is easy

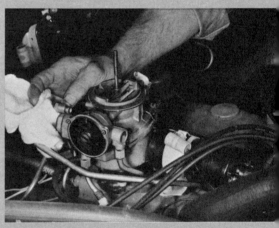

Wrap disconnected fuel line in a rag, then crank the engine. The rag will show if gas came out

Was the stall caused by a rough road or sharp bump? The lead from the distributor center tower to the coil may have jarred loose

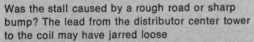

Although it's rare today, pump-to-carburetor line can clog with dirt. Disconnect the line and blow it out

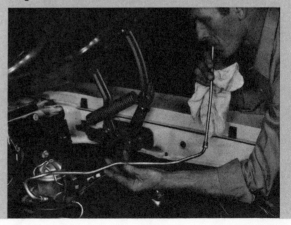

A pair of fuel line wrenches should be in your standard car kit. Here they'll expose carb inlet filter

sis is that an on-road stall is almost always caused by a malfunction in one of two systems: fuel or ignition. And the *manner* in which the car stalls is your first clue as to which system's at fault.

If the car sputtered and jerked before it seemed to give up the ghost, look first for trouble in the fuel system. Action of that kind generally comes from the fact that there was a last bit of fuel in the carburetor passages and float bowl. A few last spurts of this fuel are available to the engine before it gives up for good.

If, on the other hand, the engine conks out quietly, smoothly and completely, the problem is probably in the ignition system.

There are several preliminary steps to take, depending on the circumstances, before getting involved in details. (We're assuming that you have gas. You're not, of course, going to get the car running if the tank is empty. We're also assuming the problem is more serious than vapor lock or percolation.)

● Note the way in which the stalled engine cranks. If it doesn't crank briskly, check the battery cables. (Don't crank it for long—you don't want to add a dead battery to your problems.)

Make sure the cables are clean and tight, in that order, and don't forget to check the battery ground cable where it connects to ground.

Scrape off the inside of corroded terminals with a knife, as shown on the previous page, and clean off the battery posts. Hook everything up tightly!

If you drive an older car in which the battery cables have seen miles of use, you might want to carry a spare set—or replace them before you start out on a major trip. You never know when corrosion will eat through old cables.

● If there's a chance that the plugs have gotten wet (be especially suspicious of this on a rainy day or if you've driven through a puddle), remove each boot and wipe the entire plug, including the porcelain, with a dry rag.

● If you've been driving over a rough road or hit a bump and the car suddenly conks out, check the lead going from the center tower of the distributor to the center tower of the coil. It could have unseated itself. Push it in firmly at both the coil and the distributor. Also tighten all other electrical and ignition wires.

systematic search

If these preliminary steps don't help, you'll have to pursue a systematic search for either a fuel or an ignition failure. The troubleshooting steps are summed up in two charts, the first of which is on the next page. The ignition troubleshooting guide is on the following page. You should study the steps until you understand them thoroughly or copy the two charts to keep with you for on-the-spot reference. The photos at left are demonstrations of several steps, but you won't need them along to follow the charts' clear directions.

You'll note that the procedures are given in a logical, step-by-step order. Follow this order— it includes short cuts to a quick start wherever possible.

From these charts, you can get a good idea of those tools you should carry. You should also consider the addition of several critical spare parts to your on-vehicle inventory. This might well save you from being victimized by the spare parts racket.

The charts represent the limits to which a nonprofessional can go to start a stalled car at roadside, without a mechanic's tools and spare parts. If you happen to be unlucky and your problem goes deeper than these solutions can reach, you can console yourself (while you're walking) with the knowledge that you at least tried.

But isn't it worth the try? Who wouldn't invest the time, even with short odds, when it might mean saving a long hike and a steep roadservice charge?

Continued next page

CAUSES AND CURES OF FUEL-SYSTEM STALLS

PROBLEM AREA	HOW TO INSPECT IT	HOW TO CURE IT
Automatic choke plate stuck closed, flooding engine	Take off the air cleaner and look at the plate. If the plate is closed when the engine's warm, you've found your problem	After pushing plate open with your fingers, step down on accelerator and *keep your foot there* as you crank the engine. As soon as engine unloads itself by being diluted with influx of air, car should start. If choke refuses to stay open, indicating bad choke piston or damaged linkage, try wedging it into position—or, if there's a control cover, adjust as shown in top-right photo, p. 138. This should open the butterfly plate in carburetor
Gas not getting to carburetor	Work throttle linkage once or twice and listen. If you *don't* hear gas spitting into carburetor, there's an obstruction in the fuel system. If gas is getting to carb, stop here and begin ignition checks	Trace entire system back in a logical sequence, as explained below, until obstructed area is found
Plugged carburetor inlet filter or needle valve	Remove fuel line at carburetor (second photo at far left). Wrap end in rag and crank the engine for 2 or 3 revolutions. Inspect rag (center-right photo, p. 138). If it's wet, fuel is getting to, but not through carburetor. If dry, trouble's further back in fuel system	Unscrew fuel line inlet port nut at carburetor. Remove filter screen, if there's one there, and stick it in your pocket. Hook everything up and try to start engine. If it doesn't start, tap on carburetor bowl with screwdriver handle. This might loosen any dirt clogging needle valve. If this proves futile (and carburetor bowl is type where cover can be removed without taking carb off car) remove cover, take out float and needle valve assembly, disconnect valve, and blow it out by mouth
Loose fuel line connections	If rag is dry after above test, check for loose connection—particularly at fuel pump, which would let pump suck air, losing vacuum	Tighten all connections. If there's a sediment bowl on the fuel line, tighten that
Clogged fuel line and/or in-line fuel filter	If there's no gas on the rag, disconnect fuel line at inlet side of in-line fuel filter, if you have one. If gas pours from line, it's getting to, but not through filter. Whether or not there's a filter, fuel-pump-to-carburetor fuel line could also be clogged	*Filter:* If you have tubular type filter, take it off and blow it out. Maybe you can dislodge clogging dirt. If not, and you have no means of connecting the two ends of the lines together, there's little you can do. But even a short piece of hose wrapped tightly around ends of lines is all you need to get a flow of gas to carburetor and car running again. If you have sediment-bowl-type filter, drop glass bowl, remove ceramic filter and reconnect *Fuel Line:* Remove it and blow into it (photo at bottom-right, p. 138). Make sure it's reconnected tightly
Bad fuel pump	Disconnect fuel line from the *outlet* (carburetor) side of the fuel pump and crank engine. If gas pours out, it's getting through pump. If not, the pump is probably bad	If you have manual choke, pull it all the way out, closing choke plate. You might create enough vacuum to pull some gas into carburetor and get car running for a few miles. Failing this—or with an automatic choke—if pump goes bad you must hunt up a new one
Hot weather problems	If you can spare the time, before you do any troubleshooting let the engine cool down for about half an hour. If the problem is either vapor lock or percolation the car will then start. Leave hood up for faster cooling	

Ignition troubleshooting starts at the coil-to-distributor lead. Disconect it and hold it to a ground to check for a spark (left photo). Another vital spot is the battery side of the coil (left arrow, center photo). Disconnect the lead coming from the ignition switch and see whether it sparks to a ground; if it does, power is getting as far as the coil. Trouble could be in the coil-distributor lead (second arrow). If the condenser (on coil, right photo) is shot, replace it

CAUSES AND CURES OF IGNITION STALLS

TROUBLE AREA	TROUBLESHOOTING PROCEDURE AND REPAIR
Overall check	Pull a sparkplug wire from a plug, hold it about ¼ inch from ground and crank engine. If spark jumps to ground, trouble is *not* ignition. Ignition problems are much more difficult to repair than fuel system troubles. If a coil burns out, or if a rotor spring clip breaks off, or if a condenser goes bad or—even in some newer cars—if points should go bad, there's not much you can do unless you're prepared for it. Thus, the wise driver is one who carries spares of critical parts: points, condenser, coil (if the one now on the car has seen 30,000 or more miles of use) and just in case, a rotor. And a good spare tool is a length of ignition wire with alligator clips on each end
Bad coil or coil-to-distributor lead	Take off coil-to-distributor lead *at the distributor* and hold it to ground with ignition on, as shown below, left. If there's no spark, current is not getting to distributor and the coil-to-distributor lead, the coil, the ignition-switch-to-coil lead or the ignition switch is bad. To find which, reconnect coil-to-distributor lead and take off ignition switch-to-coil lead *at the coil* (above, center). Hold to ground with ignition on. If you get a spark, it means current is getting to coil, but not through to the distributor (see caption above). Connect one end of alligator-clipped wire to distributor pole on the coil and other to where coil-to-distributor lead attaches to distributor. Try to start car. If it starts, it means coil-to-distributor lead is bad. If it doesn't, coil is bad and must be replaced
Overall condition of distributor	Suppose, when you grounded out coil-to-distributor lead at distributor, you got a spark. This means current is getting to the distributor, but not *into* it or *through* it. Several reasons for this are listed next
Bad points	About 80 percent of all ignition stall problems lie right here. Take off distributor cap and make sure points are in good shape, if you can see them. If they are welded together, too tightly closed, pitted, burned or dirty, they can't create proper ground needed to pull current into distributor. If you have new set of points available, don't fool with old ones—replace them. If no new points are handy, insert some sort of abrasive—a nail file, or even the striking part of a matchbook cover—between them and sand them down. Do this carefully and lightly. Then wipe them clean by sliding a piece of paper between them. Now, try to set point gap as closely as possible to that recommended, which is about .018 of an inch. Use a business card, folded once, to do this. By the way, also make sure the little pigtail which attaches points inside distributor is tightly in place and hasn't broken
Other distributor problems	With current definitely going through coil and distributor, and being interrupted as it should by the opening and closing of the contact points, the car still might not start if condenser, rotor or distributor cap is bad. These are things that seldom happen, although they could. Check rotor first, particularly the spring clip. It might be missing. If so, then you must replace rotor to get started. Check distributor cap. It might be cracked. If so, start walking. If, however, contacts in cap seem to be pitted and burned, you might be able to get started by rubbing them lightly with an abrasive. Everything else ruled out, condenser must be shorted or open. This means you need a new condenser in order to get started

You can do your own body repair

BY MORTON J. SCHULTZ

Don't let the sight of your car's battered body discourage you. With modern tools and methods, you can match the job of a professional.

Your equipment can be simple and your savings will be substantial

---

autogiro model: see gyroplane model
automatic chokes: see chokes, auto
automatic garage door openers: see garages, door openers
automatic thermostat control: see thermostat control
baby shoes, preserving: see plastic forming
backpacks: see packs, camping

THINK POSITIVELY when it comes to auto body repair. The mere sight of a mangled surface on your pride and joy may produce thoughts of a brand-new fender, door panel, rocker panel, or grille, but you can smooth things over more easily than you might imagine.

Most body damage, fortunately, is minor. In some cases, you'll be able to fix it yourself as good as new, from start to finish. In others, you can do the repair work and have a professional finish the job by spray painting. Even this puts you ahead of the game financially.

The four most common body repairs are: (1) removings dents, (2) restoring rotted-out areas, (3) replacing beat-up chrome strips, and (4) replacing battered grilles. Let's examine each one in detail:

● *Dent removal.* You can repair *any* dent in the body of your car. Not necessarily an area that's folded like an accordion, but dents such as a car suffers when hit by a stone or tapped by another car. The area of the dent is no obstacle, but its depth is a consideration. An additional repair step will probably be necessary if the dent is more than half an inch deep.

1 Start dent repair by sanding to bare metal about an inch beyond the area of the depression. Ordinary drill provides power

2 Spread the plastic auto-body filler thoroughly into the dent and over all the metal area that was sanded

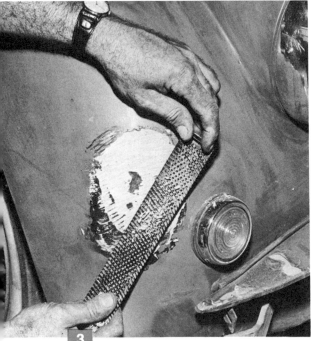

3 Shape the filler, once it has set, to the contour of the body panel. A grater does this job quickly and neatly

Unlike body repair shops, you needn't pull a dent back into shape. A pro uses a special puller, but you can do the job just as neatly with plastic body filler from an auto-parts outlet. You fill the dent instead of pulling sheet metal out.

The surface should be prepared as carefully as if you were going to paint your house. Remove old paint to the bare metal, making sure the spot you sand is at least an inch larger in diameter than the dent itself. Use a 16- or 18-grit sanding disc on a ¼-in. electric drill or power sander.

Now, this is important: If the dent is deeper than ½ in., drill ⅛- or ¼-in. holes through it half an inch apart so the plastic filler can rivet itself to the spot.

Auto-body filler comes in two parts: a black base material and a liquid hardener. Mix the hardener with the base material in the proportion specified. Use a putty knife or similar tool and apply a layer of the mixture to the entire area—that is, to the dent and the sanded surrounding area. Use a rubber squeegee to mold the filler to the contours of the area, kneading the material back and forth into the surface to assure a firm bond.

Now, let it harden. You can decrease the 20-minute drying time by holding your incandescent drop light near the spot. Heat should *not* be applied for longer than two minutes.

After the material hardens, scrape the area with a Surform grater to shape the patch and remove excess filler. Surform grater No. 294B, made by Stanley Tool Works and available at hardware stores, is ideal. As you scrape, the patch will lose its "blackness" and become white.

car body work, continued

4 Start repairing rotted areas of the body by breaking away weakened sections around the edges of the main damage

5 Press on adhesive-backed aluminum tape over the rotted-out area, then beef it up the same way you'd fill a dent

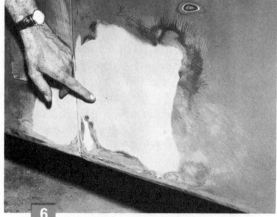

6 Ready to paint, this sizable rotted section was easily patched solid by the use of aluminum tape plus plastic body filler

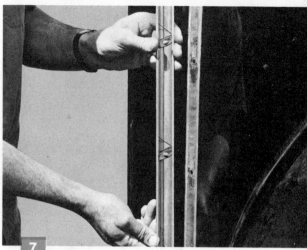

7 It's easy to remove molding held by press-on clips. And only the clips that you damage in the process need be replaced

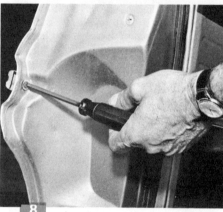

8 Door and quarter-panel molding is usually held on by screws at the ends and clips in between

After removing bolts with a wrench, pry the trim strip from a fender and the bolt-on clips will pull free with the molding

9

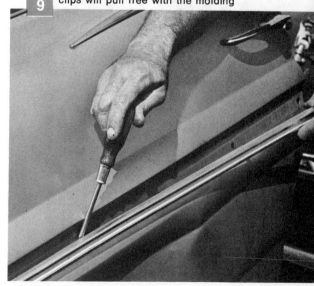

10 The first step in replacing a damaged split grille is the removal of headlight frames. A sketch noting bolt locations will help later

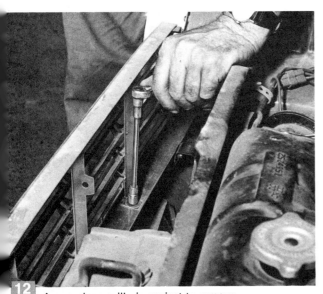

12 A one-piece grille is easiest to remove. Just go down the line and remove the bolts, one by one. Don't skip hood adjuster stops

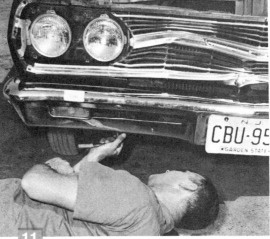

11 When you're removing the entire grille start at the bottom and work up so the grille hangs from the top while you work

This step greatly reduces the amount of sanding needed.

Now, fit a sanding block with No. 36-grit production sandpaper and sand the area smooth. Keep the paper dry. Follow with another sanding, using No. 80 or 100-grit dry sandpaper to prepare the patch for painting and to feather the patched area into the surrounding area.

Do the painting yourself with spray cans of primer and paint especially made for color-matched touch-up and available at an auto supply outlet. If more than a simple touch-up is needed, you'll have to take the car to a paint shop for spray painting. However, you've saved money by doing all preparatory labor yourself.

● Rotted-out areas. There isn't a car around which is immune to body rot or, as it's called in the trade, cancer. It can pop up in the most unlikely places, but no matter where it appears there's a simple procedure to cure it. And you don't have to use expensive and hard-to-work-with lead filler as do some body repair shops. In fact, many professional shops are now using the method described here. The patch holds just as well as lead and, if the job's done carefully, can not be detected.

Again, the first step is careful preparation. Break out weakened rotted sections, and then sand the entire area to a point slightly beyond the damaged portion, using No. 16 or 18 grit paper. What do you do with that gaping hole? Here's the trick! Available at auto supply outlets is adhesive-backed aluminum tape that sticks to a car's metal. (A leading manufacturer of the tape

145

is the 3M Co., St. Paul, Minn.) Simply cut a length of tape to cover the damage and make sure that the edges are pressed firmly into place. Now, cover the area with auto-body plastic filler —in the same manner as for filling dents—let harden, scrape and sand.

If one area of a car is subject to body rot more than any other, it's rocker panels. When one rots out, it may be easier to buy a rocker panel slip-on made for your specific car. The new panel slips over the rotted-out panel and is secured by sheet-metal screws. Spray it to match your car or attach a chrome slip-on.

● *Beat-up chrome molding.* Chrome trim on fenders and doors is subject to dents and pitting. When these moldings really get beat up, you may want to replace them. This can be rough and time-consuming, depending on the method of attachment on your car.

Moldings are held to fenders by bolt-on retainer clips or pressed-on clips. Where pressed-on retainers predominate, there is usually a bolt-on clip at either end of a molding.

exercise in identification

How can you tell what you have? Usually, bolt-on clips are used in places where you can get at them for removal. Pressed-on clips are normally used along those areas, such as doors, which are covered in back and prevent access. To check which type you have, run your hand behind a front fender. If you touch threaded bolts, the clips are bolt-ons. If not, they're pressed on. For a rear fender, lift the trunk lid and check along the sides behind the trunk liner. You'll see the bolts if the clips are bolt-on types.

To remove a battered chrome molding of the bolt-on variety, simply take a wrench to the bolts. After all bolts have been removed, pry the molding off with a screwdriver.

The bolt-on clips will come off with the molding. If they're in good shape, you can reuse them. If not, a bag of clips usually accompanies new chrome moldings. You can get replacement molding from your auto dealer or from parts and accessories dealers.

To replace the chrome, slip the clips into the molding channel, line up the threaded shanks with the holes in the fender and bolt the strip into place.

To remove a chrome molding from pressed-on clips, pry it off with a screwdriver. The clips will usually be damaged and have to be removed and replaced. Insert a screwdriver in each damaged clip and pry it out. Insert each new clip by pressing in the prongs with a pair of pliers and inserting it into the fender hole. After all clips are positioned, line up the new molding and tap it onto the clips.

Most door and quarter-panel moldings use press-on clips. Therefore, you do not have to remove the inside panels to get the molding off. The strip is held by Phillips-head screws on each end. Loosen these screws first, then simply pry the molding off.

beware threaded fasteners

Cars that have heavy-duty, die-cast molding strips on doors and quarter-panels often do not use the press-on-clip method of attachment. These moldings are usually held by threaded retainers. To get them off, the inside panels must first be removed and the clips approached from the rear. Needless to say, this is a pretty rough job and, luckily, one encountered by only a few car owners.

● *Battered grille.* There are one-piece and split grilles, and you're lucky if you have the former. One-piece grilles present no problem. They're often held in place by as few as 10 bolts. Replacing a split grille, however, can be a monumental job. Not that it's so tough, but it is time-consuming, painstaking work. Scores of attaching bolts have to be found. In some cars, you have to remove the bumper and drill out rivets.

To give you some idea of the job, let's list the major steps that you will have to perform with most cars. One word of advice: If you decide to do this job, I suggest you make a sketch of the front end. As you remove each bolt, note its location on the sketch. This will save lots of groping when you install the new grille.

1. Remove the headlight frames.

2. Remove the grille extension molding by reaching in back and disconnecting the bolt-holding clips.

3. Remove all bolts securing the grille, starting at the bottom. If you remove the top ones first, the grille could flip around while working on the bottom. Remember to remove the hood-adjuster stops.

4. Before the grille comes off, you'll have to pull the headlights from their housings. Then the guide support will come with the grille, because the two are usually riveted together. The rivets have to be drilled out, and the new grille attached to the guide support with stove bolts prior to installation.

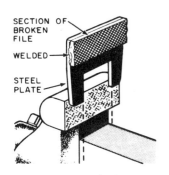

A broken file renews the grip of your vise. Weld two sections to straddle plates.

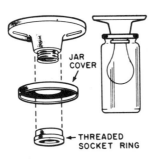

A fruit jar makes an excellent protector for exposed bulbs. Fit the cap under the screw-shell ring.

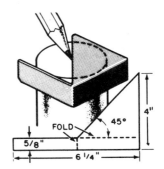

You can find the center of a dowel of any diameter by using a center finder of the dimensions shown.

Taking a "blind" inside measurement is easy if you use a coathanger wire bent to slide inside an umbrella rib.

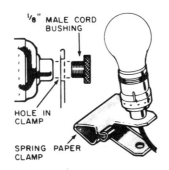

This extension cord lamp base, made from a spring paper clamp, can be clipped anywhere, or hung from a nail.

Boiler water gauges are easier to read if they are backed by a card bearing diagonal lines. Refraction does the trick.

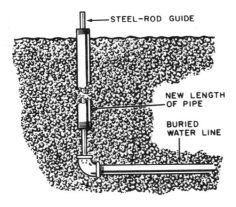

Here's how to replace a vertical buried water pipe which has frozen and burst—without digging! Remove the hydrant faucet, then thaw the pipe with hot water from a basement hose. Drop a 6-foot length of steel rod down the burst pipe until it bottoms in the elbow. By unscrewing the pipe and sliding it out over the rod, you can slide a new length of pipe down the rod, which guides it straight to the buried elbow where it can be screwed in place.

147

When nothing else works, try worms

On those days when all you can
do with an artificial lure
is beat the water to a froth—you'll
still catch fish with the lowly worm

BY STUART JAMES

■ WORM FISHING, according to the most avid anglers, is poor sportsmanship.

This is true if you are the type who wants to make his sport as difficult as possible. But if you go fishing to catch fish this is a left-handed accolade for the worm.

Competing against plugs, lures, dry and wet flies, or whatever else might come out of a tackle box, the lowly, unglamorous worm proves a time-honored fact—it will catch fish when nothing else will work.

The body wall of the worm secretes a mucus for keeping the skin soft. This has an odor that fish recognize, according to worm proponents. A worm must be fished slowly to allow the fish to get the scent. However, this scent washes off, so bait must be changed every half hour or so.

Casting a worm upstream (without a weight) permits it to drift like natural bait. Where the current eddies into a pool (right), cast above the pool and work the worm to the outer edge so it will move in a circle, presenting itself to the fish in a natural way, as if drifting

balancing wheels: see wheel alignment, auto
balancing beams: see playground equipment

Adding a small section of worm to a wet fly gives the fly an odor, and also looks as though the fly has been injured and is trailing a section of gut. This is an added incentive for the game fish to attack.

How the hook is baited with the worm depends upon the fish you wish to attract. Bluegills and crappies will nibble at the worm, so it should cover the hook with the barb going clear to the tip. For bass or trout, which are smarter and require a natural bait, you must consider the anatomy of the worm. The worm's body wall is made up of a thin layer of circular muscles and a thicker layer of longitudinal muscles that make it possible to contract and expand in moving. In the water it naturally activates these muscles, so the hook is placed through the tip to allow the worm free movement so it will appear natural to the larger fish that can take it all in one gulp.

The worm is a natural food for almost all fish. After a rain, particularly, worms are washed into streams and fish gorge themselves. To fish a worm properly, you cast above the pool where the fish lurk and let it drift down. You can check the current by tossing a twig into the water.

A light fly line or light monofilament is the best for fishing worms. It is not so easily seen, and it allows the worm natural movement.

You can cast a worm on a light line into a pool—without weight on the line—and it will slowly sink to the bottom as though it just fell from a bank.

If you encounter a pool where the current moves in a circular direction, it is ideal to bring the worm in with the current and let it swirl slowly.

It is estimated that 50,000 worms exist in an average acre of land. Only a foolish angler ignores this ready source of bait.

See also: bass fishing; fishing; fly-casting; ice fishing; lures; trolling motor.

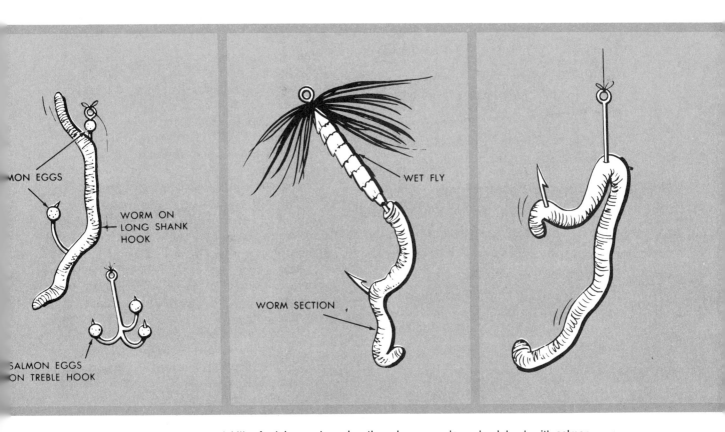

A killer for lakes and ponds—thread worm on long-shank hook with salmon eggs fore and aft; add salmon eggs on treble hook. A section of worm on a wet fly looks like trailing viscera. For bass and trout, hook a small section of worm and cast without weight, letting it wriggle naturally

149

This steering wheel is quivering like a handful of jelly. The trouble could be shocks—or front end alignment—or drive-line shimmy. Or it could mean a dying ball joint

Bad ball joints are dangerous

BY MORTON J. SCHULTZ

Nobody paid any attention when ball
joints replaced the old kingpin front
suspension, but their failure can have
horrible results. Here's how to go about
keeping an informed eye on these
critical but largely ignored components
of your suspension

---

ballast resistor: see ignition system, auto
ballistic chronograph: see chronograph
bamboo wind harp: see boys' projects

How MUCH FANFARE would the arrival of a fifth secretary to an assistant ambassador get at the Presidential Ball? Just about as much as the suspension ball joint got when it made its bow in the early 1950s.

Lincoln was the first car to hit the road with ball joints instead of kingpins—and the public greeted the innovation with supreme apathy. Yet, since then, virtually every automobile produced in this country has made the changeover.

The fact is, ball-joint front suspension has proved to be one of the most significant automotive engineering advances in a decade. They're probably more important than you realize.

Many home mechanics will be reluctant to begin a job as extensive as replacing them. Special, and often rather costly, equipment is required. Many car owners will let a professional make an honest buck out of the project.

So why this article? Four good reasons:

(1) To acquaint you with the importance of checking ball joints—or having them checked—from time to time.

(2) To let you know how to tell when they're starting to "go."

(3) To help you recognize the danger involved when trouble of this kind starts to develop.

(4) To help you understand something about

A horrible example of what happens when a ball joint lets go is shown at left (above). Had it broken at 60 miles an hour instead of in the driveway, the result could have been fatal

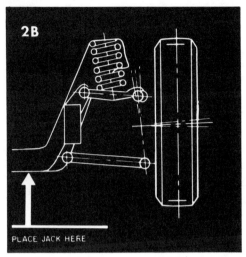

When springs are between upper and lower control arms, place jack as at left. When spring is atop the upper arm, the jack goes under frame as above

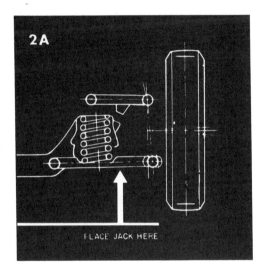

the job involved if you replace them yourself.

Lube intervals for ball-joint suspension vary from model to model. You may have heard that they should be checked and lubricated twice a year. Or you may have been told they need it only every 100,000 miles. Or you may have been told they'll *never* need lubrication.

One unfortunate result of this diversity is that many car owners feel they can pretty well ignore these vital suspension elements.

But this can be a dangerous attitude. Literally, *your life depends on your car's ball joints and their ability to hold grease.* And they can, and do, wear out—unless all driving is on excellent roads and in, above all, a *dry* climate.

The bug that infects and kills a joint faster than anything else is—*water.* So unless you live in a desert, your ball joints are not immune.

When you splatter through puddles, water can get into the joints. This will begin to dilute the grease and finally wash it out.

A new ball joint is a perfectly shaped cylinder. When water seeps in, rust begins to form on this highly polished surface—and that's all a ball joint needs to begin grinding up seals so that its life (grease-wise) literally oozes away.

Another thing affecting ball joints is the load placed on them. Suspend two tons of car on anything and run it at high speeds over bumps and ruts and *anything*—no matter how strong it is—will begin to wear.

These joints have a tremendous effect on your ability to steer and control the car. If one decides to pop at the wrong time—like when you're doing 70 per on the pike—you'll find yourself steering in one direction with the car headed in another.

Neither do you have braking action in the wheel that loses a joint. As a matter of fact, slamming on the brakes is the worst thing you could do . . . it would probably throw you into a spin as whirlish as a kid's top.

Now, knowing all this, you can see why it is important that every driver become aware of the way in which a worn ball joint will telegraph its punch. And this they do, seldom failing completely all at once or without warning.

When you drive over a bump, for instance, and the steering wheel starts to quiver in your

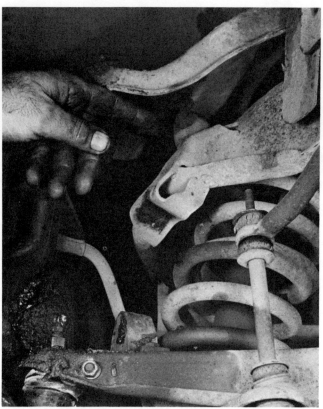

The bounce and rebound rubber bumpers (there are two to a side) must not rest on any part of the frame as you're checking out the ball joints. For some cars, special steel spacers are needed to keep them off

bad ball joints, continued

hand, it could very well be a warning sign that a ball joint's going bad.

Another sign is excessive play in the steering wheel, and wander or weave while driving.

A third telltale signal that ball joints are going bad is a noise from the front that you would generally attribute to the need for greasing. A crunching or squeaking sound when the front end is bounced up and down will alert you that these joints should be checked for excessive play.

But don't wait for these symptoms of trouble to appear. It's smart to have the ball joints inspected every time the car's oil is changed— that's every 4000 to 6000 miles in today's cars.

How ball joints are checked depends on the car's suspension system. There are two types of suspension systems:

(1) The type which has the front springs attached to the upper arms is found in Comets, Meteors, Falcons, Fairlanes and some Thunderbirds and Chevy IIs.

(2) The type where the springs are applied to the lower suspension arms. This type is com-

mon to all Chrysler products, and to most Ford and General Motors cars.

Getting an accurate indication of ball-joint wear can be done only when there is no load on the joints. On suspension system (1) the upper ball joints carry the load and thus are subject to greater wear than the lower joints. On suspension system (2) the lower ball joints take the load. Hence, to get an accurate check of ball-joint wear, you must know how to jack up your car, and this is determined by its suspension system.

To check joints of a lower-arm-spring system, the car must be supported off the floor by putting jacks or trestles beneath the lower suspension arms so that the wheels hang free. Position a dial indicator against the wheel rim, then position a pry bar between the floor and the bottom of the tire.

Keep an eye on the dial indicator, then hold your hand at the top of the tire to keep it from turning and pry upward with the bar. This is a check of ball-joint axial (up and down) play.

now check radial play

Follow this with a check of radial (in and out) play. This is done by placing your hands at the top and bottom of the tire and rocking it to and fro. In all cars, radial play should never be more than ¼ in. Every car has a specified amount of allowable axial play. The Automobile Manufacturers Association has established a set of standards for maximum allowable ball-joint wear.

To check joints of an upper-arm-spring system, place jacks or trestles under the *front cross members* and follow the same procedure described above.

When checking out ball joints, certain conditions can lead to an erroneous evaluation of ball-joint conditions. These are:

● *Wheel-bearing end play.* Wheel bearings should be properly adjusted so their play isn't added to the ball-joint reading. If you don't adjust them, then have someone apply the foot brake when checking the ball joints to keep the readings accurate.

● *Vehicle movement.* Be careful how the vehicle is jacked up. Have the car firmly supported at four points so it doesn't shift when you force the pry bar against the wheel. Shifting can cause a faulty reading.

● *Interference of rebound rubber bumpers.* Make sure the suspension arms aren't resting on the bounce and rebound rubber bumpers when

This Chevy came with riveted ball joints. After the spindle was removed from the joint, rivet heads had to be chiseled off as shown so the ball joint could be removed. Power equipment makes the job easier

Ball-joint replacement kits come with all the nuts and bolts required. But bolt holes may have to be enlarged. Be sure to use the bolts supplied; they're often of special alloy

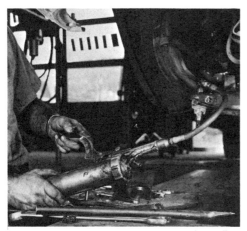

Use your grease gun as soon as you have finished the installation of replacement ball joints, but limit yourself to a manual gun so you can avoid high pressure bursting seals

readings are taken. If these bumpers flex enough, they can affect readings. In some cases, as with Chevy IIs, Falcons and Comets, it's suggested that metal spacer blocks be used to prevent this from happening.

Ball joints are positioned in their various support arms in several ways. They may be bolted in, riveted in, screwed in, pressed in, or, in some replacement cases, installed by a combination of techniques.

Units having joints which are screwed into the control arms will require large sockets (1⁹⁄₁₆ in. to 1⅝ in.) and plenty of leverage to remove them.

When replacing screwed-in ball joints, make sure you start the new ball joints straight and true into the threads in the control arm. The joints must go into the thread with a heavy drag

and be torqued to manufacturer's recommendations—at least 125 ft.-lb.

Pressed-in joints are removed with special pullers, or with special driving sleeves and a heavy hammer, *or* by pressing them into place with a hydraulic press if control arms are out of the car.

If riveted joints are used, rivets are center-punched and hollow-drilled before cutting off rivet heads with a chisel. This is done so the rivet will cut easily and not offer resistance that causes elongation of rivet holes.

If a power-operated chisel and sharp cutting blade are used, rivet heads can be snipped off without hollow drilling.

Ball-joint replacement kits contain nuts, bolts and lock washers to facilitate replacement.

With the replacement installed, check the fit of the bolt in the hole. It should fit easily, but not sloppily. The hole might require just a bit of enlarging by drilling or reaming, or by driving a pin punch into it to knock off rough edges.

As soon as new ball joints are installed, make sure they're filled with the lubricant recommended by the manufacturer. Usually this grease is a molybdenum disulfide type. Never apply it with a high-pressure gun.

When new ball joints are installed, check the front end for correct geometry. The wheels should be checked, too, for both static and dynamic balance.

In summary, a familiarity with this essential component of your car can save you money, time and trouble—and *may* even save your life!

See also: auto repairs; steering, auto; steering, power, auto; wheel alignment, auto.

Build a band grinder for your shop

It operates like a bandsaw,
but drives a belt instead of a blade.
It sharpens everything from
scissors to twist drills and makes fast
work of sanding and polishing

BY WILLIAM G. WAGGONER

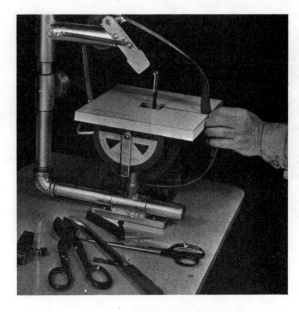

How the belt tensioner works

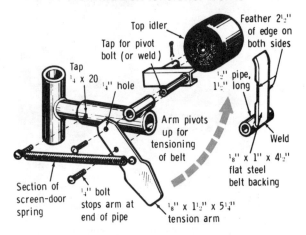

Top idler
Tap for pivot bolt (or weld)
Tap ¼ x 20
¼" hole
Feather 2½" of edge on both sides
½" pipe, 1½" long
Arm pivots up for tensioning of belt
Weld
⅛" x 1" x 4½" flat steel belt backing
Section of screen-door spring
¼" bolt stops arm at end of pipe
⅛" x 1½" x 5¼" tension arm

■ ANYONE WHO can screw pipe fittings together
can build this versatile workshop tool in a
couple of evenings. And once you learn what
it can do, you'll wonder why such a tool isn't
on the market. It not only performs the normal function of a belt sander, such as deburr-
ing, and sanding inside curves; it's the neatest
sharpener you ever used to put a quick edge
on knives, scissors, circular saw blades, twist
drills or lathe tool bits.

By taking advantage of the natural sleeve fit
of 1-in. pipe into 1¼-in. pipe, and of ⅝-in.
shafting into ½-in. pipe, you avoid extensive
machining, yet create a tool of surprising ad-
justability. The tracking pulleys can be moved
in two directions for belts of different lengths
and widths (up to 48 in. x 2 in.), and there's an
automatic tensioning device that makes it easy
to slip off one belt and insert a new one through
the table slot, as shown here. Tilting the tool
causes the belt to track.

The table tilts 20° to the back and 45° to the
front, to permit you to set any cutting bevel you
need. The belt backing plate stays rigidly vertical, aligned with the Plexiglas protractor tongue,
as the table tilts. The normal 9-in. throat clearance can be increased to 14 in. by adjusting the
bottom pipe extension back and the top pulley
sleeve forward.

And you don't even tie up a motor. By swing-

ing down the belt-tensioning arm, you can power
other tools from the opposite end of a double-
shaft motor without spinning the abrasive belt.

The table shown in the photos was salvaged
from a sink cutout of ¾-in. counter-top stock,
then edged with a plastic laminate to match the
top surface. The table can be raised—or removed altogether for large sanding jobs—by
loosening the lock screw that bears against its
vertical stem. This stem has a ¼-in. cross-rod
through it which cradles into notches at the top
of the support sheath. The easiest way to accom-
plish this is to slip the rod into an overlong ½-in.
pipe, drill a ¼-in. hole through both, separate
them, drive the ¼-in. rod through the ⅝-in. stem
and trim off the pipe right through the holes to
form the notches. The stem is then permanently
secured at right angles to the cross shaft that runs
under the table. The joint is made by concaving
the end of the stem and tapping it to take a bolt

inserted through the cross shaft. When the bolt is tight, check for squareness and weld.

The table pivots in two bearing sleeves consisting of short pieces of ½-in. pipe welded to mounting plates. When assembling the pivot mechanism, see that the ⅝-in. cross shaft running under the table extends slightly through the protractor mount that's bracketed to the table. Then, when the Plexiglas tongue is tightened against the end of the shaft with a small bolt into a tapped hole, it will sweep the protractor without binding. Note that the pivot shaft is anchored into a no-play position by means of two collars flanking the front sleeve, and cut from the same ½-in. pipe. These collars are secured by means of setscrews. The rear sleeve is equipped with a simple locking device. A ³⁄₁₆-in. rod is threaded on one end to match a heavy nut that's welded over a hole through the sleeve. For the sake of

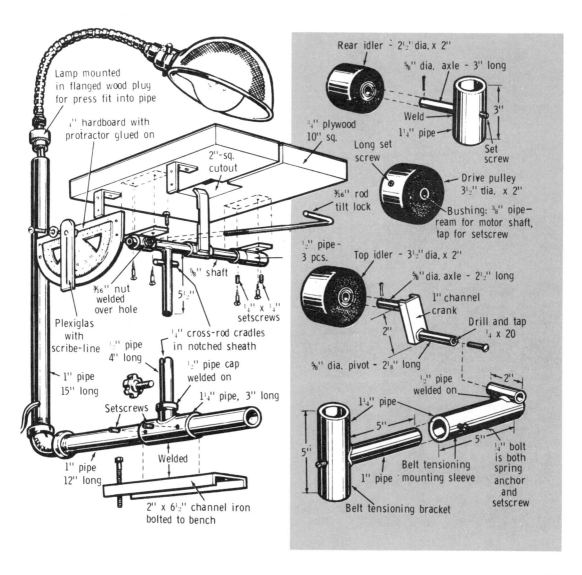

band grinder

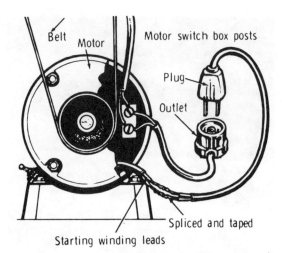

Optional reversing device lets you change direction of belt travel by reversing plug in socket mounted near on-off switch. Upward-moving belt is a boon for sharpening shears since it carries material away from cutting edges, leaving no burrs

clarity, in the drawing this lock rod is projecting toward the *front* of the table. If you prefer, it can be attached at the back of the sleeve.

The adjustable-base connection consists of a channel plate to which a sleeve of 1¼-in. pipe is welded. A pipe cap is then welded to the top of this sleeve to form a socket for the vertical support sleeve.

The photos and captions below tell you how to perform various sharpening operations. Circular saw blades can be sharpened without filing. The inside face of the belt backing plate is feathered to a knife edge at each side to give fine teeth access to the belt. Beveled teeth on combination blades are no problem, either. You just tilt the table to the proper angle for safe, precision grinding.

See also: band sander; gemstones; grinding; hand grinders; honing; power take-offs; radial-arm saws.

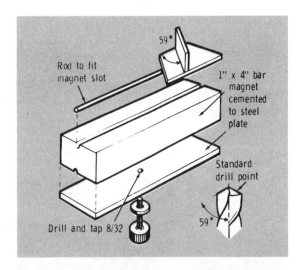

Precise angle is important for "honed" bit sharpening. Fasten upright piece of flat steel to "bed" plate, as shown, either by welding or by drilling and tapping for screws. Rod, riding in magnet's slot, holds fence at proper angle for bit

Large twist drills are held snug against fence with fingers. Small ones can be held against edge of jig, cut to same angle as fence (below, left). Knurled-head bolt passes through table slot, is tightened to hold magnet

Turn jig lengthwise and position it to serve as stop for setting perfect bevel on knives. Use magnet alone to support straight-edge tool (such as shears) while edge is drawn across magnet against belt. Tilt table for bevel angle

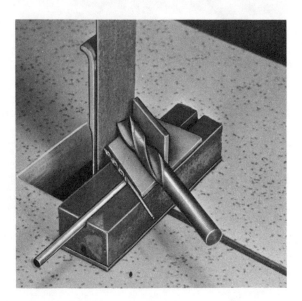

156

Clamped to saw, attachment makes use of tool's table as well as its motor. Doubled 2 x 4 base serves as backup plate for square handling

Band sander for your bench saw

BY RAY SHOBERG

This inexpensive attachment
is driven directly off
the arbor—and you can make
the pulleys right on the saw itself

WITHOUT THE COST or clutter of an extra stand and motor, you can add a flexible band sander to your shop simply by making this attachment for your bench saw. The handy little belt will whisk away burrs and smooth or polish wood, metal or plastic. The top pulley is spring-loaded to permit the belt to yield and conform to odd shapes, yet that part of the belt immediately above the table is backed up for square sanding, as shown at right.

Since the unit is so easy to attach (top left), it doesn't cut down on the convenience of your saw. You just replace the blade with the sander's drive pulley, then slip the belt over this as you lower the unit in place. A table insert positions the base, and two hook bolts anchor it firmly. To tension the belt, you merely turn the saw's blade-lowering crank.

This unit is designed for a 42 x 1-in. belt. It's an all-purpose emery cloth type, readily available since it's used on several commercial sanders; it comes in various grits for around 50 cents.

The novel aspect of this project is that you can create it on the very saw you'll use it on later. The pulleys are easier to make on a lathe, but you can turn them on the saw arbor by making

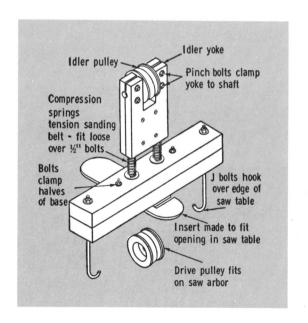

Idler yoke

Idler pulley

Pinch bolts clamp yoke to shaft

Compression springs tension sanding belt - fit loose over ½" bolts

Bolts clamp halves of base

J bolts hook over edge of saw table

Insert made to fit opening in saw table

Drive pulley fits on saw arbor

them of two pieces of 1-in. stock. In the case of the idler pulley, you turn a half at a time, as shown at the left. Most arbors aren't long enough to take both halves at once, so to make the drive pulley (which must be mounted on the arbor later anyhow) you'll have to bore a large enough

Improvised lathe results when you make a chisel rest

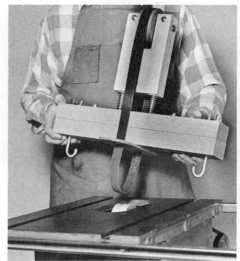

Attachment can be taken off or put on in minutes and doesn't interfere with the saw

Round or odd-shaped items are polished or smoothed with flexible section of sanding belt

hole in one half of the blank to clear the arbor's flange washer. The three other pulley halves require a hole only the size of the mandrel. Glue and screw the two halves of the drive pulley together to form the turning blank.

Although the idler pulley halves are turned separately, it's a good idea to screw them together temporarily and spin them on the idler shaft to make certain the bearing holes are aligned. Then drill a couple of ¼-in. holes

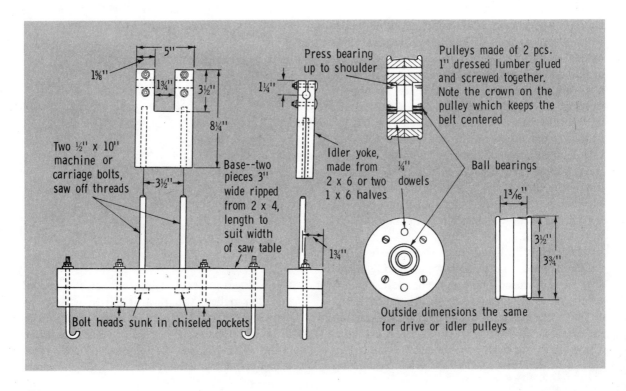

5"
1⅝"
1¾"
3½"
8¼"
3½"

Two ½" x 10" machine or carriage bolts, saw off threads

Base--two pieces 3" wide ripped from 2 x 4, length to suit width of saw table

Bolt heads sunk in chiseled pockets

Press bearing up to shoulder

1¼"

1¾"

Idler yoke, made from 2 x 6 or two 1 x 6 halves

¼" dowels

Pulleys made of 2 pcs. 1" dressed lumber glued and screwed together. Note the crown on the pulley which keeps the belt centered

Ball bearings

1³⁄₁₆"

3½"

3¾"

Outside dimensions the same for drive or idler pulleys

Driver pulley is at lower left of photo. Three sample idler pulleys show choice of bearings, including (left to right) hardwood, ball bearing, or bronze bushing. Turned halves are realigned by driving dowels flush

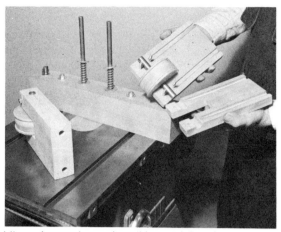

Idler yoke can be made solid as at left or in halves as at right. In split yoke, grooves replace deep drilled sockets for ½-in. upright bolts. Either way, sockets must be straight to let yoke slide freely

through both halves to facilitate realigning with dowels, after turning. You may also prefer to cut the blanks to a rough round on a jig or band saw before separating them. When turning, remember that both pulleys should be slightly crowned to keep the belt centered.

The simplest idler bearing is none at all— you simply use a shaft that will fit the holes you've drilled for the saw arbor. If the pulley is hardwood and the shaft is polished and kept well oiled, the pulley will last a long time. But you may prefer to press a bronze bushing into the center hole or—best of all—go to sealed ball bearings. If you choose the latter, buy inch-size double-shielded bearings with a bore equal to your arbor diameter and press them into sockets in the outer face of each pulley half before turning. The socket size is critical, as too tight a fit on the outer race will cause it to collapse. If you're turning the pulley on a lathe, screw the blank to a faceplate so you can turn the bearing socket at the time you true the edge.

The base consists of two 3-in.-wide pieces ripped out of 2 x 4s, long enough to extend beyond the width of the saw table. Drill half-inch holes through the top board to pass two 10-in. bolts. Cut off the threaded portion of these bolts and round the cut ends so they'll slide freely in the idler yoke. The heads of these bolts set into recesses chiseled in the bottom board, which are left a little shallow so the heads will be clamped tightly between.

If you have the equipment for drilling straight deep holes, you can make the idler yoke of a solid 2 x 6; if not, make the yoke of two 1 x 6s and cut grooves on your bench saw in the mating

faces, as is shown above. If using a solid block, you'll have to kerf it down to the idler shaft hole so you can install bolts to pinch the shaft and hold it secure. With a two-piece yoke, just drill a slightly undersized shaft hole on the joint line and use bolts above and below.

Any good hardware store carries an assortment of springs that should yield a couple about 2½ in. long, of a diameter to slip over your upright bolts, and a length that will give the right tension against the idler yoke. Steel washers prevent the spring ends from digging into the wood.

With everything assembled, it's time for your shakedown cruise. Fasten the base to the saw table temporarily with a couple of C-clamps. When you put on the belt, note the directional arrow printed inside. Now, with the belt running at proper tension, loosen the clamps and shift the base, if necessary, till the belt runs in the center of the pulleys and just skims the base. You can now properly position the hook bolts with respect to the edge of the saw table. If you can't buy such bolts, you can make them by reforming an eyebolt or bending threaded rod.

Lay out an insert to cover the saw table opening and cut it from thin plywood, hardboard or metal. Cut slots to pass the belt and mark the position of the sander base on the insert. Remove the unit and fasten the insert to the underside of the base with screws, to assure automatic realignment each time the unit is set in place on your saw table. It helps to use wing nuts on the hook bolts.

See also: abrasives; band grinder; belt-disc sander; belt sander; drill presses; lathe accessories; pad sander; sanding jig; spindle sander.

Table enlarges your bandsaw

BY MANLY BANISTER

It sets up for use in
about a minute and folds
for storage in even less
time. This 3 x 4 ft. auxiliary
plywood table gives any small
bandsaw real big-machine
capacity and flexibility

■ YOUR 12 or 14-in. bandsaw will cut anything you can get under the blade guide. The problem is to support and guide a large workpiece while it is being cut. This auxiliary table is designed for jiffy installation. It sets up ready for use in about a minute and takes down and folds for storage in even less time. Note the two photos, and then go over the detail at the right, remembering that here the table is shown upside down. The outboard side of the table is supported on short folding legs which rest on the beam of a sawhorse. In the original, the tongue cut on the lower end of each folding leg fits between the halves of the metal sawhorse leg brackets. Cleats around the auxiliary-table opening provide a means of clamping the auxiliary to the machine table.

First of all, check the height of the sawhorse to be used. Subtract this value from the height of the bandsaw table to get the distance from

the top of the auxiliary table to the bottom of the notch in the bearing blocks which are attached to the short front legs. The latter are cut about 4 in. or so longer to permit the lower ends to be clamped to the sawhorse beam. Each short leg is held by a bolt and wing nut, the latter being loosened to permit the leg to fold. The notched blocks can be attached permanently to the legs or can be attached by the alternate method detailed (shown right side up) which permits the blocks to be adjusted.

Cut the auxiliary table to size, rounding the corners as detailed, attach three aprons in the positions shown, and cut the opening for the bandsaw table; try for fit over the bandsaw table, then screw three clamping cleats around the opening.

Use 1 x 4s for the legs and cut and attach the short legs first.

It is important to note that the rear legs should

be cut just a trifle short of the measurement from the floor to the underside of the table so that you have a little room for adjustment. Don't cut any stock to the dimensions given until you are sure the parts will fit your bandsaw.

With this particular auxiliary plywood table and its adjustable components, the sliding block with the hanger bolt, washer, and wing nut, you will be able to handle very large workpieces on a stable and firm foundation.

The table top must be level with the saw table, since unevenness is likely to result in uneven cutting of the lumber.

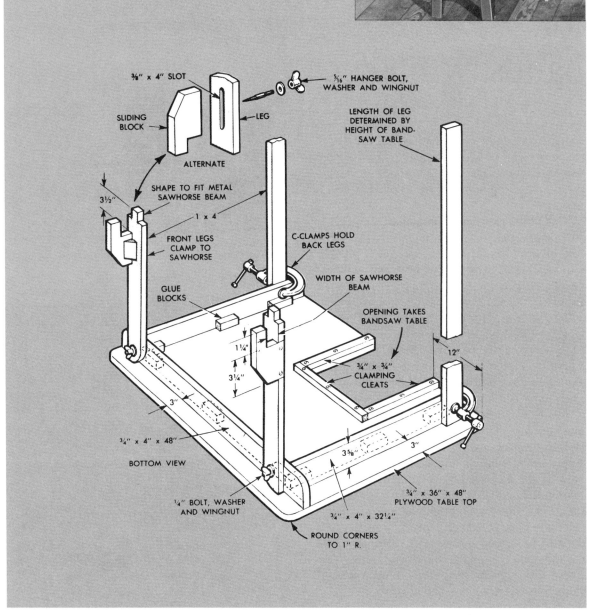

Clamp blade outer face up, apply flux to bevel and heat from beneath till solder coats it

Loosen clamp on right and bring other bevel in to overlap. Heat till solder melts, bevels join

While playing flame on joint from above, clamp on asbestos-jawed clothespin, remove heat, cool

Grind excess silver squeezed out of joint on faces. Clean gullets with three-cornered file

Brazing fixture for bandsaw blades

■ YOU CAN SAVE up to half on blade costs if you buy bulk 100-ft. rolls and make up your own bandsaw blades—either wood- or metal-cutting. But you have to know how to silver-solder the joints.

This technique is easily mastered, if you make the simple clamping fixture detailed at right. And silver-soldering has an advantage over fusion-welding: The joint can be taken apart by heating, to pass the blade through pierced work, then re-soldered.

To make the fixture, cut a 3-in. and a 4-in. length of steel angle, trim one leg of the latter as shown, then center and braze the shorter length to it. After brazing on the U-shaped rod, cut a 1-in. segment from the middle of the angles. Then both tables will be in the same plane.

A silver-soldered butt joint won't hold; you must overlap the ends with mating bevels. The steps in brazing are shown above and at right. Apply heat from below to keep the flame from blowing the flux away as it dries. If the solder balls in the first step, you used too little flux and should file the bevel bright before re-fluxing. Once the upper blade-end springs down against the lower one, you swing the torch to heat from the top until the upper end glows red and the solder melts again. The asbestos wrap on the clothespin assures slow cooling.

See also: bandsaws.

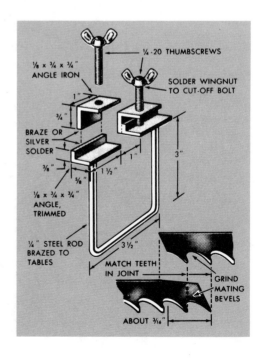

¼-20 THUMBSCREWS

⅛ x ¾ x ¾" ANGLE IRON

SOLDER WINGNUT TO CUT-OFF BOLT

BRAZE OR SILVER SOLDER

⅛ x ¾ x ¾" ANGLE, TRIMMED

¼" STEEL ROD BRAZED TO TABLES

MATCH TEETH IN JOINT

GRIND MATING BEVELS

ABOUT ³⁄₁₆"

Filing jig

■ Now you can restore the bite in the teeth of a worn bandsaw blade in jig time. As dimensioned below, the jig handles 83-in. blades from a 12-in. bandsaw. For blades of a different length, space the wheels to suit.

The stationary jaw of the blade vise is angle iron with one leg trimmed to a width of 1¾₆ in. and faced with aluminum as shown in the cross section. Three Allen screws clamp the movable jaw. After drilling through all three pieces, tap the holes in the rigid assembly and enlarge those in the movable jaw to ¹⁷⁄₆₄ in.

Use the jig across the corner of your bench so the projecting axles will clear. Or let the hubs serve as two legs, with the Allen wrench as a third.

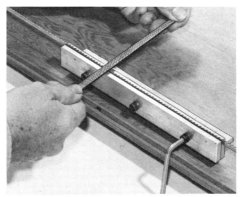

Turn blade wrong-side-out for right-hand filing with 7-in., three-corner tapered file

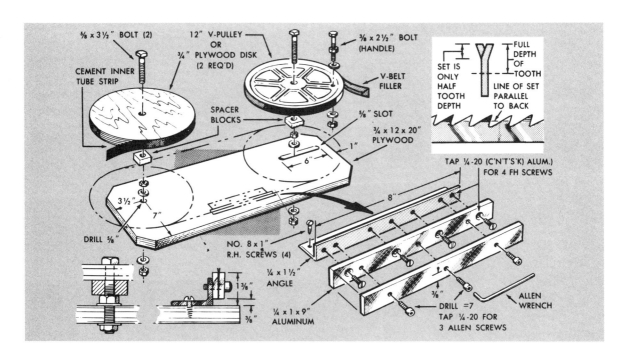

½" x 1" HARDWOOD NAILING LUG

2¼"

¾" PLYWOOD

1 SHELL-FORMING BLOCK

Make your own banjo

BY GUSTAV W. STAMM

Making a banjo is less of a challenge than most musical instruments, but it can be an intriguing test of your craft skills just the same

■ WITH THE possible exception of the finger-board, calfskin head and a few other parts which you can buy at reasonable cost, you can craft an excellent five-string banjo from hardware and lumber-store materials. With only a few hand tools and the materials at hand you're set to start from scratch.

Begin by making the form on which you laminate the shell, Fig. 1. Sandwich and clamp three pieces of ¾ x 10¼ x 10¼-in. plywood with glue in both joints. When dry, scribe a center line and bandsaw the block into two parts. Place a length of ¼-in. stock between the halves, clamp together and then screw two flat-steel cleats to each face as in the lower detail, Fig. 1.

Locate the center, scribe a circle on one face on a 4⅞-in. radius. Bandsaw just outside this line and save the waste pieces. Drill four 1¼-in. through holes located as in the lower detail, Fig. 1. Cut two ½ x 1-in. grooves 180 degrees apart in the rim for loose-fitting nailing lugs, or blocks, as in the upper detail, Fig. 1. Remove two of the steel cleats, take out the ¼-in. strip and reassemble. The opening left by removal of the ¼-in. strip allows the form to collapse sufficiently to permit its removal after the shell has been completed.

The shell consists of eight ¹⁄₁₆ x 2⅜ x 36-in. strips of maple veneer. The final finishing strip

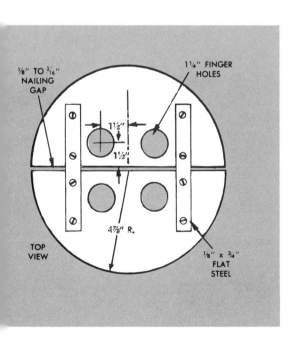

TOP VIEW

⅛" TO ³⁄₁₆" NAILING GAP

1¼" FINGER HOLES

1½"

1½"

4⅞" R.

⅛" x ¾" FLAT STEEL

Strips used in laminating the shell are soaked in water and pre-bent by forming in a ring and tying until dry

banks, piggy: see alarm, piggy bank

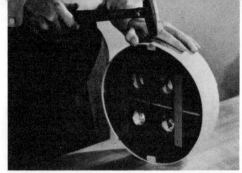

The finish end of the first laminate strip is held in place with brads. The strip is now coated with glue and the second strip is nailed to the opposite block

The first strip is started by nailing one end to the nailing block with brads. After wrapping, the ends must butt, not overlap. The finish is trimmed about $\frac{1}{16}$-in. short

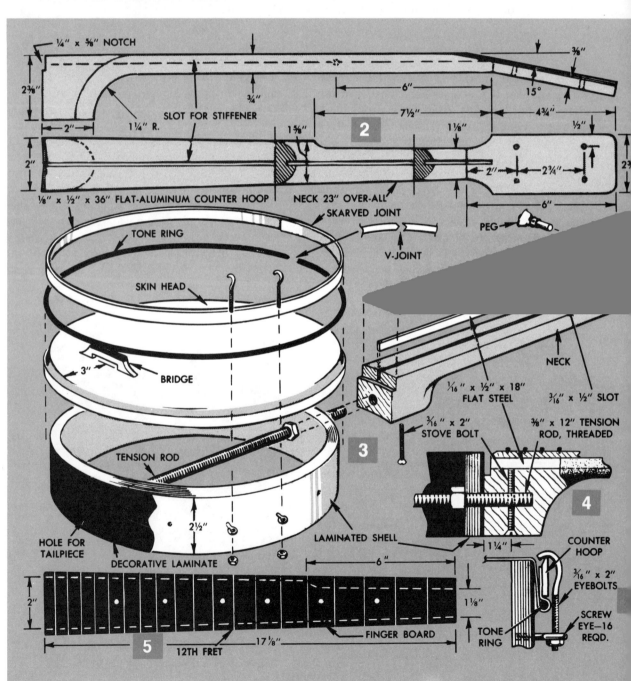

Completed head, with all parts in place. Looking at the bottom side, you see the tension rod and the rounded underside of the neck. Note the location of the tension-rod locking bolt

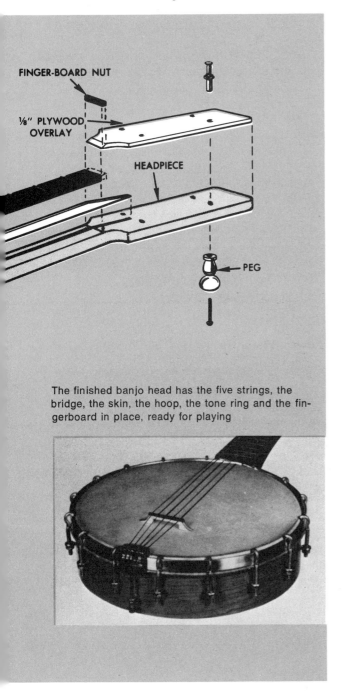

The finished banjo head has the five strings, the bridge, the skin, the hoop, the tone ring and the fingerboard in place, ready for playing

FINGER-BOARD NUT

⅛" PLYWOOD OVERLAY

HEADPIECE

PEG

is wood-grained plastic of slightly greater width and the same length. The wood strips are built up (laminated) around the form with the ends butt-joining alternately on the nailing blocks. Both ends of each strip are bradded to a nailing block to hold them in place. The result is a laminated ring with walls about $\frac{9}{16}$ in. thick.

The first step is to place the eight strips of wood laminate in soft, warm water and allow them to soak for several hours. Then you remove four of the strips, coil them into a roughly circular ring and hold in place with a cord as in the photo. Do the same with the second lot of four strips.

While the strips are drying, cut the two waste pieces you sawed from the form into four triangular blocks of roughly the same size. Saw off the right angle corner of each to give a flat about 1 in. wide. This gives you four clamping pads, or cauls, each suited to the purpose, as the curved face of each one is the same radius as that of the form. Two C-clamps can be used on each caul, the fixed pads of the clamps being inserted in one of the 1¼-in. finger holes.

now laminate the shell

The next step after the veneer is dry, or nearly dry, is to brad one end of the first strip to a nailing block on the form, using ½-in. brads. Wrap the strip tightly around the form, cut about $\frac{1}{16}$ in. short and brad the finish end to the same nailing block. Now you are ready to laminate the shell by gluing strips successively, one over the other, with the butt joints alternating on the nailing blocks. Here's how you proceed: Coat the first strip which is already on the form with glue (don't use quick-setting white glues); brad the starting end of the second strip to the nailing block opposite the one on which the butt joint of the first strip was made. Locate the first caul with its end near the starting end of the strip. Clamp the caul in place, using two C-clamps, one on each side of the form. Continue the procedure around the form until all four cauls are in place and clamped. Then brad the finish end of the strip to the nailing block, trimming the finish end if necessary to form a butt joint. Remove the clamps and cauls. The butt joints do not need to be tight, but be sure before bradding that the ends do not overlap. Continue this same procedure, step by step in sequence, until you have applied four strips. Then leave the clamped cauls in place until the glue dries thoroughly. Wipe off any excess glue with a damp cloth before it sets. Now, with the first four strips in place you apply glue to the face of the fourth strip and simply repeat the procedure just described step by step in sequence until all eight wood strips have been glued in place.

The finish strip of wood-grained plastic laminate is applied with contact cement. This strip should butt-join over one end of the gap in the form. The material must be applied with contact cement which is brushed onto the surface of the wood laminate and the inner surface of the plastic strip and allowed to dry to a stiff tacky stage (or as directed on the container). Remember that these two coated surfaces will adhere instantly on contact, so be sure you have the starting end of the strip correctly located before bradding it. When you're sure of the location, press the strip into contact about one fourth of the way around the circumference of the shell. Then clamp one of the cauls into position over the area in contact. Continue to press the strip into contact all the way around until the ends meet in a butt joint, clamping the cauls in place as you go. Leave the clamps on for a time as contact cement attains its greatest strength after it "ages" a few hours.

loosen the form

Then remove clamps, cauls and the flat-steel cleats. Loosen the halves of the form from the shell by pressing a pocketknife blade between the inner edge of the shell and the outer edges of the form halves. Once loosened all around, the halves should drop out. Pull the nailing blocks free, catch the projecting ends of the brads with pliers and pull them out of the shell, working carefully so that you do not split the wood. Snip off any brads that will not pull easily and file flush. Finish the edges of the shell to a uniform width and soften the corners with fine sandpaper.

The balance of the construction will be quite clear from Figs. 2 through 6. The neck, Fig. 2, is cut to rough form from a piece of selected mahogany about 2⅜ x 2½ x 24 in. Work the piece down to the dimensions given, paying special attention to the sectional shapes, lower detail, Fig. 2, and to the shape and finish of the headpiece, Figs. 2 and 3. Note that the neck is grooved on the top face to take a steel spine, one end of which extends past the fingerboard into the headpiece. This projection is covered with a ⅛-in. plywood overlay which is glued to, and becomes a part of, the headpiece, Fig. 3. Sand all surfaces glass-smooth.

The fingerboard, Fig. 5, is a guitar fingerboard adapted to use on a banjo by cutting it down to the size and shape indicated by the dotted lines. The fingerboard and the nut, Fig. 3, are attached to the neck with glue. Now, note closely the assembly sectioned in Fig. 4, which shows how the neck is attached to the shell.

insert the tension rod

Drill the through hole for the tension rod, which is a ⅜-in. threaded rod available from any hardware store, on the joint of the outer lamination of the shell. The hole taking the inner end of the rod is drilled only about halfway through the shell. The outer end of the rod cuts its own threads in a tap-size hole drilled in the big end of the neck.

After turning it in tightly, drill the tap-size hole for the locking bolt, Fig. 3, right through the tension rod and then tap the hole in both the wood and the metal. Countersink the hole for the locking bolt and turn the bolt in tightly. Draw the nuts on the tension rod moderately tight and nick the threads so they can't loosen.

Now, note closely the relative positions of the counter hoop, tone ring and calfskin head in Fig. 3. These parts assemble as in the sectional view, Fig. 6. Here ordinary eyebolts and screw eyes are used as counterhoop clamps, each eyebolt being altered to suit the purpose by cutting away about one third of the eye as in Fig. 6. The location of the holes for the screw eyes in the shell is not detailed in Fig. 3. The position of the holes must be determined after altering the eyebolts. You can, of course, purchase ready-made clamps, also the hoop and tone ring.

Note that the ends of the tone ring meet in a V-joint, while the ends of the counterhoop overlap and are scarved (or skived, if you like). Note also that the top edge of the hoop is beveled as in Fig. 6. This can be done quite accurately with a file. The hoop, being one of the exposed parts, should be highly polished. The wood of the neck should be finished in the natural color with several coats of violin-maker's varnish or a bar-top finish which is semigloss.

Now insert the pegs in the neck and attach the tailpiece. You can purchase banjo strings in complete sets at your local music store. Attach these strings first to the tailpiece, then to the pegs. Finally insert the bridge under the strings and you're ready to play.

See also: aeolian harp; bass fiddle; guitars; organs; pianos.

Gas-fired barbecue

BY EDWARD WIDDIS

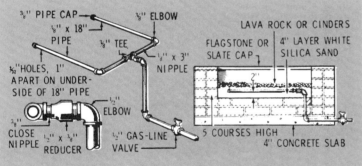

Buy white silica sand in 100-lb. sacks from sand and gravel dealers. It holds and reflects the heat

Lava rock or cinders can be used to catch meat drippings, but both must be replaced when saturated

■ YOU CAN FORGET about charcoal with this barbecue pit. It cooks with natural gas fed through burner pipes buried midway in a 4-in. layer of sand. A layer of lava rock, cinders or other porous material on top of the sand holds the heat and catches meat drippings.

Construction of the pit is detailed in the drawing. Be sure to leave small drain holes between the second and third courses of brick to allow rain water to escape. And if you want to avoid the expense of having a special grill made for your barbecue, don't make the inside width of the pit any larger than 19 in. You can purchase 22-in. grills anywhere patio supplies are sold. Larger ones are difficult to find.

In the event of chilly weather, you can use your gas barbecue as an efficient patio heater. Take off the grill and turn up the flame. It costs only pennies.

See also: brickwork; carts; high fidelity, portable; patios; patio cart; patio roof; patio screens; porch; yard lights.

169

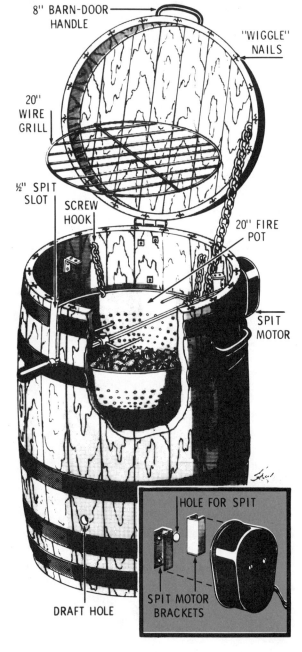

8" BARN-DOOR HANDLE

"WIGGLE" NAILS

20" WIRE GRILL

½" SPIT SLOT

SCREW HOOK

20" FIRE POT

SPIT MOTOR

DRAFT HOLE

HOLE FOR SPIT

SPIT MOTOR BRACKETS

"Old Smoky" barbecue

BY M. F. HAUSERMAN, JR.

Every backyard chef wants a new
and distinctive flavor for his favorite
recipes, and this barrel
will contribute its share

■ IF YOU'D LIKE TO TRY a new and different flavor touch for your favorite barbecue recipes, then put "Old Smoky" to work in your backyard. Smoky is an interesting and decorative barrel converted into a barbecue, but the flavor he imparts to your cooking doesn't come from

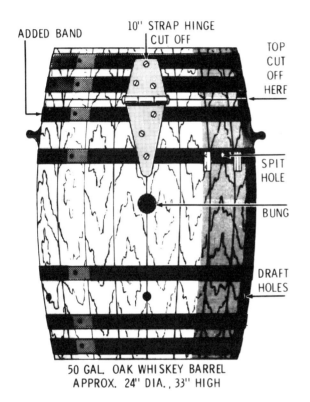

ADDED BAND — 10" STRAP HINGE CUT OFF — TOP CUT OFF HERE

SPIT HOLE

BUNG

DRAFT HOLES

50 GAL. OAK WHISKEY BARREL
APPROX. 24" DIA., 33" HIGH

There are two ways to cook in "Old Smoky"—on a grill, as above, or on a motorized spit, below. A large pan suspended on chains serves as the firepot for the spit set-up. Grill is also suspended

his looks. It comes from his charred-oak interior. Smoky started life as a barrel for aging whiskey, and his interior was charred to give flavor to the whiskey. Now, working as a barbecue, Smoky passes this fine flavor to the food.

It is not hard to convert a barrel, once you find one. If you have a liquor-bottling plant or distillery near your home, you should be able to pick up a used 50-gallon wine or whiskey barrel for a few dollars. If not, some bourbon makers will ship you a barrel. They must dispose of used ones since bourbon must be aged in a numbered oak keg which cannot be reused.

What you must do to make the barrel respectable depends on its condition. You may want to sand its weathered exterior and apply spar var-

nish. You may have to secure the hoops with screws, and you may have to add a hoop.

Ideally, you saw the barrel in two just above the third hoop. After cutting, drive corrugated fasteners into the ends of the staves, to bridge the joints between them. Locate the spit slot about 8 in. to either side of a point directly opposite the bung.

You'll have to cut this slot through the upper hoop with a hacksaw. If possible, end the slot by nicking a lower hoop with a file, to seat the spit. Then drill a hole through that same hoop, opposite the slot, to pass the spit through to its motor connection.

Pour a couple of buckets of sand into the barrel to catch embers that drop from the firepot.

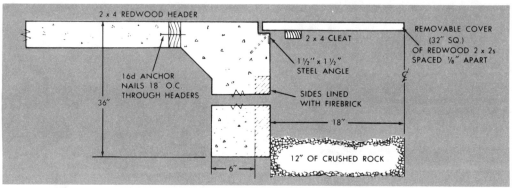

2 x 4 REDWOOD HEADER

2 x 4 CLEAT

REMOVABLE COVER
(32" SQ.)
OF REDWOOD 2 x 2s
SPACED ⅛" APART

1½" x 1½"
STEEL ANGLE

16d ANCHOR
NAILS 18" O.C.
THROUGH HEADERS

SIDES LINED
WITH FIREBRICK

36"

18"

6"

12" OF CRUSHED ROCK

Hide a barbecue
pit under your patio

BY WOODWARD RADCLIFFE

■ HERE'S A BARBECUE PIT that lives up to the name. It's a real pit sunken below the surface of the patio and concealed by a sturdy redwood cover when not in use. With it, you can entertain in true western style.

The walls of the pit are of poured concrete, reinforced around the top with steel angle. The cover is constructed of redwood 2 x 2s, spaced ⅛ in. apart for drainage, and braced across the underside with 2 x 4 redwood cleats.

The pit is lined with firebrick and floored with a thick layer of crushed rock to conserve heat. The dimensions shown in the plan drawings are only suggestions, and may be varied to suit your individual requirements.

You can attach brackets to the sidewalls to support demountable steel supports for a spit or for a grill. And if you suspend an old-fashioned iron pot over the pit, you can add some great new recipes, such as a hearty hunter's stew.

Barbecue
firemanship

To start briquets that have been placed in a coffee-can chimney, play a propane-torch flame on them. The can should have the top and bottom cut out or holes in the bottom for ventilation

■ To ENJOY your next barbecue more, start off with briquets, which are cleaner to handle and give more consistent heat than lump charcoal. But before building the fire, protect the grill with a level layer of sand, gravel or vermiculite. A 2½-in. layer of one of these will guard the grill from corrosion, absorb drippings and permit necessary air circulation.

Lighting the charcoal need not be an exasperating job. Briquets are relatively easy to start. Also, there are good, inexpensive electric fire starters as well as safe starting fluids.

If you use a fluid, presoak half a dozen briquets until they stop bubbling; build a pyramid with six or so, and then light them. Or soak an ordinary building brick with fluid and, after piling briquets around it, light the brick. Remove it after the briquets are burning strongly.

Another method is to use a coffee can as a chimney. Cut out the bottom, punch draft holes in the side and toss in six soaked briquets. Light them and, after a few minutes, add a few unsoaked ones. In about 15 minutes, remove the can and spread the briquets in a checkerboard pattern. Such an arrangement will reduce flare-ups, because drippings are more likely to fall on the firebed than on the red-hot coals.

Aluminum foil increases heat radiation, holds drippings and is easy to discard after use

The coals are ready if you hold a hand over them and must pull back within three seconds

barrel finisher: see tumbling machines
barriers, sound: see acoustics
barrow, wheel: see wheelbarrow

Throwaway bar for a one-night stand

Here's an inexpensive, easy-to-make bar you can give the heave-ho after your party

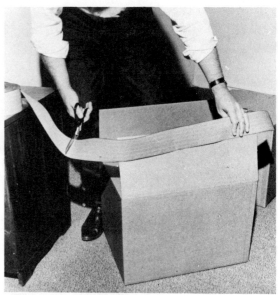

1 Tape shut the cartons to be used for this one-night stand. Use heavy paper tape. The cartons then should form rigid "building blocks." For added stability, stack some newspapers in the two boxes that will be the bar's bottom tier

2 After cutting a length of checkered oilcloth to fit completely around the stacked cartons, lay it flat on the floor and apply wallpaper paste to the back. The paste must be smooth

■ THIS COLORFUL BAR is designed to be used for one night only. It will add a touch of color to your next party and provide you with an inexpensive, practical way to serve guests.

Materials cost almost nothing. All you need are seven cardboard cartons, a large length of checkered oilcloth, a few smaller pieces of solid-color oilcloth, and a small sheet of plywood for the top.

You'll need only an hour or so to build it, and it's light enough to be carried into almost any part of the house. It has hidden spaces for holding glasses and bottles. It provides standing space for about five guests and a bartender.

The morning after the party at which this one-night stand is used, you can carry the entire construction into a storage area until your next party. Or, if you prefer, you can simply burn it or throw it away.

See also: brickwork; carts; hardboard projects; kitchens.

3 To assemble the cartons, a lot of wallpaper paste should be put on all contacting surfaces. Be sure edges are lined up to avoid seams

4 Use a paint roller to smooth out any wrinkles or air pockets you see after you wrap the oilcloth around the bar. Next, cut and apply the oilcloth covering for the plywood bar top and the footrest (a long, low cardboard carton)

5 Finally, cut access holes in the upper rear of the bar so the sides of the two top cartons will fold down against their bottoms to form oilcloth-covered shelves on which the barman can put glasses and bottles

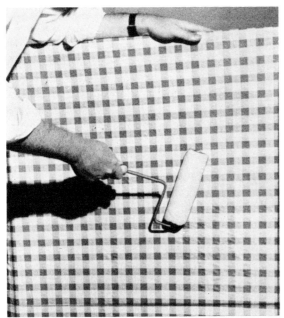

BY HI SIBLEY

Rolling patio bar

■ SURE TO LEND a touch of elegance to your next patio party, this handsome beverage center is made almost entirely of ¾-in. plywood. For convenience, the wide overhanging counter is hinged to fold over on itself, allowing you to wheel the unit through any 28-in. door. Sliding wood bars support the top when it's flipped over.

Sliding doors for the bottom compartment are slotted, top and bottom, to ride on aluminum-angle rails. As for the single drawer, use ½-in. stock for the back and sides, ¾-in. for the front, and ⅛-in. tempered hardboard set in shallow dadoes for the bottom.

Cover the top with decorative plastic laminate. Band the built-up edges first and use contact cement to bond the top.

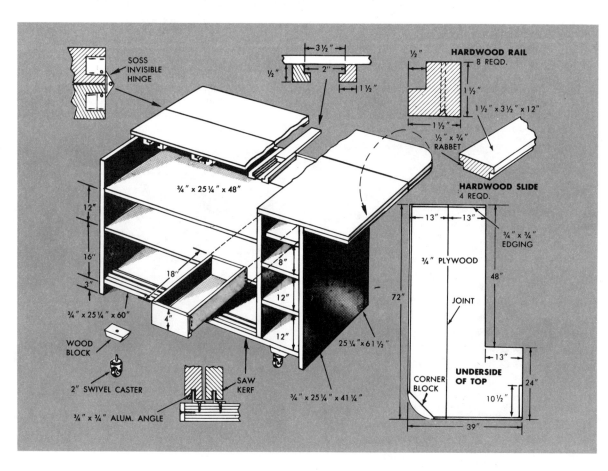

A stick dipped in a can of leftover paint and fastened to the outside shows the exact color of the paint when dry.

A facial tissue box makes a convenient cradle for your telephone receiver if you have to put it down.

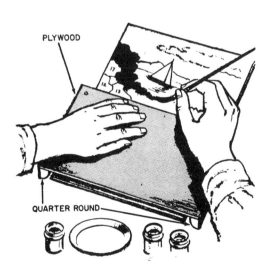

PLYWOOD

QUARTER ROUND

A handy accessory for paint-by-numbers fans is a hand "bridge" of plywood slightly wider than the picture.

Boiling clothespins in a strong salt solution will prevent them from splitting or freezing to clothes.

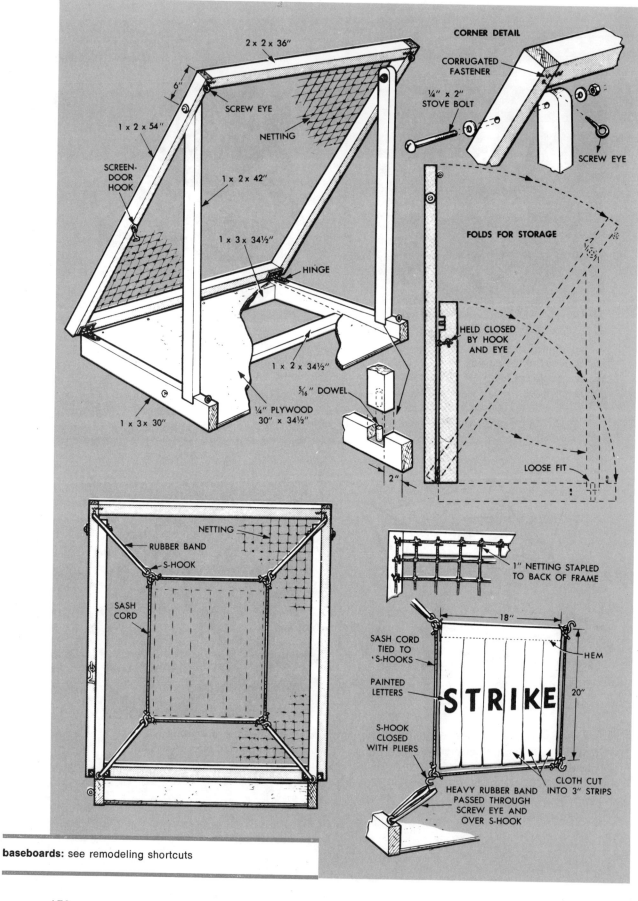

CORNER DETAIL

2 x 2 x 36"

CORRUGATED FASTENER

SCREW EYE

NETTING

¼" x 2" STOVE BOLT

6"

1 x 2 x 54"

SCREW EYE

SCREEN-DOOR HOOK

1 x 2 x 42"

FOLDS FOR STORAGE

1 x 3 x 34½"

HINGE

HELD CLOSED BY HOOK AND EYE

1 x 2 x 34½"

⁵⁄₁₆" DOWEL

¼" PLYWOOD 30" x 34½"

1 x 3 x 30"

2"

LOOSE FIT

NETTING

RUBBER BAND

S-HOOK

1" NETTING STAPLED TO BACK OF FRAME

SASH CORD

18"

HEM

SASH CORD TIED TO S-HOOKS

PAINTED LETTERS

S T R I K E

20"

S-HOOK CLOSED WITH PLIERS

CLOTH CUT INTO 3" STRIPS

HEAVY RUBBER BAND PASSED THROUGH SCREW EYE AND OVER S-HOOK

baseboards: see remodeling shortcuts

■ LITTLE LEAGUE pitchers can get their rudimentary training with this home-built pitching target. It returns the ball after each throw, and it folds into a compact bundle for handling and storing.

The backstop, detailed on the opposite page, is a rectangular frame of 1 x 2 and 2 x 2 stock over which a netting is tacked. This can be a section cut from a discarded badminton net, a fish seine, or you can use 1 x 2-in. welded-wire mesh. The backstop is hinged to a base made from 1 x 2 and 1 x 3 stock. This frames a piece of ¼-in. plywood which inclines from full frame height at the back to ground level at the front edge, and serves as the ball return.

The backstop is supported in position for use by two folding legs, the lower ends of which drop into notches cut in the frame side members. Note that a hole is drilled in the end of each leg to set over a dowel. The holes in the legs should be ⅜ in. in diameter to take the ⁵⁄₁₆-in. dowels loosely. The latter hold the legs in position when the backstop is struck by the ball. The ends of the legs should also be a loose fit in the notches, or they will be difficult to insert and remove. Hooks and eyes could be used instead of dowels.

Pitching target

BY FRANK N. STEPHANY

The target consists of a rectangle of fabric (light canvas will do) hemmed at the top edge, lettered with the word STRIKE and then cut into strips 3 in. wide to the hem. This is suspended in a "frame" made from sash cord with S-hooks at each corner. Rubber bands looped through screw eyes and attached to the S-hooks support the target in position but give readily if struck by the ball.

The center right-hand detail shows how the unit folds for carrying or storage, the dotted lines indicating position of parts when open.

See also: bicycles; boys' projects; cars, sidewalk; games, children's; playground equipment; stagecoach; stilts; train, children's.

179

Wet basement? Here's the solution

BY STEVEN J. HOWARD

Don't just sit there—
even extreme cases will
respond to treatment.
And you may be able
to effect the cure without
costly professional aid

■ How MUCH of a moisture problem can a basement have before it's beyond the skill of a do-it-yourselfer? That is, at what point would a homeowner be well advised to search the yellow pages under "Waterproofing Contractors"? Since a professional estimate will probably run several hundred dollars, it's important to recognize which *causes* of basement dampness you can combat on your own.

There are only four major causes:

1. Cracks in the foundation walls are letting water *leak* in.

2. Your area has a high water table, and hydrostatic pressure is pushing against the walls and floor, as shown in the sketch below forcing water through poor mortar joints, wall-to-floor joints, or any cracks or punctures in the concrete.

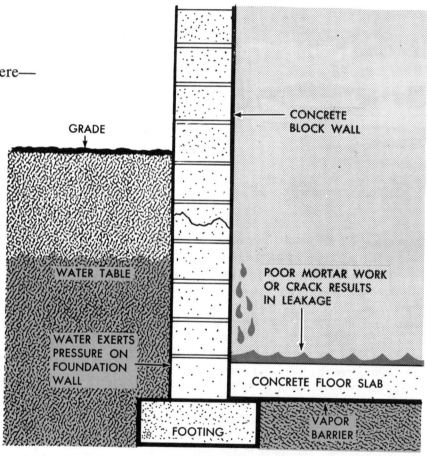

GRADE

CONCRETE BLOCK WALL

WATER TABLE

POOR MORTAR WORK OR CRACK RESULTS IN LEAKAGE

WATER EXERTS PRESSURE ON FOUNDATION WALL

CONCRETE FLOOR SLAB

FOOTING

VAPOR BARRIER

Hydrostatic pressure in the soil around a foundation, caused by a high water table, will force water through the joints of a block wall or cracks in a poured concrete wall

basketweave fences: see fences

Foundation cracks must be chiseled out to form a wedge-shaped groove that will key the repair patch into the wall. The groove, cut with a cold chisel and hammer, should be at least 1 in. deep

Loose particles must be swept out of the crack with a narrow wire brush. Then soak the crack with clear water before filling it with patching mortar

3. Your home is old, and the foundation wall (whether poured concrete or block) has become porous enough to permit *seepage*. This condition can even be found in a few newer homes where the concrete used in a poured foundation had too much sand in the mix; when the concrete breaks down with age, water seeps through it.

4. You have a condensation build-up. This has nothing to do with water entering from the outside; the problem is too much moisture in the *interior* air.

No one method of attack will solve *all* of these problems. You must determine which cause is responsible for your wet basement and select the cure to fit. Then you can decide whether it's a cure *you* can handle, or if it requires a pro.

The yellow pages for your area will probably list several different companies—all offering "sure cures." We investigated those in a typical phone book and found that the guarantees they offer range from five years to life; that the prices they charge range from $200 to $2000; and that the companies that charge the most don't necessarily provide the longest guarantees!

Almost every company touted an exclusive method. But the *product* used in each case was much the same: all methods involved a waterproofing agent. However, the *methods* fall into two general categories—solving the problem from inside the basement, or attacking it from the outside. Few advocate coming at the problem from *both* sides.

It's always worthwhile to try a few cures on

Hydraulic cement is the best patch to use if the crack is leaking at the time of the repair. Mix it with water to a thick paste and pack it into the groove. One part cement and 3 parts sand is another patch

your own, before picking up the phone. Unlike other household troubles, such as plumbing woes, you can't make a wet basement *worse* before you resort to the pro. You'll always have time to spend hundreds of dollars later, should the solution prove beyond you.

As a rule of thumb: if your problem lies mainly in the basement *walls*, chances are you can fix it yourself—if not permanently, at least well enough to last a good long time. But if the problem is affecting the concrete floor—perhaps causing it to wave, buckle, and crack—you'll most likely need professional services, unless you're handy with a jack hammer and know how to install a sump pump.

This article, then, concerns itself mainly with causes and cures you *can* handle, and with problems that are *constant,* not the rare emergency, such as backflow from overtaxed city drains. (Actually, you can usually take care of *this* emergency, too, if you keep a 3- or 4-ft. stand-pipe handy for screwing into the threaded floor drain when heavy rainfall threatens, or when you leave home for extended periods.)

Cracks in foundation walls are easy enough to spot. No matter how narrow a crack may look, it should be attended to. Small cracks can widen and eventually cause serious leakage problems. But even the narrowest crack could provide an entryway for water, since water can work its way through it by capillary action.

Inspect particularly around windows, doors and pipes. These are a foundation's weakest points, because there's an interruption in the foundation material. But be aware that a foundation can crack in other spots.

Many "experts" advocate repairing a crack from the inside. Others say it's best repaired from the outside. I can offer some solid reasons why it should be repaired from *both* sides.

Suppose you repair a crack from the inside only. If water is leaking into the cellar through that crack, it must be coming from the outside. Thus, there must be a crack on the outside that coincides with the crack inside.

If you plug up the crack from the inside only, water is still getting through the outside crack and will eventually gather enough force behind

You can buy a putty-like compound for filling cracks. You mix it with water, roll it into a ball, push it into the crack, and smooth. It dries in under 5 minutes

Exterior cracks often extend far below grade. Uncover the entire crack and patch the full length. It does no good to patch only the visible portion, as water will continue to leak through the unpatched part

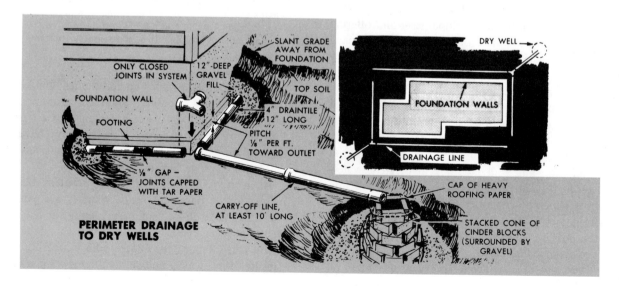

PERIMETER DRAINAGE TO DRY WELLS

ONLY CLOSED JOINTS IN SYSTEM

FOUNDATION WALL

FOOTING

⅛" GAP – JOINTS CAPPED WITH TAR PAPER

SLANT GRADE AWAY FROM FOUNDATION

12"-DEEP GRAVEL FILL

TOP SOIL

4" DRAINTILE 12" LONG

PITCH ⅛" PER FT. TOWARD OUTLET

CARRY-OFF LINE, AT LEAST 10' LONG

DRY WELL

FOUNDATION WALLS

DRAINAGE LINE

CAP OF HEAVY ROOFING PAPER

STACKED CONE OF CINDER BLOCKS (SURROUNDED BY GRAVEL)

it to weaken the patch, cause it to pop loose, and start the leak all over again. True—it could take anywhere from several months to several years for this to happen, but sooner or later the patch is going to give way.

Suppose you just patch a crack on the outside of a block wall which, admittedly, is better than the internal method. There is still water left inside that wall. Naturally, after the outside patch is in place no more will enter, but the water remaining in the wall will still have an entry into the cellar through the inside crack, and only that wall knows how much it has stored up.

A block wall, in fact, can serve as a reservoir. If the cores are full of water in the winter, a sudden freeze could result in serious damage. At any rate, water-filled blocks cause seepage so it's a good idea to drill "weep holes" in the bottom row, to drain the cores. You can do this quickly with a carbide bit in an electric drill.

There's another use for weep holes—in *both* poured and block walls. Drill one at the bottom

Use a pocket mirror with its face taped toward wall to determine if basement dampness is caused by condensation or seepage

of each large crack before you attempt to fill them. It quickly relieves water pressure around the crack and gives the patch a chance to take hold. You then plug the hole itself with a carrot-shaped plug, held in place until it starts to set.

Tackle all inside cracks first—at least you'll stop the water flow until you get around to outside repairs. The best product to use for these is hydraulic cement, because it can be used to plug up cracks even while water is leaking through them. You can, however, use a mixture of one part of regular cement to three parts of sand. If you do, wet the filled crack down every 24 hours for a week, to keep the patch from drying too quickly.

Once you've patched the *inside* crack, orient yourself so you can go outside to the same general spot. If the crack is below grade, dig down along the foundation to find if there's an outside crack which coincides with the one inside.

To repair outside foundation cracks, use either hydraulic cement or a mortar mix consisting of one part of regular cement to three parts of sand mixed with water to form a thick consistency. Again, chisel out the crack, dampen the area and trowel in the cement. As before, if you use regular cement, wet the patched area down every day for at least a week.

It's important that you chisel a crack wide and deep enough for the patching material to get a firm grip. If you simply lay cement on top of a crack, it won't adhere properly; as it dries, it will crumble and pull away, leaving you with the problem all over again. And *interior* patches have the added problem of resisting water pressures from behind; they must be keyed into

Downspout spill must be carried away from the foundation or it may seep through the basement walls. A plastic extension can be used to carry the water away from the house and distribute it over the lawn

183

To prepare the interior surface for waterproofing, roughen the concrete by means of random jabs with a pick axe or cold chisel. Sweep all loose particles from the surface with a wire brush

A waterproofing compound can be added to a mortar mix to create a trowel-on seal coat for the interior wall. Follow the instructions on the label carefully and keep the wall wet during application

wedge-shaped grooves or they'll be pushed out.

With cracks eliminated, if your basement remains wet you must find out whether the cause is water seepage through the foundation or condensation in the cellar. Tape a pocket mirror face-in to the wall overnight. If the mirror fogs, the problem is condensation. If the surface remains clear and dry while the wall around and beneath it is damp, then the moisture is coming through the wall from outside.

It is hard to tell whether this seepage is caused by porous foundation materials or by hydrostatic pressure. You can get a good idea by calling your municipal engineer and asking if your area has a high water table. If he says, "no," then you know that porous building materials are probably the problem.

You can take a chance and tackle the problem from the standpoint of porous concrete. All this costs you is some time, energy and a small expenditure for materials. Or you can call a professional immediately. He'll relieve the water pressure on the foundation, install a sump pump, or use some other means.

In any event, you should try to eliminate as much water as possible that might be accumulating around the foundation. If the problem is *porous materials*, keeping excess water away from the foundation might solve your problems.

Some 60 percent of all water seepage problems through a porous foundation can be resolved by carrying roof water away from the

foundation. Ideally, downspouts should carry water 8 to 10 feet away.

Many "experts" suggest that underground tile (if not already installed) should be laid around the outside of the foundation footing to carry away excess water that permeates the soil and sinks to the bottom of the cellar walls. These drain tiles are short lengths of 4-in. pipe that are made of clay or plastic.

Installing them is a big job. The tiles are not effective unless pitched downward along the foundation and then away from the house. The earth has to be excavated to the bottom of the foundation. Discharge lines have to be placed at opposite corners, pitched and connected to a storm sewer or a dry well. The tile then has to be covered with crushed stone or gravel that's at least 12 inches deep to insure good drainage, before you backfill the trench.

In the long run, you may have no alternative, but surely a simpler method can be tried before going through this expensive, exhausting job. One alternate is to create a waterproof liner inside the basement with waterproof mortar. We can't say such a seal will work for you, but it has worked.

Prepare the cement mixture according to the instructions on the package of epoxy, emulsified latex, or other bonding agents you add to mortar to permit the mixture to adhere properly as well as to provide a waterproof coating. Smear the stuff over the walls, but to assure proper adhesion, keep those wall surfaces thoroughly wet as the material is applied.

There are also prepared brush-on epoxy sealants. For these, you want the walls as dry as you can get them. This liquid is expensive, and is chiefly used to seal the joint between wall and floor, although you *can* coat the wall with it.

Some may tell you that interior seal coats aren't worth the time or effort because they won't work. Such "experts" advocate digging down around the entire outside foundation to the footing and coating the foundation with a watertight membrane. This is the approach usually employed in new home construction, of course, where a coat of tar is brushed on, or a layer of asphalt paper is applied with a waterproof mastic. But with an existing house it's a lot easier to put a seal coat on the *inside* rather than the *outside*. Anyway, the material used for membraning the outside of a foundation—whether it's the tar, the asphalt paper, a polyethylene film, or a waterproofing mortar such as we described above for interior use—may break down after constant exposure to moist earth. Then what? Another excavation to re-coat?

The most serious of all wet-basement-producing conditions is *hydrostatic pressure,* which results from a high water table in the area that exerts pressure on the foundation, forcing water in through cracks and the porous foundation material. If you have a wet basement for only a few months of the year, while at other times it's dry, your problem's probably hydrostatic, since the height of a water table and the pressure it exerts often vary with the seasons. The methods we spoke of thus far might keep water under hydrostatic pressure from entering a basement for all time. Then again the water table might exert so much pressure that it breaks through any watertight seal. Another danger of blocking out water is that it will then seek the line of least resistance which is beneath the home's footing and up against the floor.

If the water table exerts so much pressure it breaks through a waterproof seal, a more drastic method of stopping that water is called for. One professional drainage system, called the Vulclay process, alleviates wet basement problems that stem from hydrostatic pressure.

The process isn't cheap, running from $200 to $1000 or more, depending on the seriousness of the condition and the size of the area to be treated. It is guaranteed for 5 to 10 years, depending on the height and force of the water table in the particular area. However, no one in good conscience can guarantee a waterproofing job for a much longer time.

The process is applied to the outside of a foundation without having to excavate. Long tubes are inserted into the ground to relieve pockets of water pressure and a special material is pumped through high-pressure hoses into spuds placed about 3 feet apart along the foundation. The material fills cracks and pores in the basement wall. Its chemical makeup also enables it to absorb water like a sponge. Thus, a water-tight seal is formed around the foundation from the footing to above grade level.

If hydrostatic pressure begins to react against a basement *floor,* there is only one sure cure. A trench has to be made around the entire perimeter of the floor along the footing, which usually involves breaking up of the concrete with a jack hammer. Then, 3 to 4 inches of so-called land or weeping tile are laid at the footing. This tile absorbs moisture and drains it off to a hole where there is a sump pump. The pump in turn is connected to a dry well away from the house into which the pumped water is diverted.

Condensation, on the other hand, is an "inside job." It doesn't involve seepage of soil water. It can occur in a basement in both winter and summer. Two things are involved: cool surfaces and warm moist air. In summer, warm moist air inside the home can contact cool wall surfaces, causing the walls to sweat. In winter, the warm moist air can be provided by moisture-producing appliances in the home.

The cure for condensation lies in finding the best way to dry out the air coming into the basement. It might be as simple as providing more ventilation by opening a window or inserting vent louvers into the wall to the outside. You can often eliminate the problem by studding out the wall and putting up new walls of panel or plasterboard. The dead space provided between the finish walls and the masonry foundation walls, between which some form of waterproof aluminum-backed paper should be placed, might be just enough to make a vapor barrier. If only exposed water pipes are sweating, wrap them with insulating tape.

Severe condensation might call for the installation of a dehumidifier to "dry out" basement air before it can condense.

See also: air conditioners; building; **crawl space;** condensation; humidifiers; psychrometer.

Washtub bass fiddle carries the beat

They laughed when you brought out the old washtub, but in a moment you had them tappin' their toes

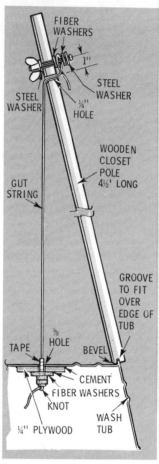

FIBER WASHERS
1"
STEEL WASHER
STEEL WASHER
¼" HOLE
WOODEN CLOSET POLE 4½' LONG
GUT STRING
GROOVE TO FIT OVER EDGE OF TUB
⅜ HOLE
TAPE
BEVEL
CEMENT
FIBER WASHERS
KNOT
WASH TUB
¼" PLYWOOD

THE OLD WASHTUB bass fiddle is making a comeback. More and more, when folks get together for a hootenanny, the thumping sound of this homemade instrument is heard, backing up the singers and git-tar pickers.

It's a toss-up as to whether the washtub bass is easier to play or to make. Playing it comes naturally to anyone with an ear for music. Hold the tub down by placing one foot on the tub rim (right foot if you're right handed, left foot if you're a lefty). Now, pluck the string in time to the music. To change notes, vary the tension on the string by shifting the top end of the neck back and forth. In no time at all, you'll be thumpin' along with the best of 'em.

When playing this washtub bass fiddle, be careful that your foot doesn't touch the bottom of the tub and deaden the sound.

Making the fiddle is just as easy. Get a No. 1 or 2 (preferably No. 1) galvanized steel tub and drill or punch a ⅜-in. hole in the center of the bottom, for the string, and another in the side, for air escape. Cut a 5-in. plywood sounding disc and drill a ⅜-in. hole in its center; then contact-cement it, plus a large fiber washer, to the underside of the tub, over the hole.

Almost any wooden pole will do for the neck, as long as it's 1¼ or 1⅜ in. in diameter. A thinner one, such as a broom handle, will tend to deaden the sound. Drill the first hole, for the ¼-in. bolt, about 4 in. down from the top. Note that the lower end of the neck is notched to fit the tub rim, and is bevelled so it can't press on the bottom of the tub.

Finally, the string, which is a standard bass-fiddle D-string, is knotted at the lower end, threaded through two fiber washers and wrapped with tape to lessen wear. Then it's threaded through the bottom of the tub, through the lower hole in the neck, and between the two fiber washers on the neck bolt (see detail). The tension created as you pull on the neck will clamp the string at the top.

See also: aeolian harp; banjo; guitars; organ; pianos.

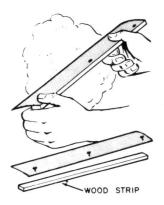

A good finishing trowel can be made by tacking a venetian blind to a wood strip.

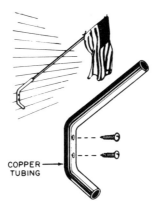

This flag socket can be made by bending and drilling copper tubing. Choose tubing just a bit larger than the staff of the flag.

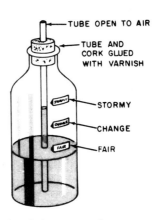

A bottle barometer forecasts the weather by the level of the colored water in the tube. High water level indicates low pressure.

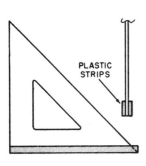

Cement ⅛-in.-thick plastic strips along one edge of a triangle to make a combined T-square and triangle.

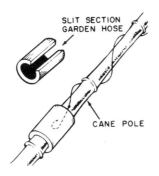

A slit piece of garden hose slipped over a cane pole protects the fisherman's hands from the hook.

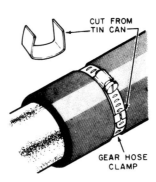

A small retainer clip made from a tin can fastens down the dangling end of a gear hose clamp.

Those plastic lids from coffee cans just fit the top of oil cans and prevent the contents from spilling.

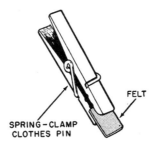

A throw-away brush for touch-up painting can be made by clamping a piece of felt in a spring-type clothespin.

Cut-up cartons make good artist's palettes because the treated cardboard won't absorb the oils in paints.

What won't catch bass?

BY LAWTON CARVER

A toothbrush, a clothespin
or even a wristwatch—
anything goes in the wacky sport
of bass fishing

■ "THE EASIEST THING in the world to make," said the late Ray Camp, a New York outdoors writer, "is a lure to catch bass.

"I know of no lure manufacturer who cannot say with impunity that his lure has caught record bass. And the reason for this remarkable success is simple. Pound for pound, a bass of any species is the hungriest, the fightin'est and downright ornery meanest thing that swims. With his usual disposition, and given a mouth large enough to swallow it, a bass would attack a lure made from a kitchen sink."

While this is a slight exaggeration, it is not far from the truth. A bass will strike anything that moves and can be swallowed, and will hit hard. It is not uncommon for a bass to hit a surface lure and carry it six feet into the air. When stuffed with food, a bass will strike just out of pugnacious anger at any movement that seems to irritate him.

On the Pascagoula River in Mississippi I

Playing tag with a bass, a lizard approaches the water, then scurries for safety when the bass lunges at him

caught a bass that had some other angler's plug still hanging by a gang hook from its mouth. On that same trip we took a bass with a cigar butt in its stomach.

It was Ray Camp who took a largemouth on a carrot rigged with a single hook, merely to prove it could be done.

A wristwatch rigged into a frog harness with a piece of pork rind on the bend of the hook will work about as well as anything—when they are hitting. The wristwatch lure, improvised out of curiosity, took a bass in New York's Ashokan Reservoir in the fall. But this can be costly fishing. A second bass made off with the watch.

Another time, just for the fun of it, I fished a transparent red toothbrush, fastening the leader to the hole in the handle and trailing the hook slightly behind and beneath the bristles. On the third cast and retrieve a bass followed it almost to the boat, as though trying to figure out what it was. Then he lunged and took it.

Largemouths are regularly caught in the south weighing up to 20 pounds, and the fishermen in that part of the country—notably Florida—have a way of doing it that would make that inveterate fly caster Izaak Walton tremble the top soil with laughter. They simply tie two or three feet of line to the end of a stout cane pole, put on a good-sized hook with a piece of pork rind attached, then row around a lake furiously jiggling the hook up and down along the edge of lily pads. This is called dibbling.

The "Doctor's Special" is a favorite with Art Smith. He has caught bass with it all over the country and wouldn't think of going on a fishing trip without a half dozen on hand.

This is an ordinary, large-size medicine capsule that is cast with a fly rod. It doesn't attract the big fish, but with a fly rod an angler will get all the action he can handle from the smaller ones.

Holes are punched in each end of the capsule, which is then strung on the shank of a hook. Glue is applied to the holes where the shank emerges. Thread is wound around the glued ends and is carried over the body of the capsule in two layers. Finally, clear finger nail lacquer is applied to make it an airtight and waterproof floating bug. The weight of the hook keeps it half-submerged on an angle, and a twitch of the rod tip gives it an action irresistible to a bass.

On a particularly frolicsome fishing trip I took a bass on a champagne cork, and another time with a yarn decorated clothespin.

The truth is, the bass is a voracious, arrogant fighter that fears nothing. A trout is shy and can be disturbed by a fine leader on the water or the unusual appearance of a lure. A bass, on the other hand, is attracted by the noise and vibration of a lure. I know a fisherman who always carried along a battered old frying pan which he banged like fury against the sides of his aluminum skiff. He said it made the bass so mad they'd strike anything; that fellow caught a lot of fish.

The average diet of a bass will include: drag-

189

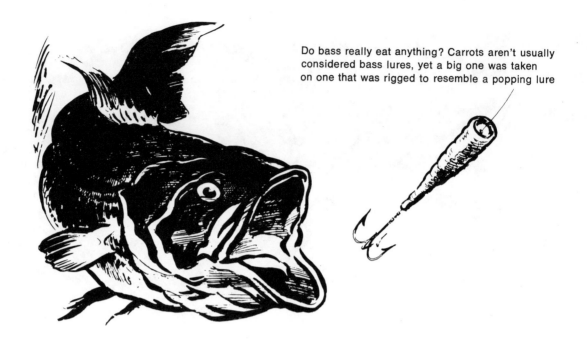

Do bass really eat anything? Carrots aren't usually considered bass lures, yet a big one was taken on one that was rigged to resemble a popping lure

snakes and—in the South—tender young cotton-mouth moccasins, smaller fish, worms and duck-lings. He'll add to this bill of fare, any delicacies that appear à la carte and are of edible size. And almost every serious fisherman has seen a bass try to take a low-flying bird out of the air.

A curious little drama takes place in the south between the chameleon and the bass that is either an age-old game or a feud. It is a common sight where the thick cypress roots arch down into the water to see a chameleon teasing a bass lying just below the water surface by running down the root dangerously close to the water, and then scurrying away when the bass leaps at the chameleon.

But just because he bites on almost anything when the mood hits him doesn't mean that the bass is easy to catch. A bass will strike a lure, taking it high into the air, and just shake it loose before he hits the water. A good-sized bass can straighten a hook so that it looks like a darning needle. And if he can't shake loose or break the line, he'll dive to the bottom and wrap himself around a stump or submerged tree.

In bass fishing you will not necessarily catch fish by thinking like a fish, though this is a highly regarded rule for fishing in general.

You can't think like a bass, because this fish doesn't seem to think at all most of the time, and when he does it is usually with the inconsistent perversity of a derby-hatted, cigar-smoking, loud-mouthed barroom brawler who is unpredictable even to those who know him best.

See also: bait, fishing; boats, buying; fishing; fly-casting; ice fishing; jet runabout; lures; pram; river-boat; trolling motor.

Project-a-plan

HOW TO USE PROJECT-A-PLANS

Here are the famous Project-a-plans—the *Popular Mechanics* system that makes you an artist in minutes. The method is simple. Cut the Project-a-plans from this page, following the dotted lines. Then coat each drawing with shellac, clear nail polish or even vegetable oil. Then mount each little drawing in a cardboard 35-mm. slide frame. Put the frame in a slide projector and project it on the material on which you want to draw—poster board, plywood, etc. Set the material up against the wall like a screen, and make certain the projector is at right angles to the board. You can make the drawing any size you wish by moving the projector. Trace the enlarged outline on the material and you're all set. You can use this system for making signs and posters, enlarging designs for jigsawing and many other projects that require artwork.

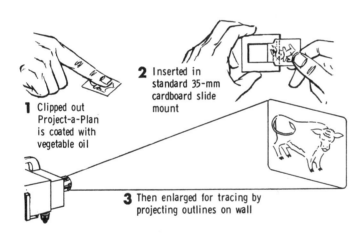

1 Clipped out Project-a-Plan is coated with vegetable oil

2 Inserted in standard 35-mm cardboard slide mount

3 Then enlarged for tracing by projecting outlines on wall

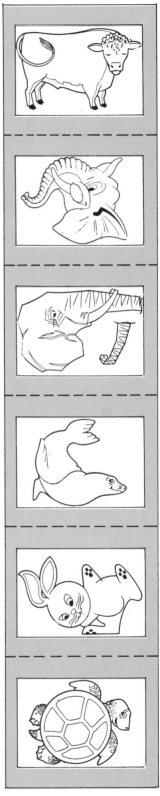

SEE "ANYONE CAN LETTER SIGNS," PAGE 68 AND "ANIMAL PLAQUES," PAGE 90.